AUDUBON GUIDE
to the National Wildlife Refuges

Alaska and the Northwest

AUDUBON GUIDE
to the National Wildlife Refuges

Alaska and the Northwest
Alaska · Oregon · Washington

By **Loren Mac Arthur
and Debbie S. Miller**

Foreword *by* Theodore Roosevelt IV

Series Editor, David Emblidge

A Balliett & Fitzgerald Book
St. Martin's Griffin, New York

Cartography: © Balliett & Fitzgerald, Inc. produced by Mapping Specialists Ltd.
Illustrations: Mary Sundstrom
Cover design: Michael Storrings and Sue Canavan
Interior design: Bill Cooke and Sue Canavan

Balliett & Fitzgerald Inc. Staff
Sue Canavan, Design Director
Maria Fernandez, Production Editor
Alexis Lipsitz, Executive Series Editor
Rachel Deutsch, Associate Photo Editor
Kristen Couse, Associate Editor
Paul Paddock, Assistant Editor
Howard Klein, Editorial Intern
Bruce B. Macomber, Proofreader

Balliett & Fitzgerald Inc. would like to thank the following people for their assistance in creating this series:
At National Audubon Society:
    Katherine Santone, former Director of Publishing, for sponsoring this project
    Claire Tully, Senior Vice President, Marketing
    Evan Hirsche, Director, National Wildlife Refuges Campaign
At U.S. Fish & Wildlife Service:
    Richard Coleman, former Chief, Division of Refuges, U.S. Fish & Wildlife Service
    Janet Tennyson, Outreach Coordinator
    Craig Rieben, Chief of Broadcasting & Audio Visual, U.S. Fish & Wildlife
        Service, for photo research assistance
    Pat Carrol, Chief Surveyor, U.S. Fish & Wildlife Service, for map information
    Regional External Affairs officers, at the seven U.S. Fish & Wildlife Service
        Regional Headquarters
    Elizabeth Jackson, Photographic Information Specialist, National
        Conservation Training Center, for photo research
At St. Martin's Griffin:
    Greg Cohn, who pulled it all together on his end, as well as Michael
        Storrings and Kristen Macnamara
At David Emblidge—Book Producer:
    Marcy Ross, Assistant Editor
Thanks also to Theodore Roosevelt IV and John Flicker.

CONTENTS

OREGON

WASHINGTON

Appendix

Foreword

America is singularly blessed in the amount and quality of land that the federal government holds in trust for its citizens. No other country can begin to match the variety of lands in our national wildlife refuges, parks and forests. From the Arctic Refuge on the North Slope of Alaska to the National Key Deer Refuge in Florida, the diversity of land in the National Wildlife Refuge (NWR) System is staggering.

Yet of all our public lands, the National Wildlife Refuge System is the least well known and does not have an established voting constituency like that of the Parks System. In part this is because of its "wildlife first" mission, which addresses the needs of wildlife species before those of people. That notwithstanding, wildlife refuges also offer remarkable opportunities for people to experience and learn about wildlife—and to have fun doing so!

The Refuge System was launched in 1903 when President Theodore Roosevelt discovered that snowy egrets and other birds were being hunted to the brink of extinction for plumes to decorate ladies' hats. He asked a colleague if there were any laws preventing the president from making a federal bird reservation out of an island in Florida's Indian River. Learning there was not, Roosevelt responded, "Very well, then I so declare it." Thus Pelican Island became the nation's first plot of land to be set aside for the protection of wildlife. Roosevelt went on to create another 50 refuges, and today there are more than 500 refuges encompassing almost 93 million acres, managed by the U.S. Fish & Wildlife Service.

The Refuge System provides critical habitat for literally thousands of mammals, birds, amphibians and reptiles, and countless varieties of plants and flowers. More than 55 refuges have been created specifically to save endangered species. Approximately 20 percent of all threatened and endangered species in the United States rely on these vital places for their survival. As a protector of our country's natural diversity, the System is unparalleled.

Setting NWR boundaries is determined, as often as possible, by the needs of species that depend on the protected lands. Conservation biology, the science that studies ecosystems as a whole, teaches us that wildlife areas must be linked by habitat "corridors" or run the risk of becoming biological islands. The resulting inability of species to transfer their genes over a wide area leaves them vulnerable to disease and natural disasters. For example, the Florida panther that lives in Big Cypress Swamp suffers from a skin fungus, a consequence, scientists believe, of inbreeding. Today's refuge managers are acutely aware of this precarious situation afflicting many species and have made protection of the System's biodiversity an important goal.

Clearly, the job of the refuge manager is not an easy one. Chronic underfunding of the System by the federal government has resulted in refuges operating with less money per employee and per acre than any other federal land-management agency. Recent efforts by some in Congress to address this shortfall have begun to show results, but the System's continued vulnerability to special interests has resulted in attempts to open refuges to oil drilling, road building in refuge wilderness areas, and military exercises.

The managers of the System have played a crucial role in responding to the limited resources available. They have created a network of volunteers who contribute tens of thousands of hours to help offset the lack of direct financing for the Refuge System. Groups like refuge "friends" and Audubon Refuge Keepers have answered the call for local citizen involvement on many refuges across the country.

I hope Americans like yourself who visit our national wildlife refuges will come away convinced of their importance, not only to wildlife but also to people. I further hope you will make your views known to Congress, becoming the voice and voting constituency the Refuge System so desperately needs.

—*Theodore Roosevelt IV*

Preface

Thank you for adding the *Audubon Guide to the National Wildlife Refuge System* to your travel library. I hope you will find this nine-volume series an indispensable guide to finding your way around the refuge system, as well as a valuable educational tool for learning more about the vital role wildlife refuges play in protecting our country's natural heritage.

It was nearly 100 years ago that Frank Chapman, an influential ornithologist, naturalist, publisher and noted Audubon member, approached President Theodore Roosevelt (as recounted by Theodore Roosevelt IV in his foreword), eventually helping to persuade him to set aside more than 50 valuable parcels of land for the protection of wildlife.

Because of limited funding available to support these new wildlife sanctuaries, Audubon stepped up and paid for wardens who diligently looked after them. And so began a century of collaboration between Audubon and the National Wildlife Refuge System. Today, Audubon chapter members can be found across the country assisting refuges with a range of projects, from viewing tower construction to bird banding.

Most recently, National Audubon renewed its commitment to the Refuge System by launching a nationwide campaign to build support for refuges locally and nationally. Audubon's Wildlife Refuge Campaign is promoting the Refuge System through on-the-ground programs such as Audubon Refuge Keepers (ARK), which builds local support groups for refuges, and Earth Stewards, a collaboration with the U.S. Fish and Wildlife Service and the National Fish and Wildlife Foundation, which uses refuges and other important bird habitats as outdoor classrooms. In addition, we are countering legislative threats to refuges in Washington, D.C., while supporting increased federal funding for this, the least funded of all federal land systems.

By teaching more people about the important role refuges play in conserving our nation's diversity of species—be they birds, mammals, amphibians, reptiles, or plants—we have an opportunity to protect for future generations our only federal lands system set aside first and foremost for wildlife conservation.

As a nation, we are at a critical juncture—do we continue to sacrifice wetlands, forests, deserts, and coastal habitat for short-term profit, or do we accept that the survival of our species is closely linked to the survival of others? The National Wildlife Refuge System is a cornerstone of America's conservation efforts. If we are to leave a lasting legacy and, indeed, ensure our future, then we must build on President Theodore Roosevelt's greatest legacy. I invite you to join us!

—John Flicker, President, National Audubon Society

Introduction
to the National Wildlife Refuge System

He spent entire days on horseback, traversing the landscape of domed and crum
bling hills, steep forested coulees, with undulating tables of prairie above. The soft
wraparound light of sunset displayed every strange contour of the Badlands and
lit the colors in each desiccated layer of rock—yellow, ochre, beige, gold.

Theodore Roosevelt was an easterner. As some well-heeled easterners were
wont to do, he traveled west in 1883 to play cowboy, and for the next eight years
he returned as often as possible. He bought a cattle ranch, carried a rifle and a six-
gun, rode a horse. North Dakota was still Dakota Territory then, but the Plains
bison were about gone, down to a scattering of wild herds.

The nation faced a new and uneasy awareness of limits during Roosevelt's
North Dakota years. Between 1776 and 1850, the American population had
increased from 1.5 million to more than 23 million. National borders were fixed
and rail and telegraph lines linked the coasts, but Manifest Destiny had a price. The
ongoing plunder of wildlife threatened species such as the brown pelican and the
great egret; the near-total extermination of 60 million bison loomed as a lesson
many wished to avoid repeating.

Despite the damage done, the powerful landscapes of the New World had
shaped the outlooks of many new Americans. From Colonial-era botanist John
Bartram to 19th-century artists George Catlin and John James Audubon, naturalists and individuals of conscience explored the question of what constituted a
proper human response to nature. Two figures especially, Henry David Thoreau
and John Muir, created the language and ideas that would confront enduring Old
World notions of nature as an oppositional, malevolent force to be harnessed and
exploited. The creation in 1872 of Yellowstone as the world's first national park
indicated that some Americans, including a few political leaders, were listening to
what Thoreau, Muir, and these others had to say.

Roosevelt, along with his friend George Bird Grinnell, drew upon these and
other writings, as well as their own richly varied experiences with nature, to take
the unprecedented step of making protection of nature a social and political
cause. Of his time in the Badlands, Roosevelt remarked "the romance of my life
began here," and "I never would have been president if it had not been for my
experiences in North Dakota." As a hunter, angler, and naturalist, Roosevelt
grasped the importance of nature for human life. Though he had studied natural
history as an undergraduate at Harvard, believing it would be his life's work,
Roosevelt owned a passion for reform and had the will—perhaps a need—to be
effective. Rather than pursuing a career as a nat-
uralist, he went into politics. His friend George

Barren-ground caribou

Bird Grinnell, publisher of the widely read magazine *Forest and Stream,* championed all manner of environmental protection and in 1886 founded the Audubon Society to combat the slaughter of birds for the millinery trade. Fifteen years later, TR would find himself with an even greater opportunity. In1901, when he inherited the presidency following the assassination of William McKinley, Roosevelt declared conservation a matter of federal policy.

Roosevelt backed up his words with an almost dizzying series of conservation victories. He established in 1903 a federal bird reservation on Pelican Island, Florida, as a haven for egrets, herons, and other birds sought by plume hunters. In eight years, Roosevelt authorized 150 million acres in the lower 48 states and another 85 million in Alaska to be set aside from logging under the Forest Reserve Act of 1891, compared to a total of 45 million under the three prior presidents. To these protected lands he added five national parks and 17 national monuments. The NWR system, though, is arguably TR's greatest legacy. Often using executive order to circumvent Congress, Roosevelt established 51 wildlife refuges.

The earliest federal wildlife refuges functioned as sanctuaries and little else. Visitors were rare and recreation was prohibited. Between 1905 and 1912 the first refuges for big-game species were established—Wichita Mountains in Oklahoma, the National Bison Range in Montana, and National Elk Refuge in Jackson, Wyoming. In 1924, the first refuge to include native fish was created; a corridor some 200 miles long, the Upper Mississippi National Wildlife and Fish Refuge spanned the states of Minnesota, Wisconsin, Illinois, and Iowa.

Atlantic puffins, Petit Manan NWR, Maine

Still, the 1920s were dark years for America's wildlife. The effects of unregulated hunting, along with poor enforcement of existing laws, had decimated once-abundant species. Extinction was feared for the wood duck. Wild turkey had become scarce outside a few southern states. Pronghorn antelope, which today number perhaps a million across the West, were estimated at 25,000 or fewer. The trumpeter swan, canvasback duck, even the prolific and adaptable white-tailed deer, were scarce or extirpated across much of their historic ranges.

The Depression and Dust-bowl years, combined with the leadership of President Franklin Delano Roosevelt, gave American conservation—and the refuge system in particular—a hefty forward push. As wetlands vanished and fertile prairie soils blew away, FDR's Civilian Conservation Corps (CCC) dispatched thousands of unemployed young men to camps that stretched from Georgia to California. On the sites of many present-day refuges, they built dikes and other

Saguaro cactus and ocotillo along Charlie Bell 4WD trail, Cabeza Prieta NWR, Arizona

water-control structures, planted shelterbelts and grasses. Comprised largely of men from urban areas, the experience of nature was no doubt a powerful rediscovery of place and history for the CCC generation. The value of public lands as a haven for people, along with wildlife, was on the rise.

In 1934, Jay Norwood "Ding" Darling was instrumental in developing the federal "Duck Stamp," a kind of war bond for wetlands; hunters were required to purchase it, and anyone else who wished to support the cause of habitat acquisition could, too. Coupled with the Resettlement Act of 1935, in which the federal government bought out or condemned private land deemed unsuitable for agriculture, several million acres of homesteaded or settled lands reverted to federal ownership to become parks, national grasslands, and wildlife refuges. The Chief of the U.S. Biological Survey's Wildlife Refuge Program, J. Clark Salyer, set out on a cross-country mission to identify prime wetlands. Salyer's work added 600,000 acres to the refuge system, including Red Rock Lakes in Montana, home to a small surviving flock of trumpeter swans.

The environmental ruin of the Dust bowl also set in motion an era of government initiatives to engineer solutions to such natural events as floods, drought, and the watering of crops. Under FDR, huge regional entities such as the Tennessee Valley Authority grew, and the nation's mightiest rivers—the Columbia, Colorado, and later, the Missouri—were harnessed by dams. In the wake of these and other federal works projects, a new concept called "mitigation" appeared: If a proposed dam or highway caused the destruction of a certain number of acres of wetlands or other habitat, some amount of land nearby would be ceded to conservation in return. A good many of today's refuges were the progeny of mitigation. The federal government, like the society it represents, was on its way to becoming complex enough that the objectives of one arm could be at odds with those of another.

Citizen activism, so integral to the rise of the Audubon Society and other groups, was a driving force in the refuge system as well. Residents of rural Georgia applied relentless pressure on legislators to protect the Okefenokee Swamp. Many other refuges—San Francisco Bay, Sanibel Island, Minnesota Valley, New Jersey's Great Swamp—came about through the efforts of people with a vision of conservation close to home.

More than any other federal conservation program, refuge lands became places where a wide variety of management techniques could be tested and refined. Generally, the National Park system followed the "hands off" approach of Muir and Thoreau while the U.S. Forest Service and Bureau of Land Management, in theory, emphasized a utilitarian, "sustainable yield" value; in practice, powerful economic interests backed by often ruthless politics left watersheds, forests, and grasslands badly degraded, with far-reaching consequences for fish and wildlife. The refuge system was not immune to private enterprise—between 1939 and 1945, refuge lands were declared fair game for oil drilling, natural-gas exploration, and even for bombing practice by the U.S. Air Force—but the negative impacts have seldom reached the levels of other federal areas.

Visitor use at refuges tripled in the 1950s, rose steadily through the 1960s, and by the 1970s nearly tripled again. The 1962 Refuge Recreation Act established guidelines for recreational use where activities such as hiking, photography, boating, and camping did not interfere with conservation. With visitors came opportunities to educate, and now nature trails and auto tours, in addition to beauty, offered messages about habitats and management techniques. Public awareness of wilderness, "a place where man is only a visitor," in the words of long-time advocate Robert Marshall of the U.S. Forest Service, gained increasing social and political attention. In 1964, Congress passed the Wilderness Act, establishing guidelines for designating a host of federally owned lands as off-limits to motorized vehicles, road building, and resource exploitation. A large number of refuge lands qualified—the sun-blasted desert of Arizona's Havasu refuge, the glorious tannin-stained waters and cypress forests of Georgia's Okefenokee Swamp, and the almost incomprehensible large 8-million-acre Arctic NWR in Alaska, home to vast herds of caribou, wolf packs, and bladelike mountain peaks, the largest contiguous piece of wilderness in the refuge system.

Sachuest Point NWR, Rhode Island

Nonetheless, this was also a time of horrendous air and water degradation, with the nation at its industrial zenith and agriculture cranked up to the level of "agribusiness." A wake-up call arrived in the form of vanishing bald eagles, peregrine falcons, and osprey. The insecticide DDT, developed in 1939 and used in World War II to eradicate disease-spreading insects, had been used throughout the nation ever since, with consequences unforeseen until the 1960s. Sprayed over wetlands, streams, and crop fields, DDT had entered watersheds and from there the food chain itself. It accumulated in the bodies of fish and other aquatic life, and birds consuming fish took DDT into their systems, one effect was a calcium deficiency, resulting in eggs so fragile that female birds crushed them during incubation.

Partially submerged alligator, Anahuac NWR, Texas

Powerful government and industry leaders launched a vicious, all-out attack on the work of a marine scientist named Rachel Carson, whose book *Silent Spring,* published in 1962, warned of the global dangers associated with DDT and other biocides. For this she was labeled "not a real scientist" and "a hysterical woman." With eloquence and courage, though, Carson stood her ground. If wild species atop the food chain could be devastated, human life could be threatened, too. Americans were stunned, and demanded an immediate ban on DDT. Almost overnight, the "web of life" went from chalkboard hypothesis to reality.

Protecting imperiled species became a matter of national policy in 1973 when President Nixon signed into law the Endangered Species Act (ESA), setting guidelines by which the U.S. Fish & Wildlife Service would "list" plant and animal species as *threatened* or *endangered* and would develop a program for their recovery. Some 56 refuges, such as Ash Meadows in Nevada and Florida's Crystal River, home of the manatee, were established specifically for the protection of endangered species. Iowa's tiny Driftless Prairie refuge exists to protect the rare, beautifully colored pleistocene land snail and a wildflower, the northern monkshood. Sometimes unwieldy, forever politicized, the ESA stands as a monumental achievement. Its successes include the American alligator, bald eagle, and gray wolf. The whooping crane would almost surely be extinct today without the twin supports of ESA and the refuge system. The black-footed ferret, among the rarest mammals on earth, is today being reintroduced on a few western refuges. In 1998, nearly one-fourth of all threatened and endangered species populations find sanctuary on refuge lands.

More legislation followed. The passage of the Alaska National Interest Lands Conservation Act in 1980 added more than 50 million acres to the refuge system in Alaska.

The 1980s and '90s have brought no end of conservation challenges, faced by an increasingly diverse association of organizations and strategies. Partnerships now link the refuge system with nonprofit groups, from Ducks Unlimited and The Nature Conservancy to international efforts such as Partners in Flight, a program to monitor the decline of, and to secure habitat for, neotropical songbirds. These cooperative efforts have resulted in habitat acquisition and restoration, research, and many new refuges. Partnerships with private landowners who voluntarily offer marginally useful lands for restoration—with a sponsoring conservation group cost-sharing the project—have revived many thousands of acres of grasslands, wetlands, and riparian corridors.

Citizen activism is alive and well as we enter the new millennium. Protecting and promoting the growth of the NWR system is a primary campaign of the National Audubon Society, which, by the year 2000, will have grown to a membership of around 550,000. NAS itself also manages about 100 sanctuaries and nature centers across the country, with a range of opportunities for environmental education. The National Wildlife Refuge Association, a volunteer network,

Coyote on the winter range

keeps members informed of refuge events, environmental issues, and legislative developments and helps to maintain a refuge volunteer workforce. In 1998, a remarkable 20 percent of all labor performed on the nation's refuges was carried out by volunteers, a contribution worth an estimated $14 million.

A national wildlife refuge today has many facets. Nature is ascendant and thriving, often to a shocking degree when compared with adjacent lands. Each site has its own story: a prehistory, a recent past, a present—a story of place, involving people, nature, and stewardship, sometimes displayed in Visitor Center or Headquarters exhibits, always written into the landscape. Invariably a refuge belongs to a community as well, involving area residents who visit, volunteers who log hundreds of hours, and a refuge staff who are knowledgeable and typically friendly, even outgoing, especially if the refuge is far-flung. In this respect most every refuge is a portal to local culture, be it Native American, cows and crops, or big city. There may be no better example of democracy in action than a national wildlife refuge. The worm-dunker fishes while a mountain biker pedals past. In spring, birders scan marshes and grasslands that in the fall will be walked by hunters. Compromise is the guiding principle.

What is the future of the NWR system? In Prairie City, Iowa, the Neal Smith NWR represents a significant departure from the time-honored model. Established in 1991, the site had almost nothing to "preserve." It was old farmland with scattered remnants of tallgrass prairie and degraded oak savanna. What is happening at Neal Smith, in ecological terms, has never been attempted on such a scale: the reconstruction, essentially from scratch, of a self-sustaining 8,000-acre native biome, complete with bison and elk, greater prairie chickens, and a palette of wildflowers and grasses that astonish and delight.

What is happening in human terms is equally profound. Teams of area residents, called "seed seekers," explore cemeteries, roadside ditches, and long-ignored patches of ground. Here and there they find seeds of memory, grasses and wildflowers from the ancient prairie, and harvest them; the seeds are catalogued and planted on the refuge. The expanding prairie at Neal Smith is at once new and very old. It is reshaping thousands of Iowans' sense of place, connecting them to what was, eliciting wonder for what could be. And the lessons here transcend biology. In discovering rare plants, species found only in the immediate area, people discover an identity beyond job titles and net worth. The often grueling labor of cutting brush, pulling nonnative plants, and tilling ground evokes the determined optimism of Theodore and Franklin Roosevelt and of the CCC.

As the nation runs out of wild places worthy of preservation, might large-scale restoration of damaged or abandoned lands become the next era of American conservation? There are ample social and economic justifications. The ecological justifications are endless, for, as the history of conservation and ecology has revealed, nature and humanity cannot go their separate ways. The possibilities, if not endless, remain rich for the years ahead.

John Grassy

How to use this book

Local conditions and regulations on national wildlife refuges vary considerably. We provide detailed, site-specific information useful for a good refuge visit, and we note the broad consistencies throughout the NWR system (facility set-up and management, what visitors may or may not do, etc.). Contact the refuge before arriving or stop by the Visitor Center when you get there. F&W wildlife refuge managers are ready to provide friendly, savvy advice about species and habitats, plus auto, hiking, biking, or water routes that are open and passable, and public programs (such as guided walks) you may want to join.

AUDUBON GUIDES TO THE NATIONAL WILDLIFE REFUGES

This is one of nine regional volumes in a series covering the entire NWR system. **Visitable refuges**—over 300 of them constitute about three-fifths of the NWR system. **Nonvisitable refuges** may be small (without visitor facilities), fragile (set up to protect an endangered species or threatened habitat), or new and undeveloped.

Among visitable refuges, some are more important and better developed than others. In creating this series, we have categorized refuges as A, B, or C level, with the A-level refuges getting the most attention. You will easily recognize the difference. C-level refuges, for instance, do not carry a map.

Rankings can be debated; we know that. We considered visitation statistics, accessibility, programming, facilities, and the richness of the refuges' habitats and animal life. Some refuges ranked as C-level now may develop further over time.

Many bigger NWRs have either "satellites" (with their own refuge names) separate "units" within the primary refuge or other, less significant NWRs nearby. All of these, at times, were deemed worthy of a brief mention.

ORGANIZATION OF THE BOOK

■ **REGIONAL OVERVIEW** This regional introduction is intended to give readers the big picture, touching on broad patterns in landscape formation, interconnections among plant communities, and diversity of animals. We situate NWRs in the natural world of the larger bio-region to which they belong, showing why these federally protected properties stand out as wild places worth preserving amid encroaching civilization.

We also note some wildlife management issues that will surely color the debate around campfires and

ABOUT THE U.S. FISH & WILDLIFE SERVICE Under the Department of the Interior, the U.S. Fish & Wildlife Service is the principal federal agency responsible for conserving and protecting wildlife and plants and their habitats for the benefit of the American people. The Service manages the 93-million-acre NWR system, comprised of more than 500 national wildlife refuges, thousands of small wetlands, and other special management areas. It also operates 66 national fish hatcheries, 64 U.S. Fish & Wildlife Management Assistance offices, and 78 ecological services field stations. The agency enforces federal wildlife laws, administers the Endangered Species Act, manages migratory bird populations, restores nationally significant fisheries, conserves and restores wildlife habitats such as wetlands, and helps foreign governments with their conservation efforts. It also oversees the federal-aid program that distributes hundreds of millions of dollars in excise taxes on fishing and hunting equipment to state wildlife agencies.

congressional conference tables in years ahead, while paying recognition to the NWR supporters and managers who helped make the present refuge system a reality.

■ **THE REFUGES** The refuge section of the book is organized alphabetically by state and then, within each state, by refuge name.

There are some clusters, groups, or complexes of neighboring refuges administered by one primary refuge. Some refuge complexes are alphabetized here by the name of their primary refuge, with the other refuges in the group following immediately thereafter.

■ **APPENDIX**

Nonvisitable National Wildlife Refuges: NWR properties that meet the needs of wildlife but are off-limits to all but field biologists.

Federal Recreation Fees: An overview of fees and fee passes.

Volunteer Activities: How you can lend a hand to help your local refuge or get involved in supporting the entire NWR system.

U.S. Fish & Wildlife General Information: The seven regional head-quarters of the U.S. Fish & Wildlife Service through which the National Wildlife Refuge System is administered.

National Audubon Society Wildlife Sanctuaries: A listing of the 24 National Audubon Society wildlife sanctuaries, dispersed across the U.S., which are open to the public.

Bibliography & Resources: Natural-history titles both on the region generally and its NWRs, along with a few books of inspiration about exploring the natural world.

Glossary: A listing of specialized terms (not defined in the text) tailored to this region.

Index

National Audubon Society Mission Statement

PRESENTATION OF INFORMATION: A-LEVEL REFUGE

■ **INTRODUCTION** This section attempts to evoke the essence of the place. The writer sketches the sounds or sights you might experience on the refuge, such as sandhill cranes taking off, en masse, from the marsh, filling the air with the roar of thousands of beating wings. That's a defining event for a particular refuge and a great reason to go out and see it.

■ **MAP** Some refuges are just a few acres; several, like the Alaskan behemoths, are bigger than several eastern states. The scale of the maps in this series can vary. We recommend that you also ask refuges for their detailed local maps.

■ **HISTORY** This outlines how the property came into the NWR system and what its uses were in the past.

■ **GETTING THERE** General location; seasons and hours of operation; fees, if any (see federal recreation fees in Appendix); address, telephone. Smaller or remote refuges may have their headquarters off-site. We identify highways as follows: TX14 = Texas state highway # 14; US 23 = a federal highway; I 85 = Interstate 85.

Note: Many NWRs have their own web pages at the F&W web site, http://www.fws.gov/. Some can be contacted by fax or e-mail, and if we do not provide that information here, you may find it at the F&W web site.

■ **TOURING** The **Visitor Center**, if there is one, is the place to start your tour. Some have wildlife exhibits, videos, and bookstores; others may be only a kiosk. Let someone know your itinerary before heading out on a long trail or into the backcountry, and then go explore.

Most refuges have roads open to the public; many offer a wildlife **auto tour,** with wildlife information signs posted en route or a brochure or audiocassette to guide you. Your car serves as a bird blind if you park and remain quiet. Some refuge roads require 4-wheel-drive or a high-chassis vehicle. Some roads are closed seasonally to protect habitats during nesting seasons or after heavy rain or snow.

Touring also covers **walking and hiking** (see more trail details under ACTIVITIES) and **biking.** Many refuge roads are rough; mountain or hybrid bikes are more appropriate than road bikes. When water is navigable, we note what kinds of **boats** may be used and where there are boat launches.

■ **WHAT TO SEE**

Landscape and climate: This section covers geology, topography, and climate: primal forces and raw materials that shaped the habitats that lured species to the refuge. It also includes weather information for visitors.

Plant life: This is a sampling of noteworthy plants on the refuge, usually sorted by habitat, using standard botanical nomenclature. Green plants bordering watery places are in "Riparian Zones"; dwarfed trees, shrubs, and flowers on windswept mountaintops are in the "Alpine Forest"; and so forth.

Wildflowers abound, and you may want to see them in bloom. We give advice about timing your visit, but ask the refuge for more. If botany and habitat relationships are new to you, you can soon learn to read the landscape as a set of interrelated communities. Take a guided nature walk to begin.

(Note: In two volumes, "Plants" is called "Habitats and Plant Communities.")

Animal life: The national map on pages 4 and 5 shows the major North American "flyways." Many NWRs cluster in watery territory underneath the birds' aerial superhighways. There are many birds in this book, worth seeing simply for their beauty. But ponder, too, what birds eat (fish, insects, aquatic plants), or how one species (the mouse) attracts another (the fox), and so on up the food chain, and you'll soon understand the rich interdependence on display in many refuges.

Animals use camouflage and stealth for protection; many are nocturnal. You may want to come out early or late to increase your chances of spotting them. Refuge managers can offer advice on sighting or tracking animals.

Grizzly bears, venomous snakes, alligators, and crocodiles can indeed be dangerous. Newcomers to these animals' habitats should speak with refuge staff about precautions before proceeding.

■ **ACTIVITIES** Some refuges function not only as wildlife preserves but also as recreation parks. Visit a beach, take a bike ride, and camp overnight, or devote your time to serious wildlife observation.

Camping and swimming: If not permissible on the refuge, there may be federal or state campgrounds nearby; we mention some of them. Planning an NWR camping trip should start with a call to refuge headquarters.

Wildlife observation: This subsection touches on strategies for finding species most people want to see. Crowds do not mix well with certain species; you

---

A NOTE ON HUNTING AND FISHING Opinions on hunting and fishing on federally owned wildlife preserves range from "Let's have none of it" to "We need it as part of the refuge management plan." The F&W Service follows the latter approach, with about 290 hunting programs and 260 fishing programs. If you have strong opinions on this topic, talk with refuge managers to gain some insight into F&W's rationale. You can also write to your representative or your senators in Washington.

For most refuges, we summarize the highlights of the hunting and fishing options. You must first have required state and local licenses for hunting or fishing. Then you must check with refuge headquarters about special restrictions that may apply on the refuge; refuge bag limits, for example, or duration of season may be different from regulations elsewhere in the same state.

Hunting and fishing options change from year to year on many refuges, based on the size of the herd or of the flock of migrating birds. These changes may reflect local weather (a hard winter trims the herd) or disease, or factors in distant habitats where animals summer or winter. We suggest what the options usually are on a given refuge (e.g., some birds, some mammals, fish, but not all etc..). It's the responsibility of those who wish to hunt and fish to confirm current information with refuge headquarters and to abide by current rules.

COMMON SENSE, WORTH REPEATING

Leave no trace Every visitor deserves a chance to see the refuge in its pristine state. We all share the responsibility to minimize our impact on the landscape. "Take only pictures and leave only footprints," and even there you'll want to avoid trampling plant life by staying on established trails. Pack out whatever you pack in. Ask refuge managers for guidance on low-impact hiking and camping.

Respect private property Many refuges consist of noncontiguous parcels of land, with private properties abutting refuge lands. Respect all Private Property and No Trespassing signs, especially in areas where native peoples live within refuge territory and hunt or fish on their own land.

Water Protect the water supply. Don't wash dishes or dispose of human waste within 200 ft. of any water. Treat all water for drinking with iodine tablets, backpacker's water filter, or boiling. Clear water you think is OK may be contaminated upstream by wildlife you cannot see.

may need to go away from established observation platforms to have success. Learn a bit about an animal's habits, where it hunts or sleeps, what time of day it moves about. Adjust your expectations to match the creature's behavior, and your chances of success will improve.

Photography: This section outlines good places or times to see certain species. If you have a zoom lens, use it. Sit still, be quiet, and hide yourself. Don't approach the wildlife; let it approach you. Never feed animals or pick growing plants.

Hikes and walks: Here we list specific outings, with mileages and trailhead locations. Smooth trails and boardwalks, suitable for people with disabilities, are noted. On bigger refuges, there may be many trails. Ask for a local map. If you go bushwacking, first make sure this is permissible. Always carry a map and compass.

Seasonal events: National Wildlife Refuge Week, in October, is widely celebrated, with guided walks, lectures, demonstrations, and activities of special interest to children. Call your local refuge for particulars. At other times of the year there are fishing derbies, festivals celebrating the return of migrating birds, and other events linked to the natural world. Increasingly, refuges post event schedules on their web pages.

Publications: Many NWR brochures are free, such as bird and wildflower checklists. Some refuges have pamphlets and books for sale, describing local habitats and species.

Note: The categories of information above appear in A and B refuges in this book; on C-level refuges, options are fewer, and some of these headings may not appear.

—David Emblidge

Alaska and the Northwest

A Regional Overview

Along America's Pacific Coast, profound forces of nature have created a wild and mutable landscape. In the perpetual dance between land and sea, rocks have been carved into fantastic shapes, sea cliffs have crumbled, and beaches are daily nibbled away by the tides. Rivers flow into the sea, carrying sediment that builds up new beaches. Inland, rain and fog dissipate, revealing a vast mountainous landscape that falls away to the high desert, shimmering under the midday sun. In the far north, wetlands and tundra stretch for a thousand miles to the Beaufort Sea. Passing over all of this is one of the world's great natural phenomena, the invisible air highway known as the Pacific Flyway, traveled twice each year by millions of birds to and from their breeding grounds in Alaska and wintering homes that spread from Washington and Oregon to South America and across the Pacific to Asia. It's a welcome habitat for any living creature: Here is the greatest accumulation of birds, fish, and wild animals in the United States.

The Northwest is an outdoor-lover's paradise, and the 38 national wildlife refuges in Oregon and Washington have made it easy for visitors—be they long-time birders working on a life list or families who enjoy stopping at a roadside nature sign—to acquaint themselves with the region's cornucopia of wildlife. There is a refuge for every temperament, from the spare, harsh beauty of Oregon's Hart Mountain National Antelope Refuge to Washington's bucolic Ridgefield NWR to the ragged, wave-washed and rocky islands of the Oregon Islands NWR. Most refuges host more than 200 bird species, from seabirds to shorebirds, raptors, and songbirds.

The Alaskan national wildlife refuges would fill almost half of Texas. Alaska's largest refuge—Arctic NWR—is bigger than the state of West Virginia, and together the state's 16 refuges account for 84 percent of our national refuge lands. All but two—Kenai and Tetlin—lack roads, and backcountry campers visiting the roadless refuges in this vast, isolated land of overwhelming beauty and wildness should be prepared for a primitive experience.

This guide also includes three refuges in California's half of the Klamath Basin, which straddles the Oregon-California border, and the sister refuge to Hart Mountain (OR), Sheldon NWR in Nevada, as well as Deer Flat NWR, on the Idaho-Oregon border.

GEOLOGY

Nothing is finished on the West Coast. Glaciers still grind out vast valleys, volcanoes spew up lava, adding tons of volcanic basalt to the landscape. Mountains increase in height as underground forces push them up. Traveling in Alaska, John Muir wrote: "Here, too, one learns that the world, though made, is yet being made; that this is still the morning of creation."

Glaucous-winged gull nest and eggs, Protection Island NWR, Washington

Earthquakes are markers for this process of creation, and the West Coast is earthquake

Barrow

3

11

6

15

9

Nome

10

Fairbanks

4

Alaska

14

12

Anchorage

13

7

Juneau

2

8

5

1

HAWAII		
1	Alaska Maritime NWR	**8** Kodiak NWR
2	Alaska Peninsula and Becharof NWRs	**9** Koyukuk NWR
		10 Nowitna NWR
3	Arctic NWR	**11** Selawik NWR
4	Innoko NWR	**12** Tetlin NWR
5	Izembek NWR	**13** Togiak NWR
6	Kanuti NWR	**14** Yukon Delta NWR
7	Kenai NWR	**15** Yukon Flats NWR

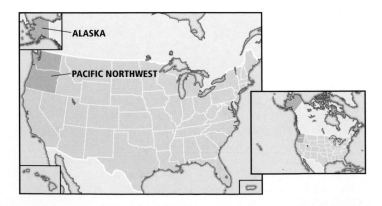

ALASKA

PACIFIC NORTHWEST

OREGON AND WASHINGTON

OREGON

16 Deer Flat NWR
17 Hart Mountain National Antelope Refuge
18 Klamath Basin NWRs (Klamath Basin NWR, Bear Valley NWR, Clear Lake NWR, Klamath Marsh NWR, Lower Klamath NWR, Tule Lake NWR, and Upper Klamath NWR)
19 Malheur NWR
20 Mid-Columbia River NWR Complex (Umatilla NWR, Toppenish NWR, McNary NWR, McKay Creek, and Cold Springs NWR)
21 Oregon Coastal Refuges Complex (Oregon Islands NWR, Bandon Marsh NWR, and Cape Meares NWR)
22 Sheldon NWR
23 Tualatin River NWR
24 Western Oregon NWR Complex (William L. Finley NWR, Ankeny NWR, and Baskett Slough NWR)

WASHINGTON

25 Columbia NWR
26 Columbia River Gorge National Scenic NWRs (Steigerwald NWR, Franz Lake NWR, and Pierce NWR)
27 Conboy Lake NWR
28 Gray's Harbor NWR
29 Julia Butler Hansen NWR
30 Lewis and Clark NWR
31 Little Pend Orielle NWR
32 Nisqually NWR
33 Protection Island NWR
34 Ridgefield NWR
35 Turnbull NWR
36 Washington Maritime NWR Complex (Dungeness NWR, San Juan Islands NWR, Washington Islands NWR)
37 Willapa NWR

country. Alaskans live on a slipping, sliding, shaking piece of the earth. Native Americans explained the frequent earthquakes that rattle America's Pacific Coast by saying that a giant tortoise supported the earth, which trembled each time the beast took a step. The giant tortoise is now explained as a series of huge tectonic plates rafting on top of the earth's molten interior, carrying islands, continents, and oceans with them, drifting at the stately pace of about 1 to 3 inches a year (about as fast as your fingernails grow). The Pacific Plate (6,000 miles long and about 50 miles thick), moving northwest and sinking below the North American Plate, is the force behind the shocks that afflict the West Coast. Earthquakes strike when growing stress wrenches apart two plates that have temporarily joined together, or when two plates collide. (These quakes account for around 90 percent

Kongakut Valley, Arctic NWR, Alaska

of the seismic activity in the United States.) Alaska experienced North America's strongest recorded earthquake (8.4 magnitude) in 1964 when a temblor hit between Anchorage and Valdez, lifting bits of Alaska 38 feet and dropping other sections seven and a half feet (and killing 131 Alaskans). The tsunami (giant wave) caused by the uplifted seabed was so powerful that it compressed the earth's atmosphere, rippling the ionosphere 50 miles above the earth's surface.

Rafting tectonic plates not only continue to shake the West Coast apart—they also created it. Two hundred million years ago Alaska didn't exist; and, farther south, the west coast of America ended in what is now eastern Washington and Oregon. The North American continent drifted west, scraping up everything in its path. The Pacific Plate rafted north, piggybacking a series of *terranes* (a giant

slab of land containing similar rocks) that eventually docked onto the continent to become Alaska and to extend the Pacific Coast westward to its present location. (Some rocks in Alaska indicate that one of its terranes rafted up all the way from the equator.)

The great western mountain ranges formed when the Pacific Ocean floor collided with the North American continent and sunk underneath it, crushing and uplifting great chunks of earth to become the West's mountains. Oregon's Wallowa, Mutton, and Jackass mountains may not be as familiar as the Cascades, but they join with Washington's Olympic range to create the mountainous terrain of the two states. In Alaska the massive Brooks and Alaska ranges, along with the Kuskokwim, Chugach, Kenai and Wrangell mountains, make up Alaska's major mountain ranges.

Mount McKinley (20,320 feet), in the Alaska Range, is the United States' highest mountain; among the 20 highest mountains in the United States, 17 are in Alaska. The Cascade Mountains in Washington, Oregon, and northern California are one segment of the Ring of Fire, a narrow zone of active volcanoes circling the Pacific Ocean basin. (Oregon's landscape was redefined when Mt. St. Helens blew its top off in 1980, sending up a black cloud of ash that floated down, coating western Montana, northern Idaho, and coastal Washington and Oregon with ash.) Alaska's section of the Ring of Fire stretches 1,000 miles along the chain of Aleutian Islands, then moves inland across the Alaska Peninsula and through the Wrangell Mountains. Along this extended sweep of islands and mainland are some 80 active volcanoes. Fourteen of those volcanoes are located on Alaska's Becharof and Alaska Peninsula refuges, and nine of them are active. The Gas Rocks near Mt. Peulik on Becharof emit a continuous stream of gases through cracks in the granite. The Ukinrek Maars craters, also near Mt. Peulik, erupted violently in 1977. A second eruption occurred in 1983 when Mt. Veniaminof, on the Alaska Peninsula refuge, erupted. The Veniaminof volcano has a summit crater that is 20 miles in circumference.

Lake Rose Tead, Pasagshack Bay, Kodiak NWR, Alaska

The Ring of Fire formed when the ocean floor slid into oceanic trenches around the edge of the Pacific Ocean, sinking beneath Asia and North, Central, and South America until it reached a depth where it heated up and became molten. As pressure built, the molten magma burst up through cracks in the earth's surface, creating volcanoes.

Ancient lava flows, so large they're difficult to comprehend, cover the Columbia Plateau. They stretch from the western edge of Idaho through the eastern half of Oregon, flow down into northeastern California, and cover Washington between the Cascade and Rocky mountains. Some of the lava oozed down an ancient valley of the Columbia River more than 600 miles to the Pacific. The basaltic rocks that formed as the lava cooled can be seen in the Columbia refuge.

CLIMATE AND TOPOGRAPHY

Wet weather is responsible for the third great force that has formed the West Coast's magnificent scenery. Glaciers, some 100,000 of them in Alaska alone, continue to scrape, grind, and cut a vast, incomparable landscape of soaring cliffs rising straight out of U-shaped valleys, narrow fjords, and sprawling moraines. Glaciers form over a period of time when more snow falls than melts. As the snow accumulates, it compresses the lower layers, changing their crystalline structure to glacial ice that reflects the most exquisite array of blues found in nature.

Alaska's glaciers are found largely in the coastal mountains of south-central and southeast Alaska, where the storms rolling in off the Pacific supply the vast amounts of moisture necessary to sustain the glaciers. (Two inland areas, the Brooks and Alaska ranges, also support glacial fields.) The North Slope (above the Arctic Circle and bounded by the Chukchi and Beaufort seas on the north and Brooks Range to the south), a place that would seem to have all the conditions necessary for the formation of glaciers, receives as little rain as Oregon and Washington's high desert, some 8 inches a year. (Cold air does not contain as much moisture as warmer air.) The North Slope stays wet only because of permafrost and poor drainage. At the other extreme, Little Port Walter, on southeast Alaska's Baranof Island, averages 223 inches of rain annually. That's 18 feet of rain! (In one really wet year Little Port Walter was inundated with 24 feet of rain.) In winter Alaska's rains fall as snow—a *lot* of snow. The United States' deepest recorded snow pack—356 inches (29 feet)—was measured on Wolverine Glacier on the Kenai Peninsula. Contrasts in the amount of annual snowfall in Alaska are enormous. Barrow, on Alaska's far north coast on the Arctic Ocean, received a low of 3 inches of snow in 1935–36, while 974 inches (81 feet) of snow fell on Thompson Pass (on Alaska Highway 4, southwest of Wrangell Saint Elias National Park) in 1952–53.

The Cascade Mountains, sprawling north to south about 100 miles inland from the Pacific from British Columbia through Washington and Oregon to northern California, control where rain falls in Washington and Oregon. As moisture-laden air blowing in from the Pacific rises over the Cascades, it expands, cools, and falls as rain and snow. By the time the air reaches the leeward side of the Cascades, most of its moisture has precipitated out. The areas in the rain shadow of the Cascades receive little rain. As rain soaks the Olympic Mountains on Washington's Olympic Peninsula with 200 inches annually, a similar rain shadow occurs. The eastern slopes of the Olympics get a scant 20 inches of rain a year.

While rain and fog often bathe the Pacific Coast of Oregon and Washington, the high desert in much of the eastern half of the two states swelters under a summer sun, and what little rain falls (between 8 to 10 inches annually) comes from November through April. The typical abrupt changes between summertime day and night temperatures may catch first-time visitors to the high desert unawares. While daytime temperatures routinely simmer from 90 to 100 degrees, night sees the thermometer dropping into the 40s and 50s.

PLANT COMMUNITIES

Desert, arctic, seashore, valley, and mountain range biotic communities are all represented in Alaska, Washington, and Oregon's wildlife refuges. Plants in these states survive temperatures ranging from minus 80 degrees to 108 degrees (all temperatures listed in this book are in degrees Fahrenheit). This amazing diversity encompasses cactus, seaweed, and ponderosa pine.

Old-growth forest, west-central Oregon

Buttercups, Arctic NWR, Alaska

As the Lewis and Clark expedition approached Washington during its epic two-year exploration in 1804–06 up the Missouri to the mouth of the Columbia River, it was the vast western pine forests here that first caught the explorers' attention. "Below this Creek the lofty Pine is thick in the bottom hill Sides on the mountains & up the runs," Captain William Clark observed in his journal, adding, a few days later: "Found the woods so thick with under growth that the hunters could not get any distance into the Isld. The red wood, and Green bryers interwoven, and mixed with pine, alder, a Specis of Beech, ash &c." To see some of the remaining vast forests of eastern Washington, visit Little Pend Oreille refuge. To see the vegetation that so impressed Lewis and Clark along the Columbia (traveling east to west), stop at Umatilla, Pierce, Franz Lake, Steigerwald, Ridgefield, Lewis & Clark, Julia Butler Hansen, and Willapa refuges.

After reaching the Pacific, the expedition explored the vast saltwater estuaries that surrounded the mouth of the Columbia. Similar estuaries stretched along the coast from Alaska to Baja California, containing a mix of plants such as pickleweed and eelgrass, both able to grow in saltwater or in salty soils. To see this coastal environment, visit Dungeness and Bandon Marsh refuges.

As Lewis and Clark approached the Columbia Plateau in eastern Washington, Captain Meriwether Lewis recorded in his journal that an Indian chief of one of the many tribes they encountered informed him that "in passing this country the feet of our horses would be so much wounded with the stones many of them would give out. the next part of the rout was about 10 days through a dry and parched sandy desert in which there is no food at this season for either man or horse, and in which we must suffer if not perish for the want of water. that the sun had now dried up the little pools of water which exist through this desert plain in the spring season and had also scorched all the grass...."

The tortured lava landscapes that the Lewis and Clark expedition crossed in southern Idaho and eastern Washington can be seen in the Columbia NWR. Both

Malheur and Hart Mountain refuges are home to the spare vegetation and long, dry vistas of the high desert.

To this mix of coastal estuary sedges and rushes, high desert sage and bitterbrush, ponderosa pine forests, and oak woodlands, Alaska adds a vast treeless plain of tundra, muskeg wetlands, far-reaching inland waters, and a 6,640-mile coastline that is rich with saltwater estuaries and marshland.

Considering its size, Alaska has relatively few species of trees and shrubs—around 133 native species. States in the Lower 48, with more favorable growing conditions, generally have twice as many native trees and shrubs as Alaska. More than half the tree species in Alaska can also be found in Washington and Oregon. Alaska's taiga (or boreal forest) of predominantly spruce, paper birch, and aspen stretches from the Kenai Peninsula to the southern slopes of Brooks Range and west nearly to the Bering Sea. Permafrost, a watertight and permanently frozen layer at various depths in the soil, holds bogs and wet areas. Moist tundra, with its low-growing shrubs, cotton grass, and tussocks of other sedges, spreads across the foothills of the Alaska Range and on the Alaska and Seward peninsulas. Low coastal marshes support wet tundra—flat areas with many shallow lakes vegetated with a mat of sedges and cotton grass. A low mat of moss campion and sedges grows between the barren rocks of the alpine tundra.

ANIMAL LIFE

For tens of millions of seabirds, waterfowl, and other species, Alaska is the Grand Central Terminal of the Pacific Flyway. More than 50 percent of the world's population of whistling and trumpeter swans, black brant, Pacific white-fronted geese, emperor geese, and cackling, Aleutian, dusky, and Taverner's Canada geese nest in Alaska. On their incredible twice-yearly migration, birds fly to Alaska in the spring from four continents, including these areas: Cape Horn, Hudson's Bay, Siberia, Argentina, the United States, Mexico, Tasmania, and South China. The waterfowl heading south in the fall from Alaska to Mexico and South America stop off at coastal Washington and Oregon, some spending the winter; others take the inland route along the flyway, where they can be seen in the Oregon and Washington wildlife refuges by the hundreds of thousands. These great migrations—early winter and spring—make the Washington and Oregon refuges a birder's paradise.

Nothing is more emblematic of the untamed West than

Pelagic cormorant, Alaska Maritime NWR, Alaska

Alaskan brown bear with captured salmon, Kodiak NWR, Alaska

the grizzly bear, and Alaska is the last place on earth where these giants roam in great numbers. (In Alaska grizzlies are called brown bears if they live along the coast, grizzlies if they live inland.) Visit Kodiak NWR to see the largest brown bears in the world—weighing in at 800 to 1,500 pounds. In the great expanses of Alaska, catching sight of the state's mammals is less predictable than in a concentrated area such as Oregon and Washington's Umatilla NWR, where a large herd of deer can often be seen browsing in the refuge meadows. Because of the harsh Alaskan climate, the resident mammals need to range over a large territory in order to find food. At least one guide company offers guaranteed brown bear viewing trips on Kodiak Island (and, presumably, a guarantee that you'll return to tell about it).

In Alaska, Oregon, and Washington you'll find many of America's largest mammals—caribou, mountain goats, pronghorn antelopes, mountain sheep, elk, moose, several species of deer, black bear (black and brown bears do not inhabit the same territory) as well as wolves, cougars, coyotes, and bobcats. You'll also find America's smallest mammals, such as the wandering shrew, weighing between a tenth of an ounce and a quarter ounce.

It is an ironic commentary on contemporary life that refuge visitors in Oregon and Washington have the best chance of seeing wildlife by remaining in their cars because refuge wildlife is more habituated to cars than to people. Exceptions exist. Your best hope for seeing mountain sheep in Hart Mountain National Antelope Refuge is to hike the wild, high backcountry where the sheep live.

OUR ALTERED LANDS

Rich in resources (but short on water, except in Alaska), the West has always been seen as prolific pickings for those who came to exploit it. The Russians colonized southeast Alaska in 1784 to form a base from which to kill sea otters (the otters, listed as a threatened species, are recovering from a century and a half of being hunted to near extinction). The next wave of white settlers went north for gold, and the next for the old-growth forests and resident salmon. Today, several salmon runs in the Northwest have been so decimated they are now protected under the Endangered Species Act. The discovery of oil on Alaska's North Slope in 1968 and the completion of the oil pipeline from Prudhoe Bay to Valdez in 1977 brought tankers to Valdez, to transport the crude oil, setting the stage for the nation's worst environmental disaster, the *Exxon Valdez* oil spill in 1989, which dumped 11.4 million gallons of oil into Alaska's pristine Prince William Sound. Some 3,500 to 5,500 otters died, along with 350,000 to 390,000 birds, uncountable salmon and other fish, and mammals and plants living along the shore.

One of the major environmental debates that will occupy the first decade of the new century concerns the continuing attempts by the oil industry to exploit Alaska's last piece of arctic coastline not dedicated for current or future oil development. This 1.5-million-acre stretch of the coastal plain of Arctic NWR, known as the 1002 (ten-oh-two) area, contains the most biologically productive section in the refuge and represents only 5 percent of the North Slope—the remainder is already open or potentially open to development.

Nowhere in Washington and Oregon is the control of nature more evident than in the fate of the once great Columbia River. Rising in British Columbia, it flows 1,996 miles, forming the border between Washington and Oregon in its final 300 miles to the Pacific. Calling it "a mighty and uproarious river," the Lewis and Clark expedition ran it in open canoes. "As the portage of our canoes over this high rock would be impossible with our Strength," wrote Captain William Clark, "and the only danger in passing thro those narrows was the whorls and

Oregon Islands NWR, Oregon

Refuge wetlands, Malheur NWR, Oregon

swells arriseing from the Compression of the water....accordingly I deturmined to pass through this place notwithstanding the horrid appearance of this agitated gut swelling, boiling & whorling in every direction, which from the top of the rock did not appear as bad as when I was in it..." More than 50 dams have reduced the wild Columbia to a series of turgid lakes and have so severely damaged the salmon runs that a plan to remove some of the dams is under consideration. However, the impounded waters now irrigate parts of eastern Oregon and Washington and have created wetlands in a desert. Ponds and marshes formed by seepage through the porous lava from water backed up by dams along the Columbia have transformed the Columbia NWR from desert to extensive wetlands.

Water is such a precious commodity in the West that several wildlife refuges have been created as "overlay refuges," meaning that the refuge sits on top of water controlled by another agency, which can take what water it needs for irrigation. The Cold Springs and McKay Creek refuges, both overlay refuges on reservoirs, lose most of their water by summer's end. In other areas, development threatens refuge water supplies. A ski resort, for example is proposed near the Klamath Basin refuges.

The use of water was not the only factor transforming the West. In eastern Oregon ranchers fenced their lands, preventing pronghorn antelopes from migrating. The environmental conflict over the cutting of old-growth forests in Oregon is well known; and, as in the entire West, a large percentage of Oregon and Washington's wetlands have been filled in.

TAKING CARE OF THE LAND

Our wildlife refuges are managed to replace the loss of natural ecosystems, although some Alaskan refuges may do less managing of their natural resources than do most NWRs. In Alaska, the U.S. Fish & Wildlife Service generally allows nature to take its course. Unlike the altered landscapes of Washington and Oregon refuges, the pristine natural ecosystems in Alaska work without a lot of help. NWR personnel in Alaska manage the vast tracts of refuge land by monitoring the refuge's natural processes.

Nine new refuges were added in Alaska and seven others enlarged following the enactment of a federal law that saw Alaskan native people compensated for the taking of their land. The Alaska Native Claims Settlement Act (ANCSA), besides awarding land and money to native tribes, also committed the federal government to withdrawing up to 80 million acres of public lands for national parks, preserves, forests, and wildlife refuges.

Nine years later, in 1980, President Jimmy Carter signed the Alaska National Interest Lands Conservation Act (ANILCA), which, among other things, created nine new Alaskan refuges and enlarged the others, adding 82,375 square miles (52,720,000 acres) to the Alaskan refuge system. The Alaska refuges now total 118,841 square miles (76,058,758 acres). ANILCA allows subsistence hunting, fishing, and trapping on Alaskan refuges, marking another difference between Alaskan and Lower 48 refuges. During big game hunting season, refuge personnel monitor hunting activities to be sure laws are observed. The changing attitudes toward fire—it is now considered a desirable natural process—underlie one management technique used in Alaskan refuges. Prescribed burning is practiced in several refuges, and fires that don't affect private land holdings within the refuges are allowed to burn.

The differences between managing Alaskan refuges and those in Washington and Oregon speak to the contrast between pristine wilderness and altered landscapes. Oregon and Washington refuges have been severely altered by human occupation and the intrusion of alien plant species. A priority is to remove what has invaded, restore what has been lost, and manage the restorations by mimicking the cycles of nature.

Prescribed burning and chemical and biological treatment help rid uplands of invasive weeds, tamarisk, and Russian olive; native species are planted in their place. Marshes are dug using laser-controlled bulldozers (allowing the leveling of the ground to exact depths), islands are built, and water-control devices are installed. The new wetlands are drained down in summer to allow food plants to grow and filled in the fall before migrating birds arrive. If the marshes can't be drawn down, they are treated with Rotenone to control invasive fish such as carp. Some refuges use dikes and levees to create wetlands; in Siletz Bay NWR the opposite occurs—breaching old levees and dikes allows the sea to flow in, re-creating former salt marshes. Cooperative farming on the refuges allows acreage to be planted in grains and alfalfa; farmers take a share and leave the rest for migrating birds. Cattle grazing encourages the growth of tender new grasses preferred by the birds. Other fields are mowed or burned to produce new grass. Refuge forests overloaded with trees caused by the suppression of fire are thinned by commercial timber sales, and then prescribed burning opens the heavily overgrown understory. Oregon and Washington's offshore islands (most are off-limits to humans) are left to nature; but chances are, when you visit a mainland refuge, you'll be seeing an artificial construct that is as intensively managed as the farm fields surrounding it.

THE FUTURE

It's obvious that our wildlife refuges are in good hands. The biologists running them are a savvy group who combine scientific expertise with experience that comes only from years of direct observation. Many of them are nomadic, moving

Shorebird festival at Grays Harbor NWR, Washington

from refuge to refuge, absorbing the sense of interdependence that binds our wildlands together. Birds may visit 10 refuges on their migration along the Pacific Flyway, and a lack of food or shelter in any one will increase the numbers in the next. Refuge staff know how to bulldoze new marshes and plant trees and set out nesting boxes that replace the natural tree cavities on trees long since felled by lumbermen. They protect the birds and animals that find refuge in our national wetlands. But the true future of our public lands lies in the hands of the public. Broad public consensus is the ultimate national policy maker. The continuing environmental battles over development versus open space, who gets the West's limited water, and whether our last great wilderness in the Arctic National Wildlife Refuge should be exploited for its oil will be determined by all of us.

Walk these refuges. Watch a hundred thousand snow geese whirl into the sky, and think about the future you want—for yourself, for your children, and for the birds.

Alaska Maritime NWR
Homer, Alaska

Common murres, Alaska Maritime NWR

A polar bear ambles along the ice-choked Chukchi Sea coast. Millions of seabirds swarm above the Pribolof Islands in the Bering Sea. Volcanoes steam along the Aleutian Islands. Whales surface and blow. Fishers cast their nets. About 1,300 miles southeast of the wandering polar bear, you'll find rhinoceros auklets building tunnel nests on wooded islands, bald eagles soaring overhead, and sea lions basking in the sun. A north-to-south glimpse of Alaska's coastline.

The most far-reaching refuge in the entire NWR system, Alaska Maritime NWR extends from the Seahorse Islands in the Arctic Ocean to Attu Island at the tip of the Aleutian Chain to Forrester Island in southeast Alaska. An extraordinary coastal triangle. This vast refuge includes more than 3,000 islands, islets, rocks, pinnacles, and headlands stretching along 4,800 miles of Alaska's coastline. Refuge habitats range from old-growth rain forests and glacial-mantled volcanoes, to windswept arctic tundra underlain with permafrost.

Alaska Maritime is so widespread that it is divided into five units. The 3.3-million-acre Aleutian Islands Unit is largest, with 200 islands, extending more than 1,000 miles Just east of the Aleutian Islands is the Alaska Peninsula Unit, including the Shumagin Islands and hundreds of smaller islands, islets, and sea stacks. The Gulf of Alaska Unit extends 800 miles from Kodiak Island to Forrester Island in southeastern Alaska. To the north, the Chukchi and Bering Sea units include many barrier islands, along with the Pribolof Islands, known for their world-famous seabird colonies and fur seal rookeries.

The keyword is *seabirds,* 40 million of them—30 species. The colorful horned and tufted puffins, auklets, and ancient murrelets, cormorants and red-legged kittiwakes, and the list goes on. Thousands upon thousands of noisy murres crowd onto narrow cliff ledges, resembling penguins from a distance. But, truth be known: There are no penguins in Alaska!

HISTORY

The 4.9-million-acre Alaska Maritime NWR was established in 1980 under the Alaska National Interest Lands Conservation Act to protect migratory birds, marine mammals, and their habitats. This act combined 11 coastal refuges into one, divided the refuge into its current five jurisdictional units, and added 1.9 million acres for good measure. If you were to place Alaska Maritime over the lower 48 states, it would stretch from Santa Barbara, California to Savannah, Georgia, an astonishing distance.

The history of Alaska Maritime is as varied as its regions and its culturally diverse Native peoples. The Inupiat Eskimos of the Chukchi Sea area have a strong connection to marine resources, such as their annual harvest of the bow-head whale. Yupik Eskimos and Aleut peoples of the Bering Sea and Aleutian Islands also depend on the marine environment; they have subsisted on marine mammals, fish, and birds for thousands of years. In the south-central and south-east regions, the rise of commercial and sport fishing and a wage-based economy have largely replaced the traditional subsistence way of life.

An important phase of World War II occurred on refuge lands. In 1942, Japanese forces took control of Attu and Kiska islands in the Aleutians. U.S. forces quickly established bases on Adak and Amchitka in response. From these bases, American forces launched a successful attack, regaining control of the occupied islands. Today, military installations are located on the islands of Adak, Shemya, and Attu, and security clearance is needed to visit these sites. Signs of the war are still evident, including dangerous unexploded ordnance.

GETTING THERE

The refuge headquarters and Visitor Center are located in Homer (451 Sterling Hwy., Suite 2), on the Kenai Peninsula. Situated on beautiful Kachemak Bay with stunning glaciated peaks rising in the distance, Homer lies at the end of Sterling Hwy., about 225 mi. south of Anchorage. To reach Homer, plan on a four-hour drive, or a one-hour regularly scheduled flight from Anchorage.

All refuge units are managed through the Homer office with the exception of Unimak Island, which is administered by the neighboring Izembek NWR. A sub-headquarters is maintained at Adak for the Aleutian Islands Unit. Since most of the refuge is very remote, access is difficult and expensive. Some islands are restricted from public use. Potential visitors should contact the refuge for specific information about particular sites.

To see world-class bird colonies and the rich diversity of other marine life, there are many regularly scheduled sight-seeing boats out of Seward, Sitka, and Homer. Charter boat trips can be arranged out of other coastal communities such as Kodiak, Nome, Unalaska, or Sand Point. Guided land tours of the remote Pribolof Islands seabird colonies are also available.

Homer and Seward are the only two communities accessible by road, but all refuge communities have scheduled air service. State ferries serve Sitka, Seward, Homer, Kodiak, and Unalaska.

■ **SEASON:** Open year-round.

■ **HOURS:** Visitor Center in Homer open daily, 9 a.m.–6 p.m., mid-April–early Oct. Guided beach walks, interpretive programs, and diverse information available. Administrative offices open 8 a.m.–4:30 p.m., Mon.–Fri. The Aleutian Island Visitor Center on Adak is open 8 a.m.–4 p.m., Mon.–Fri.

■ **FEES:** None.

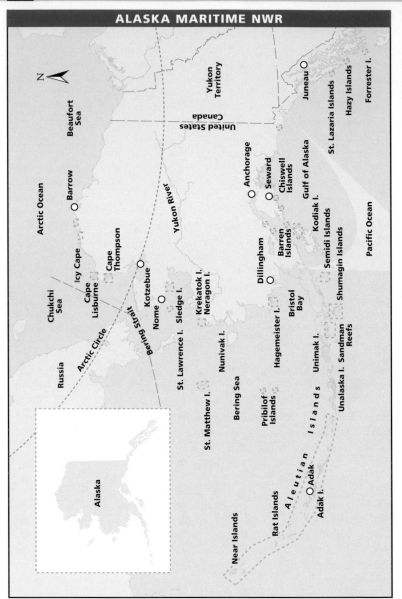

ALASKA MARITIME NWR

■ **ADDRESSES:** Alaska Maritime NWR, 2355 Kachemak Bay Dr., Suite 101, Homer, AK 99603; Aleutian Islands Unit, Alaska Maritime NWR, Box 5251, Adak, AK 99546; Unimak Island Unit, Alaska Maritime NWR, P.O. Box 127, Cold Bay, AK 99571

■ **TELEPHONE:** Alaska Maritime NWR headquarters, Homer: 907/235-6546; Visitor Center, Homer: 907/235-6961; Aleutian Islands Unit on Adak: 907/592-2406; Unimak Island Unit at Cold Bay: 907/532-2445

TOURING ALASKA MARITIME

■ **Gulf of Alaska Unit** There are a number of seabird colonies and marine mammal rookeries in the refuge that you can see via charter boat from Seward, Homer, and Sitka. Outstanding sight-seeing, birdwatching, and photographic opportunities abound. All three communities, as "basecamps," offer lodging and campgrounds.

The Chiswell Islands are 35 miles from Seward and receive the highest visitor use: More than 25,000 people on charter boats, cruise ships, and state ferries visit this popular bird colony and the adjacent Kenai Fjords National Park. Roughly 60 percent of all seabirds along the south side of the Kenai Peninsula nest on these dozen small islands.

Look for large concentrations of fork-tailed storm-petrels, small blackbird sized birds that hover and dive onto the ocean surface in search of small fish and other prey. Watch for rhinoceros auklets tunneling into their burrows. These long-billed birds have a short, pale upright horn at the base of their yellowish-orange beak. In addition to the petrels and auklets, colorful tufted puffins, murres, kittiwakes and cormorants nest on the cliffs and ledges in abundance. Chiswell Island also has a substantial sea lion rookery. This cluster of islands is one of the few places in the refuge where abundant marine birds and mammals can be seen without great cost.

Tufted puffins, Alaska Maritime NWR

Roughly 55 miles from Homer, visitors can see the seven Barren Islands, beyond the tip of the Kenai Peninsula, with the largest aggregation of nesting seabirds in the northern Gulf of Alaska. About one-half million seabirds, representing 18 species, nest on the cliffs, ledges, or in crevices of these rugged islands. More than half of the area's birds use East Amatuli Island. Commonly sighted seabirds here include fork-tailed storm-petrels, tufted puffins, murres, and kittiwakes. The second-largest sea lion rookery in the region is located on Sugarloaf Island, in this group.

In the southeastern part of the Gulf of Alaska Unit, you can visit 65-acre St. Lazaria Island, 15 miles from Sitka. Charter boats and cruise ships come out to view this productive island where one-half million seabirds nest. Here, you might see Leach's storm-petrels, rhinoceros auklets, and ancient murrelets, birds that lay their eggs in crevices or burrows. Defying any fear of heights, common and thick-billed murres nest on precipitous cliff ledges.

The largest seabird colony in southeast Alaska is located on the more remote Forrester Island where more than a million seabirds breed. Large concentrations of rhinoceros auklets, storm-petrels, and five species of nocturnal seabirds use this southernmost island.

Arctic fox, Alaska Maritime NWR

On the water at least seven species of whales might be seen near refuge lands: beluga, humpback, minke, fin, gray, killer, and pilot. During the summer, humpbacks are the most commonly seen. The only large terrestrial mammals on refuge lands are occasional brown or black bears and Sitka black-tailed deer. Smaller mammals that inhabit some islands include arctic fox and mink.

■ **Alaska Peninsula Unit** More than 700 islands, islets, and rocks on the south side of the Alaska Peninsula make up the Alaska Peninsula Unit. While many of these islands are tiny, such as the Semidi Islands and Sandman Reefs, they support some of the highest densities of nesting seabirds in the world. Suklik Island in the Semidis chain is home to 250,000 nesting horned puffins, perhaps the largest colony for this species anywhere.

While wildlife observation use has increased in this region, most visitors primarily hunt and sport fish on the Alaska Peninsula, and there are no game species on the refuge islands. Adventure cruise ships sometimes visit islands such as the Shumagins, and occasionally sea kayakers or backpackers explore the islands. State ferries travel the length of the Alaska Peninsula with stops at Chignik Bay and Sand Point.

■ **Aleutian Islands Unit** Bridging two continents, this thousand-mile string of islands offers vital habitat for more than 250 species of birds—a staggering 10 million seabirds alone—and marine mammals such as the once-endangered sea otter, endangered Steller's sea lions, harbor seals, and the northern fur seal. There are more salmon-spawning streams in the Aleutians, some 360 waterways, than on any other refuge in the United States.

These islands offer opportunities to see birds seldom found anywhere else in North America. Whooper swans, tufted ducks, Siberian rubythroats, wood sandpipers, Far Eastern curlews, and common black-headed gulls are a few of the *Asiatic* visitors. In addition to these Far East birds, the Aleutians have spectacular seabird colonies, such as Kiska Island, with the largest-known colony of crested and least auklets in the world. Whiskered auklets and red-legged kittiwakes are two other seabirds that nest only on the Aleutian and Pribolof islands.

While the weather here can be forbidding and unpredictable, the landscape is strikingly beautiful. Cushioned by flower-specked tundra, 57 volcanoes rise up along the chain, and many are active. Like the Hawaiian Islands, the Aleutians are the peaks of an underwater mountain range. The flora is rich and unique. You can see plants from both Asia and North America. Abundant wildflowers include chocolate lilies, delicate bell-shaped flowers whose bulbs were once harvested, dried, and pounded into flour by some Native groups. While the blossoms have an unpleasant scent, they are truly as chocolate in color as a candy bar. You can also see several species of orchid, monkshood, lupine, buttercup, and iris. To spot wild monkshood, look in the thickets and meadows for blue flowers with an upper hood (sepal) over a lower portion, about 1 inch wide.

Because of the remoteness of these places, the rough seas and winds, the rocky shorelines, and the expense of getting there, it is difficult to visit many of the (mostly uninhabited) islands. Some have restricted access to protect wildlife. Birdwatching groups visit Attu every spring, and the occasional adventure cruise ship comes to the area. Some sight-seeing occurs on the state ferry serving Unalaska from Seward once a month from May to October. A few adventurous people have been known to visit the Aleutians by sailboat, yacht, or sea kayak. Still, by and large, the area receives very few outside visitors.

■ **Bering Sea Unit** The famous Pribolof Islands, sometimes referred to as the "Galapagos Islands of the North Pacific," are part of the Bering Sea Unit, which also includes several islands and headlands on Norton Sound, St. Matthew Island, and Hagemcister Island. About 1,000 people visit the Pribolofs each year, serious birders from all over the world. Guided tours of refuge bird cliffs are available on both St. Paul and St. George islands. Lodging and food are also available.

On the Pribolofs, more than 2,500,000 seabirds nest, including the largest red-legged kittiwake colony in the world and Alaska's largest murre colony. Ten other species of seabirds are found on the islands in high concentrations, such as St. George's colony of parakeet auklets. You can also get a glimpse of a number of Asiatic migrant birds frequenting the area. Some 20 shorebird species and many of the more than 50 passerine migrants here are of Asiatic origin.

The largest northern fur seal rookery in the world can be seen here. You might also spot two unique small mammals.

Parakeet auklets, Alaska Maritime NWR

The Pribolof shrew is found only on St. Paul, and the St. George lemming can be spotted on both islands. Arctic foxes and introduced reindeer can also be observed.

■ **Chukchi Sea Unit** These northernmost refuge lands include many barrier islands, the high escarpments of the Lisburne Peninsula, and a number of islands in Kotzebue Sound. The seabird colonies at Cape Thompson and Cape Lisburne are known for their high concentrations of nesting murres, kittiwakes, and horned puffins. Unlike other seabird nesting sites in the refuge, here you will find a much greater diversity of land mammals in the surrounding area. You might see caribou from the Western Arctic herd, polar and grizzly bears, muskoxen and Dall sheep, wolverine and arctic fox. Several hundred walrus may haul out at Cape Lisburne in late summer when the sea ice has receded farther north.

However, public use in this region is limited due to inaccessibility and isolation. The closest large communities are more than 100 miles to the south in Kotzebue, or nearly 300 miles to the northeast in Barrow. Air charters and guided trips are available; still, very few people visit these refuge lands.

ACTIVITIES

■ **HIKES AND WALKS:** There are no established hiking trails in the refuge with the exception of a short 1-mile developed trail in Homer that extends from the beach to the uplands. The trail begins within a few blocks of the Visitor Center.

Hiking on many of the islands in Alaska Maritime refuge is difficult because of thick, dense vegetation. On Unimak Island there are a number of game trails to follow, but proceed with caution: You are in bear country.

■ **SEASONAL EVENTS:** May (mid-month): Shorebird Festival, held in conjunction with International Migratory Bird Day. Activities in Homer include bird walks, shorebird viewing, workshops, educational exhibits, and other local events. October: National Wildlife Refuge Week

■ **PUBLICATIONS:** Brochures and bird checklists available through the Visitor Center bookstore in Homer. *Islands of the Seals: The Pribolofs,* vol. 9, no. 3, by Alaska Geographic Society (Anchorage, 1982). *The Aleutian Islands,* vol. 22, no. 4, by Alaska Geographic Society (Anchorage, 1995). *Where the Sea Breaks Its Back: The Epic Story of Early Naturalist Georg Steller and the Russian Exploration of Alaska* by Corey Ford (Alaska Northwest Books, Anchorage, 1992).

HUNTING AND FISHING Given the size and diversity of this refuge, hunting and fishing opportunities vary considerably. Many of the waters adjacent to refuge islands offer good saltwater fishing for species such as **halibut** and **salmon**. There are limited opportunities for hunting of **waterfowl** and **big-game mammals** due to access and cost. **Caribou** hunting, for example, is allowed on Adak Island, but special permits are needed. Contact the USFWS Adak field office for current information (907/592-2406).

Alaska Peninsula and Becharof NWRs

Southern Alaska

Mt. Peulik volcano on the Becharof refuge

The haunting call of a red-throated loon echoes across the lake as you follow a fresh set of brown bear tracks along the shore. Suddenly, you hear a strange bubbling: gas rocks. Beneath Becharof Lake, carbon dioxide gases seep through fractured rocks, rising to the surface. Behind you, a majestic volcano rises abruptly more than 4,800 feet. The Yupik Eskimos call the mountain Peulik, or "one with smoke."

The Alaska Peninsula and Becharof refuges offer memorable scenery and a rich diversity of wildlife and topography: alpine tundra, huge lakes, salmon-packed rivers, fog-shrouded beaches, and rocky sea cliffs crowded with seabirds. Brown bears, caribou, moose, and wolves roam a pristine wilderness that has changed very little over the millennia.

HISTORY

Alaska Peninsula and Becharof refuges were established under the 1980 Alaska National Interest Lands Conservation Act to protect the region's diverse habitats and rich array of wildlife. Together these refuges encompass about 5.5 million acres. Approximately one-third (400,000 acres) of Becharof refuge is designated wilderness. Nearly 24,000 visitors come here each year, including local residents.

GETTING THERE

These refuge lands are accessible only by small aircraft, boat, or backcountry hiking. There are no roads or maintained trails. Becharof NWR is located approximately 295 air mi. southwest of Anchorage and 10 mi. south of King Salmon, a small community with lodging, recreational supplies, and guiding and air taxi services. There are daily flights from Anchorage to King Salmon, the main access point for both refuges. From King Salmon, visitors can charter an aircraft into remote locations of both refuges.

ALASKA PENINSULA AND BECHAROF NWRS

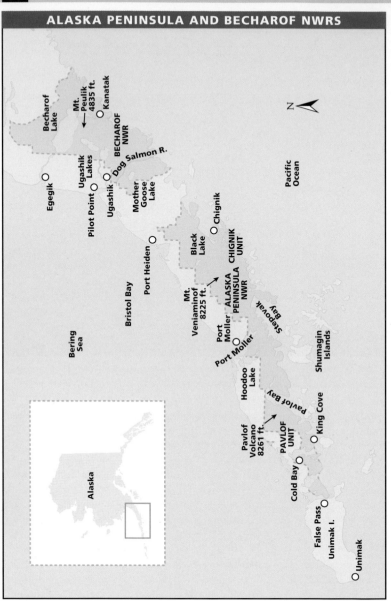

■ **SEASON:** Open year-round. May through Sept. is the most desirable time of the year for visitation and wildlife viewing.

■ **HOURS:** Open 24 hours; refuge headquarters: Mon.–Fri., 8 a.m.–4:30 p.m.

■ **FEES:** None.

■ **VISITOR CENTER:** The King Salmon Visitor Center offers a trip-planning desk, exhibits explaining natural and cultural resources, wildlife films, and a bookstore, making this the best place to begin your visit to the Alaska Peninsula. Visitor Center (at King Salmon Airport): open daily, 8 a.m.–5 p.m., May–Sept., and Mon.–Sat., during the rest of the year.

■ **ADDRESS:** King Salmon Visitor Center, P.O. Box 298, King Salmon, AK 99613.

Alaska Peninsula/Becharof NWR, Headquarters, P.O. Box 277, King Salmon, AK 99613

■ **TELEPHONE:** King Salmon Visitor Center: Voice, 907/246-4250; Fax, 907/246-8550; Headquarters: Voice, 907/246-3339; Fax, 907/246-6696

TOURING ALASKA PENINSULA/BECHAROF

Many parcels of land within the boundaries of the refuges belong to Native American corporations and private individuals. Some, but not all, owners have marked their property boundaries. Most cabin sites are private property. Visitors should always get a landowner's permission to visit. When planning a trip, consult the refuge manager about private lands.

■ **BY FOOT:** There are no established trails. Good opportunities exist for rugged cross-country hiking in the refuges, particularly in well-drained upland areas. Views of the dramatic scenery are far-reaching because of the broad, windswept tundra, large lakes, and open sea.

■ **BY CANOE, KAYAK, OR RAFT:** The refuges are open to boating. It is possible to float some of the rivers, although remote locations and related travel expenses can make this difficult. There are, however, two world-class rivers that are popular for floating near the refuge. Aniakchak River, located in Aniakchak National Preserve, and the Alagnak River in Katmai National Park, are wild rivers that offer excellent float trips.

WHAT TO SEE

■ **LANDSCAPE AND CLIMATE** The Alaska Peninsula and Becharof NWRs share similar characteristics. Both are fringed by the turbulent Pacific Ocean, with its rugged sea cliffs, misty fjords, and long beaches. Huge, pristine lakes and their tributaries offer superior habitat for fish, bears, and migratory birds. Becharof Lake is the second largest lake in Alaska and covers a quarter of Becharof refuge. Ugashik Lakes in the Alaska Peninsula NWR are well known for their healthy populations of salmon, grayling, and brown bears.

Volcanic activity along this Pacific "Ring of Fire," coupled with glacial activity, has shaped and reshaped the landscape. Fourteen major volcanoes, of which four on the refuges are active, rise up dramatically along the peninsula.

Mt. Veniaminof (8,225 feet) is a huge smoldering volcano and the most

Red-throated loon

Lapland longspur at nest

prominent mountain on the Alaska Peninsula refuge. This massive volcano has a base almost 30 miles wide, greater than any active volcano on record. The summit crater is more than 20 miles in circumference and has a 25-square-mile glacier. This is the most extensive crater-glacier in North America. Named for a Russian Orthodox priest, Mt. Veniaminof was designated as a National Natural Landmark in 1970.

The Ukinrek Maars (craters near the south shore of Becharof Lake near Mt. Peulik) formed as a result of a violent volcanic eruption in 1977. The largest maar is about the same diameter as three football fields (900 feet), and roughly 200 feet deep. In recent years groundwater has filled the huge depression to form a beautiful maar lake. Visitors should use extreme caution when approaching the maars because the ground surface is very fragile, and a fall would be life threatening because of the vertical drop.

Be prepared for strong winds, rain, and frequent cloud cover. Rainfall varies dramatically in the refuges. Western sections receive less than 20 inches of rain annually, while the eastern Pacific side may be saturated with as much as 160 inches. July is the warmest month, with an average daily temperature of 54 degrees. January and February temperatures drop to a chilly 14 degrees on an average day.

■ **PLANT LIFE** A variety of plant life can be discovered along the rolling tundra hills, alpine ridges, and wetlands that characterize the refuges. With the exception of willows and alder thickets and one scenic stand of cottonwoods in the Mother Goose Lake area, refuge lands are largely treeless. Grasses and sedges dominate the landscape. Flowering plants, such as Labrador tea and lousewort, are interspersed with lichens, mosses, crowberry, or blueberry bushes.

■ **ANIMAL LIFE**
Birds A birder's paradise, these two refuges lay claim to more than 250 species of birds. Within the wilderness area of Becharof NWR, the steep, rugged cliffs near Puale Bay offer excellent habitat for large concentrations of seabirds. Thousands of cormorants, kittiwakes, murres, and puffins nest here. The Pacific coastline is also

home to about 300 nesting pairs of bald eagles. A few peregrine falcons also nest on the cliffs and offshore islands of the peninsula.

On many lakes throughout the refuges, you are likely to see resident common and red-throated loons. Other breeding waterbirds and shorebirds to look for include tundra swans, red-necked grebes, least sandpipers, black turnstones, common snipe, greater yellowlegs, short-billed dowitchers, and wandering tattlers. Rock sandpipers and black oystercatchers are year-round coastal residents.

Where there is shrub habitat, look for yellow and Wilson's warblers and common redpolls. Listen for the three-note melody of the golden-crowned sparrow on the tundra. The most abundant passerine is the Lapland longspur. In June you can watch the males claim their breeding territories as they hover briefly, then glide gracefully to the tundra singing a beautiful melody.

In the fall watch for hundreds of thousands of geese as they migrate through or near the refuges. Tundra swans, white-fronted geese, Canada geese, and sandhill cranes stage in large numbers along the Bristol Bay side of the refuges.

Land mammals Brown bears are abundant along the Alaska Peninsula. Some of the highest concentrations of bears in North America occur in the southern Chignik unit of Alaska Peninsula NWR. An average of one bear every 2 square miles inhabits the Black Lake area. Island Arm on Becharof Lake is another extremely important area for brown bears. As many as 200 to 300 bears congregate on streams around Becharof Lake to feed on salmon during the spawning season. Occasionally bears are known to den on islands in Becharof Lake, a rare phenomenon, as bears usually den at higher elevations.

The Alaska Peninsula caribou herd is one of Alaska's major herds. The northern portion of this migratory herd travels more than 150 miles each spring from wintering grounds near King Salmon to calving grounds south of Port Heiden.

Other land mammals ranging throughout the refuges include wolverine, river otter, beaver, red fox, hare, arctic ground squirrel, hoary marmot, weasel, and porcupine. Wolves and moose are also present.

Marine mammals Coastal areas provide important habitat for several marine mammal species. Harbor seals, Steller sea lions, and sea otters can be spotted along the coast. Many haul out on offshore islands beyond refuge boundaries. Gray and killer whales migrate through the area, while beluga whales often swim up refuge rivers to feed on salmon in the spring.

Sea otter

Fish All five common species of Pacific salmon (sockeye, coho, king, pink, chum) inhabit the major rivers and lakes of the refuges during a portion of their life cycles. Becharof Lake is home to the second largest run of sockeye salmon in the world. Four to six million wild salmon are produced annually from the lake and its tributary rivers and streams. The Ugashik Lakes support large concentrations of salmon, lake trout, and Arctic grayling. Numerous other lakes, rivers, and creeks support healthy populations of salmon, Dolly Varden char, northern pike, and Arctic grayling.

ACTIVITIES

■ **CAMPING:** Primitive camping is allowed throughout both refuges. There are no designated campgrounds within refuge boundaries, but there are two privately owned campgrounds, both in King Salmon. Brooks Camp in the neighboring Katmai National Park also has a limited number of campsites (reservations required).

Be prepared for wet, foggy, and windy weather and transportation delays. Campers are advised to have tents that can withstand winds of 50 to 75 mph and heavy rains.

■ **WILDLIFE OBSERVATION:** The Alaska Peninsula and Becharof refuges offer outstanding opportunities to see some of the nearly 275 species of resident and migratory wildlife. Brown bears can be observed throughout the region, but precautions should be taken to avoid close encounters. (See sidebar in Kodiak NWR) During the summer months you may see caribou, moose, wolves, many small mammals, and a variety of breeding birds. The birding is outstanding here.

HUNTING AND FISHING Hunting and fishing are the primary user activities for both refuges. **Caribou** can be hunted Aug. through Oct., and **moose** can be hunted in Sept. Hunting for **brown bears** is permitted in spring on even years and in fall on odd years.

Fishing opportunities are outstanding for **king and silver salmon, arctic char, lake trout, northern pike,** and **grayling.** Catch-and-release fishing is recommended for most lakes, streams, and rivers.

Note that local Native peoples commonly practice subsistence hunting and/or fishing on this refuge.

■ **PHOTOGRAPHY:** The Alaska Peninsula has spectacular scenery and opportunities for photographing many wildlife species. Avoid sensitive nesting areas and approach wildlife with caution. Keep a respectful distance from animals with young, to avoid dangerous conflicts.

■ **HIKES AND WALKS:** For an extended backpacking trip, the Gertrude Lake Route in the wilderness area of Becharof NWR is a fairly easy 27-mile hike that can be walked comfortably in five days (by people in good physical condition with proper equipment). The route involves three major, but not difficult, river crossings, and gradual elevation changes that follow Gertrude and Bible creeks. The hike offers beautiful vistas of the volcanic mountains and good opportunities for observing wildlife.

There are a number of areas in both refuges suitable for cross-country hiking. Contact the King Salmon Visitor Center or refuge headquarters for information and maps.

■ **SEASONAL EVENTS:** May: International Migratory Bird Day/Refuge Open House; October: National Wildlife Refuge Week

■ **PUBLICATIONS:** Free brochures, pamphlets, and information sheets available, including "Bear Facts" pamphlet with safety tips, bird checklist, and community maps. *Katmai National Park/Becharof National Wildlife Refuge* by Jean Bodeau (Alaska Natural History Association, Anchorage, 1996) *The Alaska Peninsula*, vol. 21, no. 1, by Alaska Geographic Society (Anchorage, 1994).

Arctic NWR
Northeastern Alaska

Tundra lowlands against Brooks Range foothills, Arctic NWR

Awakening you is a steady sound of clicking hooves. You step outside your tent to witness tens of thousands of caribou walk in procession across a vast sweep of flower-specked tundra. Grunts, bellows, and bleats fill the air, creating a caribou symphony. It is midnight on the coastal plain of Arctic NWR, yet the sun rolls along the northern horizon, hovering above the ice-mantled Arctic Ocean. Under a salmon sky, you are standing near the top of the world in one of the greatest wilderness areas left on the planet.

Arctic refuge is the largest and most northerly refuge in the NWR system. South Carolina could almost fit inside its borders. Kaktovik, a small Inupiat Eskimo village, fringes the Beaufort Sea on the northern border. Arctic Village, an Athabascan Gwich'in Indian community, hugs the shore of the Chandalar River on the southern boundary. Between these two settlements are hundreds of square miles of spectacular wilderness, the majestic Brooks Range, and countless rivers, streams, and lakes.

But a visitor won't find any man-made trails here, only the ancient paths of the caribou. Of the nearly 20 million acres of refuge lands, 8 million are designated wilderness, more than on any other refuge. Here, you meet nature on its own terms. Hiking for days in Arctic refuge without seeing a trace of any other human is entirely possible, despite the refuge's annual visitation of around 10,000 people.

HISTORY

In the early 1950s, several visionary conservationists launched a campaign to provide pernament protection for the northeast corner of Alaska. Leaders such as George Collins, Lowell Sumner, and Olaus and Margaret Murie worked together to inform Americans about the unique features of the Arctic. In 1960, after a decade of dedicated rassroots efforts, the 9-million-acre Arctic National Wildlife Range was established by executive order of the president.

SAFE HIKING When trekking the Arctic NWR wilderness, avoid brushy areas where visibility is poor and you might surprise a bear. If you do walk through such areas, make noise so that bears will hear you. Proper planning and good equipment will make your trip more enjoyable. Topographic maps, a compass, and emergency supplies are essential. You must be prepared to handle any situation completely on your own. Guides are recommended for those who are not experienced backcountry travelers.

Twenty years later, Congress changed the name from *range* to *refuge* and more than doubled its size under the 1980 Alaska National Interest Lands Conservation Act (ANILCA). Arctic refuge is the only protected area in America that encompasses a full spectrum of arctic and subarctic ecosystems. ANILCA also designated three National Wild and Scenic Rivers within the refuge: the Ivishak, Sheenjek, and Wind.

GETTING THERE

Hard as it is for visitors from the lower 48 to imagine, the refuge is roadless. The main access is by air. Most visitors fly regularly scheduled flights from Fairbanks to Fort Yukon, Kaktovik, Arctic Village, or Deadhorse. From these points, several charter operators can fly visitors to remote river gravel bars or tundra landing sites. Weather can delay flights, so it's important to take along extra food.

It is possible to drive approximately 300 mi. north of Fairbanks along the Dalton Hwy. and then hike into Arctic refuge along rivers such as the Ivishak and Ribdon near the western boundary. However, travel along this gravel road can be rough on vehicles, and there are few facilities en route.

■ **SEASON:** The refuge is open year-round, although most people visit the area during the summer months. Snow blankets the ground from Sept. through May.

■ **HOURS:** Open 24 hrs. Arctic NWR maintains a well-staffed office in Fairbanks at the federal building. Office hours: Mon.–Fri., 8 a.m.–4:30 p.m.

■ **FEES:** None.

■ **ADDRESS:** Arctic National Wildlife Refuge, 101 12th Ave., Box 20, Fairbanks, AK 99701

■ **TELEPHONE:** 907/456-0250

TOURING ARCTIC

■ **BY FOOT:** A vast wilderness awaits the adventurer. There are numerous river valleys and countless peaks to explore or climb. Arctic refuge contains the highest glaciated peaks in Brooks Range, and glacier climbing is also possible. Following rivers or existing animal trails is often easier than taking shortcuts across a marshy stretch of tundra. In the lowlands, much of the terrain is covered with cotton-grass tussocks. These 1-to-3-feet-high spongy bumps make walking difficult. Some of the worst mosquito conditions can be found in marshy, tussock-studded areas. No doubt, stick to the riverbanks and alpine tundra ridges, and you'll enjoy the hiking more.

■ **BY KAYAK OR RAFT:** Rafts are recommended because they can be transported easily by aircraft. Collapsible kayaks are another option. Water levels are generally adequate on major rivers from mid-June to mid-August. By late-July the sea ice is usually open enough to allow travel through coastal lagoons on the Arctic Ocean shore. There are 18 major rivers in the refuge, with each drainage offer-

ARCTIC NWR

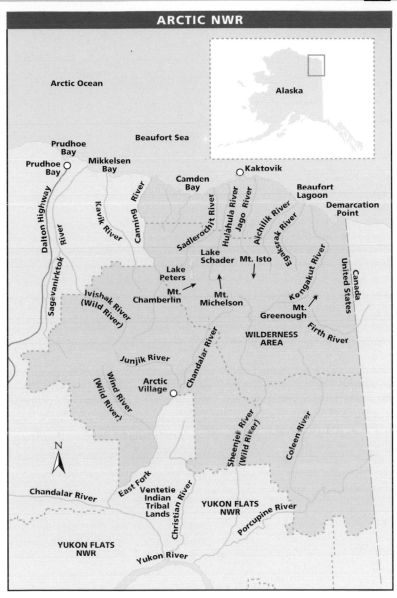

ing outstanding wilderness and wildlife opportunities. Consult refuge staff to learn more about planning an expedition. There are a number of commercial guides who lead float trips in the refuge. Ask the refuge office for a current list.

WHAT TO SEE

■ **LANDSCAPE AND CLIMATE** Arctic refuge encompasses a wide range of landscapes and wildlife habitats. It contains the greatest variety of plant and animal life of any conservation area in the circumpolar north. The coastal plain, Brooks Range, and boreal forest are three zones that each contain distinct arctic and subarctic habitats.

The coastal plain is part of Alaska's North Slope, bordered by the Arctic Ocean on the north, and Brooks Range to the south. This 10-to-40-mile-wide treeless plain of tundra is characterized by dwarfed plants and shrubs, far-reaching wetlands, dry upland tundra areas, and numerous stream and river corridors. Fringing the shoreline are a number of barrier islands and productive lagoons.

Rising dramatically above the coastal plain is Brooks Range. These rugged mountains, foothills, and alpine tundra ridges extend more than 200 miles, running west to east across the refuge; the range's highest peaks (topping 9,000 feet) and its only active glaciers are within the refuge.

On the south slopes of Brooks Range, evergreen trees and a patchwork of lakes and rivers begin to appear. Spruce, poplar, and willow trees shelter the land.

The weather varies considerably depending on your location in this huge refuge. Summer temperatures average in the 30s along the foggy Arctic coast, and winds can be fierce. Moving inland, temperatures can rise dramatically, often into the 70s and occasionally the 80s. Sunscreen is a necessity because of lack of shade. The climate south of Brooks Range is more typical of Alaska's interior, with higher rainfall, warmer temperatures, and lighter winds.

■ PLANT LIFE

Tundra Beneath much of the refuge, the ground is permanently frozen—1,000 feet thick or more in some areas. During the summer the top 2-foot active layer of ground thaws. This fragile blanket of peat and densely matted plants, known as tundra, protects the underlying layer of impenetrable permafrost. If this mossy blanket is disturbed, it is like an open wound. The unnatural melting of the permafrost layer causes continued thawing and slumping of the earth, which creates permanent scars on the land.

Coastal plain wildflowers and pack ice, Arctic NWR

Tundra plants have adapted to this environment by developing shallow root systems and short reproductive cycles. Mosses, cotton grass, sedges, dwarfed willows, blueberry bushes, and other shrubs dominate the tundra, providing an important food source for many arctic animals, such as caribou, moose, musk ox and grizzly bears. Numerous species of wildflowers thrive here on the arctic and alpine tundra. Lavender lupine, white dryas, and pink moss campion explode with color in June and July.

Forest The boreal forest on the south side of Brooks Range is largely characterized by black spruce in the lowlands and by white spruce in more well-drained areas. Willows shrubs, poplars, and birch skirt the many rivers and lakes, creating a spectacular autumn tapestry in August and September. The boreal forest provides important habitat for many birds, furbearers, and other mammals. Residents of Arctic Village and other neighboring communities rely on spruce wood as their major winter fuel source. Spruce is also used for constructing cabins and for building toboggans.

■ ANIMAL LIFE

Birds The Arctic refuge is the perfect place to see and admire birds that make some of the longest migrations in the world. The American golden plover winters on the pampas of Argentina and travels roughly 10,000 miles to nest on the tundra. Several hundred tundra swans, the largest breeders in the refuge, migrate from the Carolinas and Chesapeake Bay. They build large nests by tundra lakes and ponds, often near river deltas along the coastal plain. Hundreds of thousands of snow geese visit the refuge while en route to their wintering grounds in California's Central Valley and other points in the western United States. The geese use the coastal plain of the refuge as a vital rest stop, foraging on cotton grass.

These are examples of some of the 180 species of birds, 134 of which are breeders, that have been identified in the refuge. In addition to many shorebirds, ducks, and waterfowl, there are numerous songbirds to be found here. Some that you might see or hear include Lapland longspurs, common and hoary redpolls, snow buntings, Savannah sparrows, and even the occasional American robin. Birds of prey such as golden eagles, rough-legged hawks, and peregrine falcons also visit the refuge. Few birds, however, are year-round residents. Among those adapted to the arctic winter are willow and rock ptarmigan, ravens, gray jays, pine grosbeaks, black-capped chickadees, and American dippers.

Mammals Arctic refuge is the only conservation area in America where you may see all three species of Alaska's bears: polar, grizzly, and black. Magnificent polar bears amble along the coastline, and are sometimes spotted when they come into shore to scavenge on whale carcasses that Inupiat people have hunted. While they spend most of their lives offshore, the coastal plain of the refuge has the highest density of land-denning polar bears in America. Pregnant female bears dig snow dens in November and give birth to one or two cubs in January. Grizzly bears roam throughout the refuge, but black bears are found only in the more southern areas of the boreal forest.

The refuge is also home to 31 other species of land mammals. The Central Arctic and Porcupine caribou herds both spend part of their year in the refuge. The Porcupine herd, one of the larger migratory herds, visits the coastal plain

Polar bear

CARIBOU IN THE ARCTIC NWR Thousands upon thousands of caribou grace Alaska's vast landscape. They journey across sweeping plains of tundra, over glacial-mantled mountains, and along braided rivers reaching the sea. More caribou than people live in Alaska. About a million of these majestic animals can be found in more than 30 herds.

The Porcupine caribou herd is one of the largest migratory herds in North America. Numbering as high as 180,000, this herd is shared by Canada and the United States. Studies show that caribou in this herd are among those traveling farther than any other terrestrial mammals, about 3,000 miles annually. During the winter months, they live in scattered groups in the Yukon and Northwest Territories, and in Alaska. In March or April the herd begins a dramatic northern procession to its calving grounds on the coastal plain of Arctic NWR, following trails thousands of years old.

The birthing grounds of the Porcupine caribou herd, and many other species, have been threatened with proposed oil development for the past two decades. Pending federal legislation would protect this extraordinary area within Arctic NWR as wilderness, making it off-limits to any industrial development.

each summer, giving birth to as many as 50,000 calves in some years. Another herbivore living on the coastal plain year-round is the muskox. Inupiat people call the muskox *omingmak,* or "the bearded one." More than 300 of these shaggy, ancient creatures live year-round on the coastal plain. The musk-ox, caribou, and Dall sheep are the only arctic ungulates that survived the most recent Ice Age.

In the Brooks Range you are likely to see America's northernmost Dall sheep. These sure-footed animals live above the timberline on rugged ridges and valley slopes. In the mountain valleys you might encounter a number of different mammals such as moose, caribou, and gray wolf, as well as smaller animals like the porcupine, arctic fox, or arctic ground squirrel.

Farther south, a different array of mammals is associated with the boreal forest: marten and mink, lynx and snowshoe hare, beaver and muskrat.

Fish Arctic refuge is home for numerous species of freshwater, anadromous, and marine species. Arctic grayling, Arctic char, northern pike and lake trout are among the 14 species of freshwater fish. A dozen species of anadromous fish (those that swim upriver to spawn) spend part of their life cycles in refuge waters. The coastal lagoons provide nutrient-rich habitat for 17 species of marine fish such as Arctic cisco and cod.

ACTIVITIES

■ **CAMPING:** There are no designated campsites. The Arctic refuge offers a wilderness camping experience that is unsurpassed. Gravel bars make good campsites—they are durable, flat, and have fewer mosquitoes. The worst mosquito season usually occurs in late June through July. Avoid pitching a tent near a game trail where you might encounter bears, and store food away from sleeping areas in airtight containers. Trees grow slowly in the Arctic, and wood can be scarce in some areas. Gas or propane stoves are recommended for cooking.

■ **WILDLIFE OBSERVATION:** The Arctic refuge contains the greatest wildlife diversity of any protected area in the circumpolar north. Brooks Range and tree-

Caribou, Arctic NWR

less coastal plain offer wonderful opportunities for viewing wildlife. June is an ideal month for witnessing the gathering of the Porcupine caribou herd on the coastal plain and in the northern river valleys of Brooks Range. June and July are desirable months to see some of the many breeding birds that visit the refuge. On the coastal plain you might be lucky enough to see a small group of muskoxen grazing a north-flowing riverbank or bears and wolves following their prey.

You may get to see some animals at close range if you are patient and avoid making sudden movements or noises. A good rule of thumb: Let the animals come to you (with the exception of a bear or moose!). A second universal rule: Never feed any of the animals or leave food available in your camp.

■ **PHOTOGRAPHY:** The scenery here is breathtaking and the vistas far-reaching. Bring a zoom lens and light filters. Photography in the early morning or late evening light can make for a long day here, in the land of endless summer light. Approach wildlife quietly and with respect.

■ **HIKES AND WALKS:** The Arctic refuge offers an unlimited number of day hiking and backpacking opportunities.

■ **SEASONAL EVENTS:** October: National Wildlife Refuge Week

■ **PUBLICATIONS:** Brochures; bird, mammal, and fish checklists; and information sheets on species such as wolves and caribou. *Midnight Wilderness: Journeys in Alaska's Arctic National Wildlife Refuge*, by Debbie Miller (10th Anniversary Edition, Alaska Northwest Books, Anchorage, 2000); *Arctic National Wildlife Refuge*, vol.20, no. 37, by Alaska Geographic Society (Anchorage, 1993); *Two in the Far North*, by Margaret E. Murie (Alaska Northwest Books, Anchorage, 1997).

HUNTING AND FISHING Grizzly bear season is April, May, and Sept. **Caribou** and **Dall sheep** may be hunted Aug. and Sept., and **moose** can be hunted in Sept.

Fish such as **grayling, northern pike**, and **Dolly Varden** are in a number of the rivers. The refuge office has a list of licensed hunting and fishing guides. Subsistence hunting and/or fishing is commonly practiced by local Native peoples on this refuge.

Innoko NWR
McGrath, Alaska

Green-winged teals

An iridescent green head slips beneath the surface of a glassy lake. After a few moments of underwater foraging, the greater scaup reappears, beads of water glistening on its brightly colored feathers. Across the lake, a beaver carefully repairs its dam with freshly cut saplings. Along the marshy shore, deep indentations reveal the footsteps of a moose, which likely visited the lake to feed on aquatic plants.

A relatively flat land of lakes and ponds, wetlands and bogs, slow-moving rivers and sloughs, Innoko NWR is home to a wide range of wildlife. Located in west-central Alaska along the Yukon River, Innoko refuge is one of the NWR system's more remote conservation areas. Several Yukon River villages depend on Innoko's wildlife and plant resources to sustain their subsistence way of life.

HISTORY

Innoko NWR was established in 1980 by the Alaska National Interest Lands Conservation Act. Congress set aside 3.8 million acres to protect extensive wetlands that offer prime nesting and breeding habitat for at least a quarter-million waterfowl and other migratory birds. The area also features excellent moose and beaver habitat and approximately 1.2 million acres of designated wilderness.

In the early 1900s gold strikes in the refuge and adjacent lands created a boom of activity in what became known as the "Inland Empire." The gold-mining support communities of Dikeman and Dishkakat flourished on what are now refuge lands. Signs of these abandoned communities are still present.

A segment of the Iditarod National Historic Trail passes through the refuge as well as a small portion of the world-famous Iditarod Sled Dog Race.

About 2,500 people visit Innoko refuge each year, including local residents from nearby villages and hunters and anglers. For geographic reasons, the 750,000-acre Northern Unit of Innoko NWR is managed by the Koyukuk NWR.

For information regarding the Northern Unit, contact the refuge manager of Koyukuk NWR (P.O. Box 287, Galena, AK 99741; 907/656-1231).

GETTING THERE

Innoko NWR is located about 300 mi. northwest of Anchorage. Refuge headquarters for the Southern Unit is in McGrath, a community on the Kuskokwim River about 70 mi. east of the refuge's boundary.

Regularly scheduled flights are available to McGrath from Anchorage. Most visitors charter a floatplane from McGrath to access the refuge. There are no communities or facilities within the boundaries of the refuge, but limited accommodations are available in McGrath. This small town has four established bed-and-breakfasts and no campgrounds.

■ **SEASON:** The refuge is open year-round. The greatest visitor use is in Sept. during moose-hunting season. This is a land of extremes, where temperatures range from 85 degrees F. in summer to minus 60 in winter.

■ **HOURS:** Refuge open 24 hours. Visitor contact station in McGrath open Mon.–Fri., 8 a.m.–4:30 p.m.

■ **FEES:** None.

■ **ADDRESS:** Innoko NWR, P.O. Box 69, McGrath, AK 99627

■ **TELEPHONE:** 907/524-3251

WHAT TO SEE

■ **PLANT LIFE** About one-half of the refuge is covered with a mix of stunted black spruce, muskeg, wet meadows, or marsh. Plants associated with these poorly drained areas include sedges, horsetail ferns, lichens, and mosses. In very boggy areas you might spot the delicate sundew, an insectivorous plant. Willow and alder frame most of the rivers and streams, with leaves that create meandering paths of gold in the fall. White spruce, paper birch, and aspen cover well-drained hills and slopes.

Meadow vole

■ **ANIMAL LIFE**

Birds Innoko NWR is a haven for breeding and nesting ducks and other waterfowl, including large concentrations of white-fronted and Canada geese. The seasonal flooding of the Innoko and Iditarod rivers creates fertile habitat for invertebrates and aquatic plants. Such plant life along these river corridors offers a round-the-clock buffet for visiting birds. Green-winged teal, American wigeon, shoveler, pintail, scaup, and mallard are some of the more abundant duck species that you are likely to see here. But be prepared for lots of mosquitoes.

Mammals The drier parts of the wetlands provide good habitat for small mammals like the meadow, red-backed, and yellow-cheeked voles. Many birds of prey thrive on these rodents and other small mammals. You might see red-tailed or sharp-shinned hawks and owls like the great horned or the more elusive great gray. Bald eagles, peregrine falcons and goshawks are also present.

The Innoko River corridor offers prime habitat for moose. Seasonal flooding coupled with wildfires in the region help to promote the growth of willows, a major food source for moose. A healthy population of moose also means that large numbers of predatory black bears and wolves are present.

Numerous beaver lodges and food caches can be found on many of the rivers and streams and most lakes. Other furbearers include marten, lynx, red fox, river otter, and wolverine. A small herd of caribou uses certain areas of the refuge, particularly during light snow years when they are not restricted to the wind-blown slopes of nearby mountains to access food.

HUNTING AND FISHING Residents from five communities regularly hunt, fish, and gather berries for subsistence use. Nonlocal visitors also have the opportunity to hunt and fish. **Moose** can be hunted in Sept., and visitors enjoy **pike** fishing during the summer. Most hunters and anglers access the refuge by floatplane.

ACTIVITIES

■ **BOATING:** When flying in by floatplane, you are permitted to bring in a raft, canoe, or kayak. You can also use a motorized boat when coming in via the Yukon River.

■ **SEASONAL EVENTS:** October: National Wildlife Refuge Week

■ **PUBLICATIONS:** Literature for planning trips, bird checklist. *The Middle Yukon* (vol. 17, no. 3) by Alaska Geographic Society (Anchorage, 1990).

Izembek NWR
Cold Bay, Alaska

Ahgileen Pinnacles, Izembek NWR

Facing the Bering Sea in a relentless wind, you've reached an international cross-road for migratory birds. Beginning in late August, a quarter-million birds stop at Izembek refuge to fuel up for their journeys south. Izembek Lagoon contains one of the largest eelgrass beds in the world and hosts the world's entire population of black brant, along with thousands of Canada and emperor geese. While the geese feast upon the eelgrass, shorebirds probe the mudflats for invertebrates. At high tide the shorebirds gather in such huge concentrations that in flight they resemble smoke clouds.

Beyond the lagoon, smoking volcanoes rise to heights of 9,000 feet along with the stunning Ahgileen Pinnacles. Between the highlands and the lagoon lies a beautiful array of lakes, rivers, glacier-carved valleys, snowfields, and hot springs.

HISTORY

Historic village and cultural sites suggest that a large number of Native people inhabited these lands for thousands of years. When the Russians wintered near the area in 1827, they named Izembek Lagoon after Karl Izembek, the ship's surgeon. During World War II, Cold Bay served as an important military site, with as many as 20,000 troops based there.

Originally established as a wildlife range in 1960, Izembek NWR has long been recognized as a critically important area for migrating and wintering waterfowl. Izembek Lagoon, also known as Izembek State Game Refuge, was the first wetland site in America to receive global recognition by being designated as a Wetland of International Importance. Under the 1980 Alaska National Interest Lands Conservation Act, the range was reclassified as a refuge, and 300,000 of its acres were designated as wilderness. Today, the U.S. Fish & Wildlife Service administers the 2.9-million-acre Izembek NWR as a complex, including Unimak Island of the Alaska Maritime Refuge and the Pavlof/North Creek Units of Alaska

Peninsula Refuge. These areas receive roughly 4,000 visitors a year, including local residents.

GETTING THERE

Izembek NWR is located near the tip of the Alaska Peninsula, about 600 mi. southwest of Anchorage. The refuge office is in Cold Bay (0.5 mi. north of Cold Bay's airport), a small community accessible only by air or ferry. Regularly scheduled flights are available from Anchorage 6 days a week. The state ferry serves Cold Bay once a month from May through Oct. Some cruise ships also stop at Cold Bay.

■ **SEASON:** Open year-round.
■ **HOURS:** 24 hours.
■ **FEES:** None.
■ **ADDRESS:** Izembek National Wildlife Refuge, PO Box 127, Cold Bay, AK 99571
■ **TELEPHONE:** 907/532-2445

TOURING IZEMBEK

From Cold Bay there is limited vehicle access on approximately 40 miles of gravel and dirt (4WD) roads. A few rental cars are available. Charter aircraft or boats are required for access to other areas within the refuge.

WHAT TO SEE

■ **LANDSCAPE AND CLIMATE** The refuge is treeless and windswept. Ground-hugging plants are well adapted to frequent strong winds and a short growing season. Freshwater lakes and ponds glisten across the tundra while glaciated volcanoes form a spectacular backdrop. On a clear day you can see the 9,372-foot Shishaldin Volcano on Unimak Island. This heavily glaciated volcano recently erupted in 1999 and is one of many active volcanoes of the Aleutian Islands and the Alaska Peninsula. But don't count on getting a good look at the volcano: This region averages only 12 clear days per year.

Black brants, Izembek NWR.

■ **PLANT LIFE** Wildflowers, grasses, shrubs, and lichens predominate the dry tundra. Look for a great variety of berries. Salmon berries, blueberries, mountain cranberries, strawberries, and crowberries are plentiful on the refuge from mid-July through September.

■ **ANIMAL LIFE** Along streams you might see brown bears feeding on salmon. Hundreds of thousands of salmon (four species: red, silver, pink and chum) spend part of their lives in the freshwater lakes and streams. The salmon runs begin in June and continue into September.

Surrounded by the turbulent waters of the Bering Sea and the Pacific Ocean, the refuge provides habitat for seven species of marine mammals and many seabirds and shorebirds. Along the coast you can spot harbor seals, sea otters, sea lions, and the occasional walrus. Thousands of gray whales migrate along the coast in spring and fall. Killer whales may also be observed. Many seabirds, including storm-petrels, cormorants, puffins, oystercatchers and terns, nest on the rocks and islets near the shore.

ACTIVITIES

■ **CAMPING:** There are no campgrounds at Cold Bay. Backcountry camping is permitted. Be aware that you are in bear country. Keep a clean camp and store food properly away from tent.

■ **WILDLIFE OBSERVATION:** The best time to view birds and other resident wildlife is between late August and October. Be prepared for cool temperatures, high winds, rain, and fog. Waterproof footwear, gear, and layered clothing to combat the wind are essential.

The road system provides access to a portion of the refuge, including the shorelines of Izembek Lagoon and Cold Bay, plus Russell Creek and the foothills of the 6,000-foot Frosty Peak. These areas offer excellent wildlife viewing, hiking, photography, hunting, and fishing opportunities.

Much of the land embraced by the refuge complex is in private ownership. If you are planning a trip, be sure to contact the refuge manager regarding the status of these lands.

When visiting Izembek, you may discover unexploded ordnance from WWII. If you see something in the ground that looks suspicious, do not disturb it: It may be highly dangerous. Report any findings to refuge staff.

■ **HIKES AND WALKS:** There are no established hiking trails. Walking can be difficult because of the uneven terrain associated with tundra; the best opportunities are along the shorelines and in upland areas. You can also follow good bear trails along the streams, but be wary of bears and make noise to let them know of your presence. (See sidebar in Kodiak NWR.)

HUNTING AND FISHING
Sept. and Oct. bring many **waterfowl** hunters to the area. **Caribou** and **brown bear** may also be hunted in the fall.

Anglers enjoy good **salmon** fishing from July through Sept.

■ **SEASONAL EVENTS:** September: Izembek NWR participates in the Silver Salmon Derby held over Labor Day weekend; October: National Wildlife Refuge Week

■ **PUBLICATIONS:** Brochures, bird checklist. *The Alaska Peninsula* (vol. 21, no. 1) by the Alaska Geographic Society (Anchorage, 1994).

Kanuti NWR
Central Alaska

Northern pintails, female and male

In the heart of Alaska's interior is a vast wetland basin formed by the Kanuti and Koyukuk rivers. A striking patchwork of lakes, ponds, rivers, and forest, Kanuti NWR welcomes a rich diversity of wildlife. Each summer thousands of white-fronted and Canada geese, along with many other species of waterfowl, nest in this productive habitat. In the scenic Kanuti River canyon, you might see nesting peregrine falcons or rough-legged hawks. The Koyukuk River, the third-longest river in Alaska, meanders through the refuge on a path that eventually merges with the Yukon River. While floating this peaceful river in the midnight sun, your chances are good for seeing moose, bears, or wolves along its banks or red-throated loons and beavers in its waters.

HISTORY

Under the 1980 Alaska National Interest Lands Conservation Act, this 1.4-million-acre refuge was established primarily as a waterfowl breeding area. Slightly larger than the state of Delaware, Kanuti is a roadless area bounded by the foothills of Brooks Range to the north and Ray Mountains to the south. While there are no communities within the refuge, Athabascan Indians from nearby villages have used the resources within the refuge for their subsistence way of life for thousands of years. During the late 1800s gold mining was widespread in the area. Today, there are active gold placer mines upstream from the refuge on tributaries of the Koyukuk River. (Placer mining involves digging up sand and gravel deposits, washing away the sediments, and trapping the heavier gold that settles at the bottom.)

GETTING THERE

Kanuti NWR is 130 air mi. northwest of Fairbanks. No roads lead to the refuge; however, the Dalton Hwy. and Trans-Alaska Pipeline corridor are located as little as 8 mi. east of Kanuti, and it is possible to hike into the refuge. Still, with no established trails, it is recommended that only experienced backcountry hikers attempt the trip. Most visitors access the refuge by air or float rivers that flow through the refuge. Daily flights are available from Fairbanks to Bettles and to the villages of Alatna and Allakaket. Air charters are available in Bettles if you wish to fly to a remote refuge lake. Guides can be hired in Bettles / Evansville, Fairbanks, and Anchorage.

■ **SEASON:** Open year-round, although most visitors fly to the area during the summer. If you enjoy dogsledding, cross-country skiing, or snowmobile trips, visit during the winter.

■ **HOURS:** Open 24 hours, Kanuti NWR maintains a well-staffed office in Fairbanks. Office hours are Mon.–Fri., 8 a.m.–4:30 p.m. A subheadquarters and Visitor Center is shared with Gates of the Arctic National Park in Bettles. The Visitor Center is open Mon.–Fri., 8 a.m.–5 p.m., from June through Labor Day.

■ **FEES:** None.

■ **ADDRESS:** Kanuti NWR, 101 12th Ave., Rm. 262, Fairbanks, AK 99701

■ **TELEPHONE:** Fairbanks office: 907/456-0329; Visitor Center in Bettles (summer only): 907/692-5494

TOURING KANUTI

Rivers flowing through the refuge offer excellent opportunities for float trips through a wilderness region that few outsiders ever see. Hiking trips are more difficult because of the nature of the terrain. Be prepared to battle mosquitoes in this water-dominated environment.

About 200,000 acres of private property lie within the boundaries of Kanuti NWR. These lands contain numerous cultural sites, including Inupiat Eskimo hunting sites, Athabascan Indian fish camps, burial sites, and turn-of-the-century gold-mining camps. Check with the refuge manager about the status of private lands in the area you plan to visit.

WHAT TO SEE

■ **LANDSCAPE AND CLIMATE** This region is a land of extremes: Temperatures can range from more than 90 degrees in the summer to minus 70 degrees during the winter.

Much of the refuge is comprised of muskeg and low-lying lakes and ponds. The Kanuti Flats dominate the central part of the refuge. This major wetland area was formed 50,000 years ago from a 200-square-mile ice-dammed lake. Old signs from at least three glacial periods can be

Moose

seen in the refuge. The gently rounded uplands between Kanuti River canyon and Allakaket, and moraines along the Koyukuk River valley are two examples. Some drainages have backwater sloughs that flow in the opposite direction of the main flowing stream or river. Such drainage patterns are a result of old ice-dammed lakes and glacial deposits that shaped the land.

■ **PLANT LIFE** The boreal forest covers much of the refuge. White spruce mixed with paper birch occurs in the uplands, while poorly drained lowlands support open black spruce forests with an understory of mosses, sedges, and grasses. White spruce and cottonwoods line the Koyukuk River, along with tall shrub thickets. Wet muskeg covers much of the lower valleys, with common plants such as willow, dwarf birch, blueberry, cranberry, and Labrador tea.

■ **ANIMAL LIFE**

Birds Nearly 160 species of birds are found in the refuge, including 64 species of waterfowl and shorebirds. Ducks, such as lesser scaup, American wigeon, and northern pintail, breed on the many lakes and ponds in the lowlands. The larger lakes, such as Old Dummy Lake, provide important rest stops and staging areas for countless migratory waterfowl. Ducks banded on the refuge migrate along all four North America flyways.

Mammals You are likely to see signs of recent forest fires in the area. More than one-third of the refuge has burned since 1990. Lightning-caused fires create diverse habitats that support a wide variety of wildlife on the refuge. Mammals such as moose benefit from new vegetation associated with fire-burned zones.

Fish The Koyukuk River system provides important habitat for spawning chinook and chum salmon. Beginning in early July the chinook salmon arrive, spawning in many tributaries. Eggs hatch in the early spring, and young salmon spend up to two years in the refuge before they travel out to sea.

ACTIVITIES

■ **CAMPING:** Camping is allowed, although there are no designated campsites or campgrounds. Limited food and camping equipment are available in nearby villages. When camping, be aware of bears. Keep a clean campsite and store food outside of tents and out of a bear's reach. Dead or downed trees may be used for firewood. Contact the refuge manager regarding the status of private property that might relate to your planned trip.

■ **SEASONAL EVENTS:** October: National Wildlife Refuge Week.

■ **PUBLICATIONS:** Refuge brochure. *Up the Koyukuk* (vol. 10, no. 4) by Alaska Geographic Society (Anchorage, 1983). *Journey to the Koyukuk* by J.N. Wyman (Pictorial Histories Publishing Co., Missoula, Mont., 1988).

HUNTING AND FISHING
Local residents of four nearby villages regularly use the refuge for subsistence hunting and fishing. Most of the Kanuti refuge is a controlled-use area, which means that only local residents can hunt for **moose** in the fall. There is good **grayling** and **pike** fishing in many of the refuge streams and rivers.

Kenai NWR
Soldotna, Alaska

Kenai NWR

Known as Anchorage's 2-million-acre playground, Kenai NWR is a splendid mix of spectacular scenery, glacier-filled highlands, and almost every kind of wildlife found in Alaska. Kenai welcomes an astonishing 300,000 visitors each year, but in a space this vast, you can walk into the wilderness and not see anyone for days. There is room for all sorts of activity: Two oil and gas fields are active on the refuge (they're in a corner of the refuge not often explored by visitors), and during the sockeye salmon run, it's difficult to find parking space along the Russian River. Alaska's only refuge with a road cutting through its heart, Kenai is also the state's most popular and heavily used recreational fishery.

HISTORY

Kenai is the one place in the United States where the size of a moose's antlers helped lead to the creation of a national wildlife refuge. During the 1930s, hunters from the Lower 48, overly eager to bag a trophy rack that stretched more than 5 feet, tip to tip, were responsible for a serious decline in the peninsula's moose population. In 1941, only two weeks after the bombing of Pearl Harbor, President Franklin Roosevelt issued an executive order establishing the Kenai National Moose Range. Its purpose was to manage the moose so that they didn't suffer the fate of Kenai's caribou, which by 1910 had disappeared from the peninsula because of overhunting and man-caused fires. In 1980, 39 years later, the range became Kenai NWR when President Jimmy Carter signed the Alaska National Interest Lands Conservation Act, which increased the refuge from 2,700 square miles to its present size of 3,078 square miles, about three times the size of Rhode Island.

GETTING THERE

Kenai NWR is located on Kenai Peninsula, south of Anchorage. From Anchorage drive south on the Seward Hwy. (AK 1). Stay right on AK 1 at the Y and continue

MOSQUITOES You won't need to go looking for what Alaskans call their second state bird—the mosquito. It will find you. Volunteers helping the U.S. Air Force School of Aerospace Medicine to find the perfect mosquito repellent agreed to stand around in an Alaskan marsh—some wearing repellent, some without—and let mosquitoes bite them. If they'd stayed out an hour, those without repellent would each have received a staggering 1,188 to 3,360 mosquito bites (this statistical tidbit was arrived at by counting the number of mosquito bites each volunteer received during several two-minute periods). Those using repellent with 33 percent DEET (the standard chemical used to repel mosquitoes) escaped with an average of 3.5 bites per hour.

It's probably not paranoia that has you believing mosquitoes bite you more than they do your friends. You may just have stronger natural secretions—lactic acid, produced by muscle movement, and carbon dioxide, formed when you breathe—known to lure hungry female bloodsuckers. Most female mosquitoes need a blood meal to produce eggs, which they lay in water or on ground that has previously been flooded—where the eggs can survive three to five years awaiting another flood.

When visiting Kenai's marshes and ponds, consider that there are more than 2,600 species of mosquitoes, and some of them are sure to be there. So don't forget your repellent. You'll need it.

on the Sterling Hwy. through Sterling to Soldotna. Continue through Soldotna and turn left on Funny River Rd. after crossing the Kenai River bridge, then turn right (before the hardware store) on Ski Hill Rd. to the Visitor Center. The drive from Anchorage is 110 mi. The northeast corner of the refuge can be reached by trail from Hope.

■ **SEASON:** Open year-round.

■ **HOURS:** Refuge open 24 hours. Visitor Center open Memorial Day–Labor Day, Mon.–Sun., 8 a.m.–6 p.m; open Sept.–May, Mon.–Fri., 8 a.m.–5 p.m.; Sat.–Sun., 10 a.m.–5 p.m.

■ **FEES:** None.

■ **ADDRESS:** Kenai NWR, P.O. Box 2139, Soldotna, AK 99669-2139

■ **TELEPHONE:** 907/262-7021

TOURING KENAI

■ **BY AUTOMOBILE:** The 18.5-mile Skilak Lake loop road turns south off Sterling Hwy. about 5 miles after the east entrance to Kenai and rejoins Sterling Hwy. about 7 miles east of Sterling. The road passes five trailheads (for short hikes into the refuge), four overlooks, and five campgrounds.

■ **BY FOOT:** More than 100 miles of trails lace the refuge, ranging in length from the 0.3-mile Egumen Lake Trail (trailhead, Sterling Hwy., mile 70.4) to the 20.8-mile Funny River Trail, which has an elevation gain of 1,950 feet.

■ **BY BICYCLE:** Bicyclists may ride any refuge road.

■ **BY CANOE, KAYAK, OR BOAT:** Two world-class canoe trails follow 140 miles of lakes, rivers, creeks, and portages within the refuge.

■ **BY HORSEBACK:** Trails in the refuge are open to horseback riders.

WHAT TO SEE

■ **LANDSCAPE AND CLIMATE** Kenai is a land of water—1,200 lakes nestle

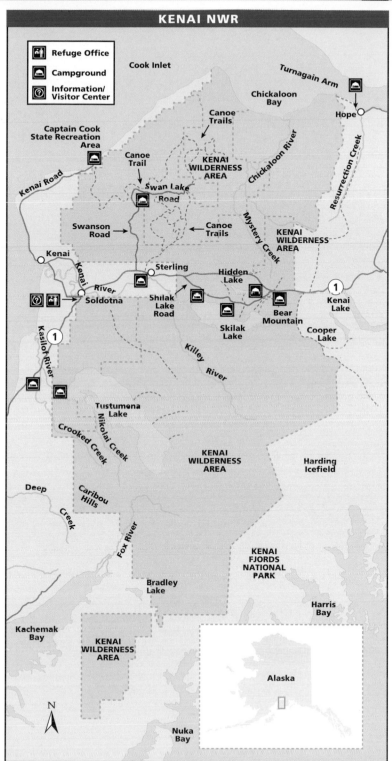

KENAI NWR

- Refuge Office
- Campground
- Information/ Visitor Center

Cook Inlet

Turnagain Arm

Chickaloon Bay

Hope

Canoe Trails

Captain Cook State Recreation Area

Canoe Trail

KENAI WILDERNESS AREA

Kenai Road

Swan Lake Road

Chickaloon River

Resurrection Creek

Swanson Road

Canoe Trails

Mystery Creek

KENAI WILDERNESS AREA

Kenai

Sterling

Hidden Lake

Kenai Lake

Kenai River

Soldotna

Shilak Lake Road

Skilak Lake

Bear Mountain

Cooper Lake

Kasilof River

Killey River

Tustumena Lake

Nikolai Creek

Crooked Creek

Caribou Hills

KENAI WILDERNESS AREA

Harding Icefield

Deep Creek

Fox River

KENAI FJORDS NATIONAL PARK

Bradley Lake

Harris Bay

Kachemak Bay

KENAI WILDERNESS AREA

Alaska

N

Nuka Bay

Willow ptarmigan, the state bird of Alaska

in the low rolling hills and muskegs. Nine river systems flow through the refuge, emptying into Cook Inlet on the peninsula's northern and western shores. The rivers, choked with salmon during spawning season, support 40 percent of the commercial fishing done in the inlet. The refuge is divided into two distinct areas, the lowlands and the Kenai Mountains, rising from sea level to 6,000 feet along the southeastern boundary of the refuge and providing a stark, barren backdrop to the dense spruce and birch forest that covers much of the lowlands. Glaciers flowing from the Harding Icefield high in the mountains continue to deposit glacial silt into the rivers, coloring the water a distinct and milky light jade green.

Expect rain (20 inches annually in the lowlands) and cool weather in Kenai's maritime climate, with July temperatures averaging 48 to 63 degrees F.; in January temperatures range from a frigid minus 30 to 30 degrees.

■ PLANT LIFE

Wetlands Pondweeds, grasses, sedges, and horsetail growing in the shallow ponds of Kenai's wetlands are the preferred food of moose. Gigantic stands of densely packed pond lilies on the Upper Swanson River can make canoeing difficult in summer when the lilies are at their full growth—it is best to canoe this stretch in spring or fall.

Forest Those accustomed to the parklike forests of the Cascades and Sierra Nevada, with plenty of trails and open space, will need an attitude adjustment when they first encounter Alaska's rain forests. The hemlock-spruce forest grows so tightly packed that there is no easy way through. Even at forest's edge, where there is more light, dense, impenetrable thickets of alder and willow interspersed with devil's club—a pernicious, spiny shrub—spell slow going for those determined to fight their way through. Many of the trails through the forest are narrow wooden walkways that skim the top of the muskeg, built to prevent hikers from sinking in.

The tree line at Kenai begins at around 900 feet; above this altitude, hiking in the open subalpine terrain is exhilarating. Look for fireweed, the beautiful lilac-purple flower that grows from 1 to 7 feet and is one of the first plants to establish itself in ground uncovered by receding glaciers (its seeds are blown by the wind).

■ ANIMAL LIFE

Birds Expect the unexpected when you're birding in Kenai. Birds easily recognized in the Lower 48 often change their feathers when they arrive in Alaska—and you may discover them in unfamiliar terrain. Sandpipers and other shorebirds abandon the beaches to nest in the mountains. More than 170 species of birds have been seen in the refuge; of those, 112 species nest in Kenai, including the rare and graceful trumpeter swan. Indeed, one of the great experiences at this refuge is hearing a swan trumpet its cry from lake to lake.

Bald eagles are common on the peninsula; during salmon spawning, watch for the spectacular sight of an eagle diving to grasp a salmon in its talons. Birders have a good chance of seeing the downy, hairy, and three-toed woodpeckers—all common in the refuge. Alaska's state bird, the willow ptarmigan, can be seen in the treeless areas of the high mountains. (Miners wanted to name their community Ptarmigan, but no one could figure out how to spell it. That's why Alaska has a town named Chicken.)

Mammals If you're a moose in Alaska, somebody will probably be gunning for you. Moose are the most hunted of big game species in the state—each year around 6,000 to 8,000 of them are killed, both for their meat and trophy-size antlers, which can reach 5 feet tip to tip. Moose are one of the mammals you'll be most likely to see on the refuge, which is home to around 3,500 head. There are an estimated 7,500 moose on the entire Kenai Peninsula.

The cantankerous moose looks so absurd it seems improbable that some Alaskans consider this big-nosed, droopy-lipped animal to be more dangerous than a brown bear—but while a brown bear is often satisfied establishing territory with a false charge, an agitated moose is more likely to carry through with an attack. Fierce defenders of their calves, female moose should be given a wide berth, especially from mid-May to mid-June when the females have recently dropped calves.

Dall sheep live on the steep slopes and alpine ridges of the refuge and may be seen from the Skyline and Fuller Lakes trails. Massive curling horns distinguish the mature rams, with the horns taking seven to eight years to form a full circle. The horn-clashing practiced by the rams establishes order in the bands of adult rams that live together and occurs throughout the year.

Beluga whales follow the salmon runs, and there's a chance of seeing one at the mouth of the Kenai River during incoming tides June through September.

Fish Four species of salmon—king, silver, red, and pink—are found in Kenai's

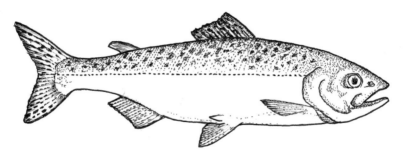

King salmon

waters; and arctic char, grayling, Dolly Varden and lake and rainbow trout are found in refuge lakes. Salmon runs on the Kenai River (the four species of salmon run the river at various dates from mid-May through September) and on the Russian River (red salmon, mid-June through late July), attracting fishing enthusiasts from throughout the states.

After several years at sea, and having traveled thousands of miles, salmon return to spawn in the exact stream in which they were born. They find their way using a magnetic map in their heads; and once in their nursery river, they use their sense of smell to find their birth stream. Watching thousands of salmon working their way upstream is one of the great sights of the refuge.

ACTIVITIES

■ **CAMPING:** The refuge has 13 campgrounds with 301 campsites. Only 3, Kenai-Russian River, Upper Skilak Lake, and Hidden Lake, charge fees (generally $10 or less). Wilderness camping is allowed, but don't try it unless you practice minimum-impact camping and know how to camp safely in bear country.

■ **WILDLIFE OBSERVATION:** Brush and dense timber obscure viewing along much of the refuge road system. Your best bet for observing wildlife is to take a hike in the early morning or late evening when the animals are most active. View salmon at Russian River Falls (on the Russian Lakes Trail), songbirds on the Visitor Center nature trail, and trumpeter swans, loons, and grebes along the canoe trail. Caribou may be seen on the Kenai River Flats along Bridge Access and Marathon roads. If you see a wolf, consider yourself very lucky. Sightings are few.

Dall sheep

■ **PHOTOGRAPHY:** There is plenty of spectacular scenery at Kenai, with rugged mountains towering over the wetlands, but the atmosphere is often misty. Most likely animal photos are of moose, seen along the roads; remember that the refuge is 2 million square miles, and resident animals are likely to be where you aren't.

■ **HIKES AND WALKS:** Kenai NWR is an outstanding exception to the general lack of trails in Alaskan refuges, where muskeg and dense, rootbound forests make trail building a difficult—and expensive—proposition. For the truly ambitious, a trail follows the refuge boundary southward from Hope, continuing out of the refuge to Seward. But casual day hikers will find plenty to do along the Skilak Lake loop. Kenai River Trail (0.5 mile) leads to a scenic view of the Kenai River Canyon. On Skilak Lake's rocky islands, gull and cormorant rookeries can be seen by hiking the 2.5-mile Skilak Lookout Trail. For a strenuous workout, Cottonwood Creek Trail gains 2,000 feet in a mere 4.5 miles.

KENAI HUNTING AND FISHING SEASONS

Hunting
(Seasons may vary)

	Jan	Feb	Mar	Apr	May	Jun	Jul	Aug	Sep	Oct	Nov	Dec
geese									■	■	■	■
duck									■	■	■	■
sandhill crane									■	■	■	■
grouse	■	■	■					■	■	■	■	■
ptarmigan	■	■	■					■	■	■	■	■
moose								■	■			
Dall sheep								■	■			
mountain goat								■	■			
caribou								■				
grizzly bear										■		
wolf	■	■	■	■					■	■	■	■
black bear	■	■	■	■	■	■	■	■	■	■	■	■
snowshoe hare	■	■	■	■	■	■	■	■	■	■	■	■
squirrel	■	■	■	■	■	■	■	■	■	■	■	■

Fishing

	Jan	Feb	Mar	Apr	May	Jun	Jul	Aug	Sep	Oct	Nov	Dec
red salmon						■	■	■				
silver salmon						■	■	■				
king salmon					■	■	■					
pink salmon								■				
grayling					■	■	■	■	■			
trout	■	■	■	■	■	■	■	■	■	■	■	■
char	■	■	■	■	■	■	■	■	■	■	■	■

Fishing at the confluence of the Kenai and Russian rivers is famous for its salmon runs and its hordes of fishermen, so be prepared for crowded conditions.

■ **CANOEING:** The Swan Lake canoe trail covers 60 miles, connecting 30 lakes with access to the 17-mile Moose River. The most popular of the two canoe trails, it has shorter portages and can be used for day paddles, a weekender, or longer trips.

The Swanson River canoe trail has longer portages, but the difficulties mean it's less likely to be crowded. Trips usually last a weekend to more than a week. In the trail's remote areas, the routes are often indistinct and require wilderness skills for a successful paddle.

For information, contact the refuge office, and remember that trips are limited to 15 people.

■ **SEASONAL EVENTS:** October: National Wildlife Refuge Week

■ **PUBLICATIONS:** *Kenai National Wildlife Refuge/Chugach National Forest Trail Map* (Trails Illustrated/National Geographic Maps, Evergreen, Colo., 1996). *Kenai Pathways/a guide to outstanding wildland trails of Alaska's Kenai Peninsula* by David Allen (Alaska Natural History Assn., Anchorage, 1995). *The Kenai Canoe Trails* by Daniel L. Quick (Northlite Publishing Co., Soldotha, Alaska, 1995). *55 Ways to the Wilderness of Southcentral Alaska* by Helen Nienhueser and John Wolfe (Mountaineers Books, Seattle, 1994).

Kodiak NWR
Kodiak, Alaska

Glacial lake at Kodiak NWR

Poised to chomp on a salmon, an enormous Kodiak brown bear wades into the rushing river. In the early morning light the largest land omnivore on earth catches a 5-pound red salmon with one big bite. High above, a majestic bald eagle fills the sky with grace. Talons outstretched, the eagle swoops down and deftly plucks a salmon from the water.

This is Kodiak Island, where the land belongs to the creatures of the wild. Kodiak Island is the largest island in the Gulf of Alaska (3,588 square miles) and the second largest island in the United States; only the island of Hawaii is bigger. Yet no matter where you stand, you are never more than 15 miles from the surrounding turbulent sea. The 30-mile-wide Shelikof Strait, known for its treacherous waters, separates the island from the Alaska mainland.

Kodiak NWR encompasses about two-thirds of the island, along with the adjacent islands of Uganik, Afognak, and Ban. Known as the Kodiak Archipelago, these islands contain a variety of landscapes, including 4,000-foot rugged mountains, glacial valleys, thick spruce forests, tundra uplands, 11 large lakes, 14 major rivers, and 117 streams that run thick with Pacific salmon.

HISTORY

In 1941, President Franklin Roosevelt established Kodiak NWR by executive order to preserve the feeding and breeding grounds of the brown bear and other wildlife. Congress added an additional 50,000 acres to the refuge under the 1980 Alaska National Interest Lands Conservation Act, making it slightly larger than the state of Delaware, encompassing all told about 1.8 million acres. It is a popular place by Alaska standards: Around 42,000 people visit the refuge each year, most of them hunters and anglers. This figure includes some of the 14,000 residents of the Kodiak Island Borough who use the refuge.

GETTING THERE

Regularly scheduled flights are available to the town of Kodiak from Anchorage. Kodiak is also served by ferry from Homer and Seward several times per week. Contact the Alaska Marine Highway System in Juneau for the current ferry schedule.

Once you've reached Kodiak Island, you can charter a floatplane or a boat with guides into the refuge's many recreational sites. There are no roads within the refuge.

■ **SEASON:** Open year-round. Summer and fall seasons are the two most popular visiting periods.

■ **HOURS:** Visitor Center, in Kodiak, open Mon.–Fri., 8 a.m.–4:30 p.m., and seasonally noon–4:30 p.m. on Sat.–Sun. (May–Oct.). Administrative offices open Mon.–Fri., 8 a.m.–4:30 p.m.

■ **FEES:** There are no fees except for public-use cabin rentals.

■ **ADDRESS:** Kodiak NWR, 1390 Buskin River Rd., Kodiak, AK 99615. The administrative office and Visitor Center are at this location about 1 mile north of the state airport.

■ **TELEPHONE:** 907/487-2600; Fax: 907/487-2144

TOURING KODIAK

■ **BY AUTOMOBILE:** There are no roads in Kodiak refuge.

■ **BY FOOT:** Much of the refuge is covered with dense brush that makes hiking difficult. The best walking terrain is in the northern half of the refuge, above tree line. At this latitude (57 to 58 degrees), you need only reach elevations of 1,200 to 1,500 feet to encounter alpine tundra and good walking—which brings rewards of scenic vistas.

■ **BY KAYAK OR RAFT:** Several rivers, such as the Uganik, Ayakulik, and Karluk, offer good float-trip opportunities. Portions of the rivers and some access points are on private and Native-owned lands. Contact refuge staff regarding the status of these properties. In some cases permits and fees are required to access private lands.

WHAT TO SEE

■ **LANDSCAPE AND CLIMATE** Rugged mountains, glacial lakes, fjords, and salmon-filled streams: Kodiak NWR has magnificent scenery and rich habitat that supports the highest concentration of brown bears on earth.

Salmon leaping upstream toward spawning grounds

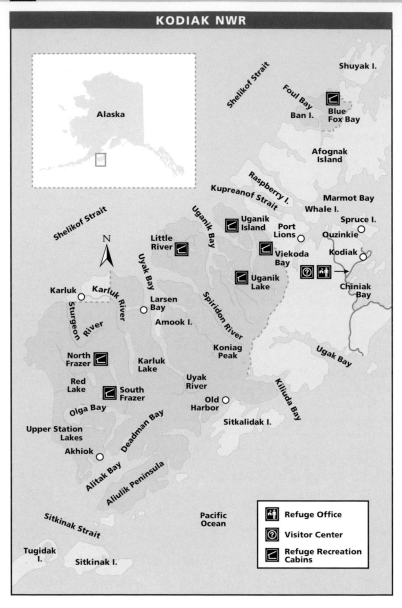

KODIAK NWR

Alaska

Shuyak I.

Shelikof Strait

Foul Bay

Ban I. Blue
Fox Bay

Afognak
Island

Raspberry I.

Kupreanof Strait

Marmot Bay
Whale I.

Uganik Bay

Uganik
Island
Port
Lions
Spruce I.

Quzinkie

Little
River
Viekoda
Bay
Kodiak

Shelikof Strait

N

Uyak Bay

Uganik
Lake

Chiniak
Bay

Karluk   Karluk River

Sturgeon River

Larsen
Bay

Spiridon River

Amook I.

Koniag
Peak

Ugak Bay

North
Frazer
Karluk
Lake
Uyak
River

Red
Lake
South
Frazer
Old
Harbor

Kiliuda Bay

Olga Bay
Sitkalidak I.

Upper Station
Lakes
Deadman Bay

Akhiok
Alitak Bay

Aliulik Peninsula

Sitkinak Strait

Pacific
Ocean

Refuge Office

Visitor Center

Refuge Recreation
Cabins

Tugidak
I.
Sitkinak I.

During the late-Pleistocene period, about 10,000 years ago, ice sheets covered much of the Kodiak Archipelago. Today, only remnant glaciers remain, but signs of the Ice Age are everywhere: glacier-gouged rivers and lakes; ancient moraines that are now covered with a flower-specked tundra; and fjords that finger into the sea.

Four major drainages support large runs of Pacific salmon and high concentrations of wildlife: the Karluk, Ayakulik/Red, and Sturgeon rivers, and Dog Salmon Creek. The scenic headwater lakes of these rivers offer prime spawning conditions, outstanding habitat for bears and eagles, and recreational opportunities for anglers, hunters, and campers.

The weather on Kodiak Island is usually cool and wet. Flying can be hazardous, and flights may be delayed for days. Visitors should take extra supplies as a precaution.

■ PLANT LIFE

Shoreline Kodiak's coastline features scenic, rocky cliffs, exposed to wind and surf. Hardy plants, such as villous cinquefoil and roseroot, grow in pockets of soil along the rugged shoreline. Beach pea grows on many of the sand and pebble beaches, producing an edible pod that is a good source of vitamin C.

Forest Much of the northeastern part of Kodiak and Afognak islands is covered with a dense forest of Sitka spruce. Beneath this conifer canopy are shade-tolerant plants such as devil's club (a tall, huge-leafed plant with sharp spines that can penetrate leather) and salmonberry, which produces large, tasty red berries in midsummer. The foothills and steep slopes are covered with dense alder thickets that form a belt around the mountains. Elderberry shrubs grow along the edges of alder thickets and in subalpine meadows, offering a good food source for brown bears. High-bush cranberries also offer excellent browse for Sitka black-tailed deer.

Tundra Treeless tundra covers most of the southwestern portion of the refuge. Similar to arctic regions in Alaska, this bumpy landscape is characterized by hummocks. These 2- to 3-foot-high vegetated mounds make walking difficult.

Lowbush cranberry, blueberry, wild geranium, and dwarf birch are common plants on the tundra. If you smell something extremely fragrant, it might be the flowers of Labrador tea. This small shrub produces miniature bouquets of white blossoms. The dried flowers and leaves can be brewed to make a strong tea. In boggy areas you might see sundew, an insectivorous plant. Its sweet, sticky leaves attract insects. Once stuck on the leaf, the insect is dissolved and absorbed by the plant.

Labrador tea

Meadows and alpine tundra On south-facing slopes you'll find lush meadows with a colorful array of wildflowers. Lupine, Indian paintbrush, shooting star, monkshood, and chocolate lilies form a beautiful tapestry among the grasses, sedges, and mosses. Above the alder belt, generally 1,200 to 1,500 feet, alpine tundra is covered with crowberry, dwarf alpine bearberry, mosses, and lichens. The ground is often laced with Aleutian heather, mountain saxifrage, and lavender cushions of moss campion. These plants hug the ground to withstand cold, windy conditions.

■ ANIMAL LIFE

Birds Look for soaring bald eagles. Kodiak NWR supports one of the largest

Kodiak brown bear

concentrations of nesting bald eagles in the United States. At least 400 pairs of these magnificent birds nest year-round on the refuge's coastal pinnacles, cliffs, and cottonwood trees.

During the summer or winter you'll likely see some of the hundreds of thousands of seabirds along the 800 miles of rugged refuge coastline. More than 140 seabird colonies occupy the refuge, including abundant numbers of breeding tufted puffins and black-legged kittiwakes. An estimated 1.5 million seabirds winter in the refuge bays and nearshore waters, including common murres, crested auklets, three species of cormorants, pigeon guillemots, and marbled murrelets. Kodiak Island has the greatest diversity of wintering birds in Alaska, due to its varied habitats and moderate temperatures.

Moving inland you'll find some of the 237 species that have been identified in the Kodiak Archipelago, from black-billed magpies and fox sparrows to Wilson's warblers and golden-crowned kinglets. In upland areas, listen for the gregarious cackling of willow and rock ptarmigan.

Land mammals In contrast to the birds, only six species of land mammals are native to Kodiak Island: brown bear, red fox, river otter, short-tailed weasel, tundra vole, and little brown bat. These animals are common throughout the refuge, as are introduced Sitka black-tailed deer.

"Bear Island" might better describe Kodiak (an Alutiiq Native word that means "island"). An estimated 2,500 of these giant omnivores live on the island,

KODIAK BROWN BEAR The enormous brown bears of Kodiak Island are considered a unique geographic subspecies, *Ursus arctos middendorffi*. The largest land omnivore in the world, males (boars) can weigh as much as 1,500 pounds, while females range from 400 to 600 pounds. The skulls of Kodiak bears tend to be larger and more dome shaped than those of other brown/grizzly bears (*Ursus arctos horribilis*), perhaps because of thousands of years of evolutionary isolation on Kodiak Island.

These powerful creatures are often referred to as carnivores—when in fact much of their diet is grasses, forbs, and berries. Beginning in late June, brown bears congregate on streams to fish for salmon, their most important food during the summer. Many bears leave the streams from mid-August to mid-September to feast on red elderberries, devil's club berries, blueberries, and salmon berries.

Bears begin entering their dens in late October, although some boars remain active all winter. Pregnant sows give birth to one, two, three, or occasionally four cubs in their dens in late January. At birth the tiny cubs weigh less than a pound. When they emerge from the den in late May, the cubs weigh 15 to 20 pounds. They remain with their mothers for two to three years.

Human encounters with bears are common on Kodiak Island, and bears can be dangerous, particularly when protecting their young. To avoid possible bear conflicts, be sure to observe animals from a distance. Avoid coming between or disturbing female animals and their young. Don't surprise bears at a close distance—make noise to let them know of your presence.

While there have been several documented maulings, no one has been killed by a bear in more than 30 years. Ask refuge managers for further advice and information sheets about dealing with bears.

about one bear per 1.5 square miles! They are most active in the morning and late evening hours, spending much of their time foraging in alder thickets. Beginning in July, bears begin to congregate on streams and fish for salmon. Watch for high densities of bears along most major drainages with salmon runs.

Marine mammals Whales, porpoises, sea otters, and sea lions can be spotted off the refuge coast. Fin, humpback, and killer whales can be seen feeding in the bays and coastal waters. Dall porpoises and harbor seals are also present.

Fish Kodiak NWR offers ideal spawning and rearing habitat for six species of Pacific salmon: pink, chinook, chum, sockeye, silver, and steelhead (the latter was recently reclassified from a trout to a Pacific salmon species). Adult salmon begin returning to Kodiak's streams and rivers in late May. Approximately 25 million salmon utilize the island's waterways. By October, salmon runs are on the decline. About two-thirds of the salmon harvested by commercial fishermen in the Kodiak area originate from the streams on the refuge.

Other fish residing in refuge waters include rainbow trout, Dolly Varden, and arctic char. Adjacent bays and inlets offer prime habitat for halibut, other bottomfish, and crab.

ACTIVITIES

■ **CAMPING:** There are no designated campgrounds in the refuge. It is important to follow bear safety rules when camping. Keep a clean camp. Cook, clean, and store food away from sleeping areas. Bearproof food containers are desirable.

Bear and deer hunting seasons occur in spring and fall. If you are seeking solitude and optimal wildlife viewing, plan to visit during the *summer* season.

Public-use Cabins: There are seven public-use cabins that can be reserved in advance by lottery. All cabins are accessible by floatplane, and three are reachable by boat. Each one- or two-room cabin has a kerosene heater and at least four sleeping platforms, a pit toilet, and a meat cache. None of these primitive cabins have electricity, running water, or even cooking stoves. Depending on the season, cabins can be rented for a maximum of 7 to 30 days, for $20 to $30 per night.

All of these cabins offer good hunting, fishing, hiking, and

HUNTING AND FISHING Many refuge visitors are **deer** or **bear** hunters. All hunting on the refuge requires access by floatplane or boat. Nonresident bear hunters are required by state law to hire one of the many registered big-game guides. Contact refuge staff for the current guide list and regulations. Bear populations have been stable or increasing throughout the refuge's recent history.

Fishing opportunities abound. The refuge has 90 drainages that support populations of anadromous or resident fish. Anglers visit the refuge to fish for the six species of **Pacific salmon**, **Dolly Varden**, and **rainbow trout**. Summer use of the refuge's seven recreational cabins is primarily for sportfishing. Commercial guides are also available. Contact refuge staff for further information.

wildlife viewing opportunities, as well as beautiful scenery. Contact the refuge office for details about specific cabins and the lotteries that are scheduled four times per year.

■ **WILDLIFE OBSERVATION:** Kodiak NWR has many excellent locations for viewing brown bears and other wildlife. A number of guide services are available for wildlife viewing/photography. Many guides and air taxis offer guaranteed

Uganik Bay, Kodiak NWR

Kodiak bear mother and cubs

bear-viewing excursions during the summer months. (For advice on avoiding conflicts with bears, see sidebar.)

■ **PHOTOGRAPHY:** Beginning in July and continuing through early October, photographers have the best opportunity to view and photograph brown bears congregating at salmon streams. The summer season also offers the best weather (less rain and fog) for photographing birds, bears, and other wildlife. Commercial photographers and filmmakers require a special-use permit from the refuge staff.

■ **HIKES AND WALKS:** There are no designated human trails in the refuge, but lots of bear trails can be followed, with caution.

■ **SEASONAL EVENTS:** May: International Migratory Bird Day (2nd weekend of May); Crab Festival (end of May); Monthly: Families Understanding Nature Program, presented every Saturday during the summer, and on the last Saturday of each month during remainder of year.

■ **PUBLICATIONS:** Brochures; public-use cabin information; bear facts pamphlet; bird and wildlife checklists; list of many guides for big-game hunting, sportfishing, and wildlife viewing/photography.

Koyukuk NWR
Galena, Alaska

Female moose and calf

Rounding a bend of the Koyukuk River, you hear the gargling calls of sandhill cranes winging their way across the vast wetland basin. Near the river's edge a cow moose with her twin calves nibbles on willow leaves. Farther downstream, a Koyukon Athabascan Indian family sets a net to catch northern pike, whitefish, or salmon. To the west, the gentle Nulato Hills rise in the distance to heights of 4,000 feet.

Koyukuk NWR is dominated by water. An estimated 15,000 lakes, 14 rivers, and thousands of streams form a major part of this productive wetland basin in west-central Alaska. Fringed by the boreal forest, these lakes, marshes, and waterways provide important habitat for breeding waterfowl, fish, bear, and one of the highest densities of moose in the state.

HISTORY

Under the 1980 Alaska National Interest Lands Conservation Act, the 3.5-million-acre Koyukuk NWR was established to protect its rich wetlands for migratory waterfowl and other wildlife. The boundaries of the refuge encompass an area slightly smaller than New Jersey. Approximately 400,000 acres of the refuge are designated wilderness, including the unusual Nogahabara Sand Dunes.

Koyukon Athabascan Indians have long used refuge lands to sustain their subsistence way of life. The local residents of six nearby villages rely heavily on area resources such as moose, fish, caribou, and berries. About 1,600 people visit the refuge each year.

GETTING THERE

The remote Koyukuk NWR is located about 270 air mi. west of Fairbanks. Refuge headquarters are in Galena, a community on the north bank of the Yukon River, 7 mi. south of the refuge's southern boundary. Regularly scheduled flights to

Galena leave from Fairbanks or Anchorage. Visitor accommodations are available in Galena, as well as fuel and food supplies.

■ **SEASON:** Open year-round. Although most visitors make trips to the refuge during the summer and fall, the refuge is also accessible in winter (see Touring Koyukuk, below).

■ **HOURS:** Refuge office in Galena open Mon.–Fri., 8 a.m..–4:30 p.m. This office also administers Nowitna NWR and the Northern Unit of Innoko NWR.

■ **FEES:** None.

■ **ADDRESS:** Koyukuk NWR (office and visitor contact station), 101 Front St., P.O. Box 287, Galena, AK 99741

■ **TELEPHONE:** 907/656-1231

TOURING KOYUKUK

■ **BY AUTOMOBILE:** There are no roads out of Galena to access the refuge, but you can charter small aircraft into the refuge from this town.

■ **BY BOAT OR RAFT:** Regular flights are available from Galena to the villages of Hughes and Huslia, two Athabascan communities that offer good launching points for floaters. Koyukuk village, near the confluence of the Yukon River, is a common takeout point. Floating the Koyukuk River offers excellent opportunities for hunting and fishing, observing wildlife, and experiencing solitude. For the adventuresome and hardy, visitors can plan for a 10-day or 2-week trip along this scenic 200- to 300-mile stretch of river. Local guides are available.

■ **WINTER TRANSPORTATION:** Hardy visitors can access the refuge in winter with the help of a local guide—by snow machine, dog team, or charter aircraft.

WHAT TO SEE

■ **LANDSCAPE AND CLIMATE** The Koyukuk River, Alaska's third longest, meanders through the refuge for more than 300 miles from the northeast to the southwest, where it joins the Yukon River. A land dominated by water and buffeted by the boreal forest, Koyukuk Flats offer little change in relief. Elevations range from 100 feet above sea level near the Yukon River confluence to 300 feet where the Koyukuk enters the northeast corner of the refuge. The Koyukuk River floodplain is 5 to 20 miles wide and often experiences heavy spring flooding.

The Nogahabara Sand Dunes are a striking geological phenomenon within the Koyukuk wilderness area. One of Alaska's largest active sand dunes, these windblown ridges were formed during the Pleistocene period and cover about 25 square miles.

Belted kingfisher

Sparsely vegetated with small shrubs and trees, the dunes are always shifting with the wind. Access is difficult, although it is possible to land a charter floatplane on a nearby lake and then hike into the area.

■ **PLANT LIFE** The vegetation pattern of the refuge reflects the high incidence of wildland fires caused by lightning. Fires help create a succession of abundant shrubs and plants that support moose and other browsing mammals. Blueberrries provide a good food source for black bears.

The refuge includes a diversity of vegetative zones, from black and spruce forests along the rivers to moist tundra dominated by plants such as Labrador tea, crowberry, and dwarf birch.

■ **ANIMAL LIFE**

Birds Surrounding wetlands include many river-flooded lakes that offer nutrient-rich habitat for breeding waterfowl and fish. Trumpeter and tundra swans, sandhill cranes, and white-fronted geese are abundant. More than 400,000 ducks and geese migrate south from the refuge each year. Along the river you are likely to see Canada and white-fronted geese, swallows, and belted kingfishers nesting in the cutbanks, or yellow warblers flitting through the willow bushes.

Mammals Moose and black and grizzly bears are resident species, and a portion of the Western Arctic caribou herd sometimes winters in the refuge.

Fish The Koyukuk River and its tributaries offer prime habitat for spawning salmon, in particular chum salmon, an important resource utilized by local residents. Northern pike, sheefish, and grayling offer additional fishing opportunities.

ACTIVITIES

■ **CAMPING:** Camping on the refuge is allowed, although there are no designated sites. Backcountry visitors should note that

> **HUNTING AND FISHING**
> **Moose** hunting is popular in Sept.
>   Visitors can fish for any of several species, including **northern pike**. In July and Aug., local residents are busy with their subsistence harvest of **salmon**.

there are a number of private inholdings in the refuge; please respect the hunting and fishing camps of local residents. If you are planning a trip, check with the refuge office on the status of private lands.

Galena has public showers and a few bed-and-breakfasts but no public campgrounds.

■ **SEASONAL EVENTS:** October (first weekend): Yukon Jamboree, a community festival in Galena with activities such as skin sewing, beadwork, and Athabascan fiddle dancing.

■ **PUBLICATIONS:** Refuge brochure; bird and wildlife checklists. *Up the Koyukuk* (vol. 10, no. 4) by Alaska Geographic Society (Anchorage, 1983). *Make Prayers to the Raven: A Koyukon View of the Northern Forest* by Richard Nelson (University of Alaska Press, Fairbanks, 1986). *On the Edge of Nowhere* by Jimmy Huntington (Press North America, Sunnyvale, Calif., 1992).

Nowitna NWR
Central Alaska

Tundra swan on nesting grounds

On the edge of a crescent-shaped lake, trumpeter swans paddle and probe for vegetation in the nutrient-rich waters. Nearby, a beaver pushes a freshly cut sapling toward the weak spot in its dam. Beyond the spruce forest you can hear the steady murmur of the Nowitna River, a stream that once carved out this lake during spring flooding. The river later changed its course, leaving behind what is known as an oxbow lake. Such lakes are scattered throughout the meandering Nowitna River lowlands, providing some of the best habitat for nesting waterfowl, such as the elegant trumpeter swan.

HISTORY

The 2-million-acre Nowitna NWR was established to protect its productive habitat for breeding geese, ducks, and other waterfowl—thanks to the 1980 Alaska National Interest Lands Conservation Act. Because of its remote, roadless character, the refuge receives only about 800 visitors each year, largely local users.

GETTING THERE

Nowitna refuge is about 200 mi. west of Fairbanks in the central portion of the Yukon River valley. The closest human settlement is Ruby, a small Athabascan Indian Village on the Yukon River, some 35 river mi. west of the mouth of the Nowitna River. Galena, a larger communty, is 55 river mi. down the Yukon.

The refuge office is in Galena, where there are small stores, bed-and-breakfast facilities, and two small restaurants. Regularly scheduled flights to Galena or Ruby are available from Fairbanks and Anchorage. Visitors can charter small aircraft to reach the refuge from Galena or Fairbanks. Some visitors, mostly moose hunters, take a long boat trip down the Yukon River from the Dalton Hwy. bridge or the Tanana River bridge at Nenana to reach the refuge area.

■ **SEASON:** Open-year round.

■ **HOURS:** Refuge office in Galena open Mon.–Fri., 8 a.m.–4:30 p.m. This office also administers Koyukuk NWR and the Northern Unit of Innoko NWR.
■ **FEES:** None.
■ **ADDRESS:** Nowitna NWR, 101 Front St., P.O. Box 287, Galena, AK 99741
■ **TELEPHONE:** 907/656-1231

TOURING NOWITNA

■ **BY AUTOMOBILE:** There are no roads in Nowitna refuge.
■ **BY FOOT:** There are no established trails.
■ **BY BOAT:** Local residents travel extensively up and down the Yukon and Nowitna rivers in the summer and fall in motorized boats.
■ **WINTER TRANSPORTATION:** Snowmobiles and dogsled teams are the common means of transportation for local people in the winter.

WHAT TO SEE

■ **LANDSCAPE AND CLIMATE** The Nowitna River is the main artery flowing through the heart of the refuge from the highlands of the Kuskokwim Mountains into a broad wetland plain of lakes, marshes, and streams. This nationally designated Wild and Scenic River flows north for 300 miles and eventually merges with the Yukon River.

An unusual feature of the refuge is the Boney Creek Dissected Benchlands. The benchlands feature canyonland topography, with flat-topped mesas and plateaus that are covered with vegetated dunes. Small streams carve paths across the mesas, forming unusual drainage patterns. The benchlands cover 26 square miles and are located in the east-central portions of Nowitna refuge.

■ **PLANT LIFE** The boreal forest dominates much of the refuge. Open stands of black spruce are common in low-lying areas. White spruce, birch, and aspen can be found on better-drained slopes. Willow, lingonberry, blueberry, Labrador tea, and alder are some of the common plants found in the understory. Above the tree line, plants such as crowberry, white mountain-avens, and dwarf birch predominate.

■ **ANIMAL LIFE**
Birds The lower Nowitna offers the best opportunity to see a diversity of breeding birds. The most striking waterfowl are the trumpeter and tundra swans, with the trumpeter being the more abundant. Larger than the tundra swam, the trumpeter swan has a 6- to 8-foot wingspan and nests on water by making a platform of dense vegetation. Tundra swans usually nest on dry, upland sites or on islands, and their call is higher pitched than the hornlike call of the trumpeter.

White-fronted and Canada geese and numerous species of ducks breed on the many lakes and ponds that dot the landscape. Some of the more common nesting ducks include American wigeons, mallards, northern pintails, northern shovelers, green-winged teals, common goldeneye, and greater and lesser scaup. Nowitna's varied forest and wetland habitats support more than 125 bird species.
Mammals Along the river you are likely to see moose, a common resident of the Yukon and Nowitna floodplains, and an important resource for local residents. You might encounter wolves, black and grizzly bears, and smaller predators such as the wolverine, lynx, and red fox. Old-growth white spruce forests along the river provide some of the best marten habitat in Alaska.

Small mammals play a significant ecological role. One such animal is the abundant red-backed vole, which grows to only a few inches long. Yet the combined weight of these blunt-nosed, mouselike creatures exceeds that of all large animals, including the many predators whose lives depend on small rodents. This vole's dark olive-brown sides and chestnut back camouflage well against rocks and logs.

Fish There are many popular sport fish in the Nowitna River and its tributaries; one, the northern pike, can grow to over 20 pounds. Arctic grayling, burbot, least cisco, and several species of whitefish are also present. Sheefish are another excellent sport fish that are prized for their sweet, white flesh. The Nowitna River supports one of the few known resident populations of sheefish in Alaska. Most sheefish spend their lives in both freshwater and saltwater, but the Nowitna sheefish do not migrate.

ACTIVITIES

■ **CAMPING:** Camping is allowed in Nowitna refuge, although there are no designated campsites or campgrounds. If you float through the refuge, gravel and sandbars offer good camping sites, and you might pick up a river breeze to help combat the mosquitoes. Ruby, the village nearest to the refuge, has a public campground.

■ **WILDLIFE OBSERVATION:** If you visit the refuge in late May or early June, or in August and September you'll avoid the worst of the mosquitoes. July generally brings the best weather, but the insects peak at this time.

The Nowitna and Yukon rivers offer outstanding opportunities for wildlife observation, fishing, boating, and camping. A 223-mile segment of the wild Nowitna River flows through the refuge, and a 100-mile stretch of the Yukon River forms the northern boundary. Both rivers can be floated by raft, canoe, or kayak.

The upper Nowitna features a canyon area where steep hills and bluffs rise 200 feet above the river. Keep in mind that the river corridor through the canyon area is a main thoroughfare for local grizzly and black bears.

Along the Yukon River you will have a chance to reflect on a prehistoric Alaska. The Palisades, also known as "the Boneyards," are an impressive series of 100-foot bluffs extending for 7 miles. The bluffs contain numerous Pleistocene vertebrate remains, including mammoth, bison, beaver, and elk. Many scientific and nonscientific groups have examined these sites. State and federal laws prohibit the collecting of fossils on the refuge and state lands.

> **HUNTING AND FISHING**
> **Moose** hunting along the rivers is a popular fall activity.
>
> During the summer you can fish for several species of freshwater fish, including **northern pike** and **grayling**.

■ **PUBLICATIONS:** Refuge brochure. *The Middle Yukon* (vol. 17, no. 3) by Alaska Geographic Society (Anchorage, 1990).

Selawik NWR
Kotzebue, Alaska

Asiatic whooper swans

The Inupiat Eskimos of the region call the river *siilivik,* meaning "place of sheefish." "Selawik" is merely an English alteration. An important subsistence resource, this large species of whitefish is commonly found in the rivers throughout Selawik NWR.

Nestled between Kobuk Valley National Park and Koyukuk NWR, the tundra wetlands of the refuge provide important habitat for an abundance of wildlife including many species of waterfowl, songbirds, moose and grizzly bears, and furbearers. The Western Arctic caribou herd, Alaska's largest, migrates through the refuge in the spring and fall, and some groups occasionally winter in the area. The broad Selawik River valley and delta, along with the even larger Kobuk River delta, straddle the Arctic Circle and contain most of the refuge's more than 20,000 lakes and wetlands. This important habitat comprises the most extensive arctic tundra lake system of all the Alaska refuges.

HISTORY

Selawik NWR was established by the 1980 Alaska National Interest Lands Conservation Act. Its boundaries encompass 3.2 million acres (about 4,700 square miles, roughly the size of Connecticut), two-thirds of which are in federal ownership. Much of the coastal region of the refuge is comprised of Native selected or conveyed lands, including the Inupiat Eskimo villages of Selawik and Noorvik. About 10,000 people visit the refuge each year, largely the local residents of Kotzebue and six nearby villages, who come to hunt and fish.

A 240,000-acre area of the remote Waring Mountains was also designated as wilderness under the Lands Act. These mountains form the northern boundary of the refuge near Kobuk Valley National Park.

The Selawik Wild River corridor contains many significant archaeological sites, dating back to the late Pleistocene era when the Bering Land Bridge connected Asia to North America. This corridor served as one of the important trading routes between interior Indian groups and Eskimos of the coastal areas.

GETTING THERE

Located approximately 350 mi. northwest of Fairbanks, Selawik refuge receives relatively few nonlocal visitors because of its remoteness and the cost of transportation.

Most visitors travel to Kotzebue to access the refuge. Regularly scheduled flights are available from Anchorage; another access point for Selawik visitors is on the lower Yukon River. Regularly scheduled flights to Galena are available from Fairbanks and Anchorage. From Galena, it's possible to charter smaller planes to reach the refuge.

■ **SEASON:** Open year-round, although most visitors travel to the refuge during summer and the fall hunting season.

■ **HOURS:** Refuge office, Kotzebue, open 8 a.m.–4:30 p.m., Mon.–Fri. Kotzebue Public Lands Information Center, open mid-May–mid-Oct.

■ **FEES:** None.

■ **ADDRESS:** Refuge office: Selawik NWR, Box 270, 160 Second Ave., Kotzebue, AK 99752 (within walking distance of airport; taxis available)

■ **TELEPHONE:** 907/442-3799 or 800/492-8848

TOURING SELAWIK

■ **BY AUTOMOBILE:** There are no roads in Selawik refuge.

■ **BY FOOT:** Upland areas in the Waring Mountains offer good hiking along rolling foothills of alpine tundra and ridgelines rising to 1,200 feet. The Selawik sand dunes in the northeast corner of the refuge, adjacent to the Waring Mountains wilderness, provide the best summer hiking and some of the most beautiful scenery in the refuge. Access to these areas is limited.

WHAT TO SEE

■ **LANDSCAPE AND CLIMATE** The refuge contains a variety of landscapes, including extensive wetlands, large river deltas, arctic and alpine tundra, low-lying mountains, and sand dunes. In th summer temperatures range from the 50s to the 70s, with 24 hours of sunshine in June. During the winter, sheefish swim beneath frozen lakes, while temperatures may drop to minus 60 degrees F. On the shortest day of the year in December,

Wolverine

the area receives only one hour and 43 minutes of direct sunlight.

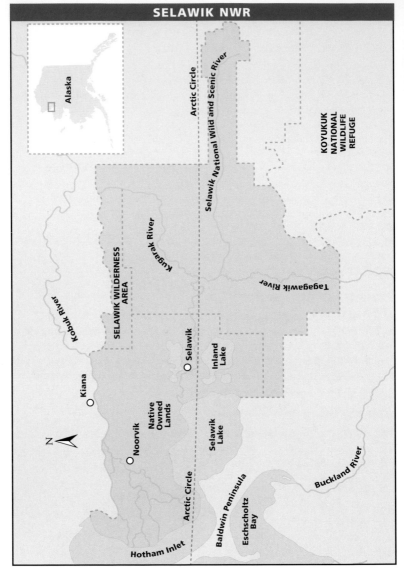

SELAWIK NWR

■ **PLANT LIFE** A mosaic of tundra plants and taiga dominate Selawik refuge. Cotton-grass tussocks cover much of the land, along with plants such as blueberry, Labrador tea, dwarf birch, and an array of spongy lichens and mosses.

■ **ANIMAL LIFE**

Birds The surrounding wetlands on the lower Selawik support one of the highest breeding densities of waterfowl in the northwest region of Alaska, with birds from all four North American flyways. Approximately 1,000 pairs of tundra swans nest on the wetlands, along with other abundant species such as the Pacific loon, sandhill crane, and red-necked grebe. These wetlands also host the Asiatic whooper swan, one of few places in North America where this species is known to nest. In the fall the Selawik delta serves as an important staging area for hundreds of thousands of ducks, geese, and shorebirds.

Tundra swan cygnets in nest

Mammals You may find moose browsing on willows, caribou migrating through the valley, or wolves in search of their prey. To the north, the weathered limestone ridges of the Waring Mountains rise to heights of 1,000 to 2,000 feet above rolling ridges of alpine tundra. This extremely remote and rugged wilderness area is seldom visited. The Waring Mountains are home to the elusive wolverine, along with hundreds of thousands of migratory caribou, whose trails crisscross most of the area.

Fish Sheefish, grayling, northern pike, and whitefish are some of the common resident fish in the Selawik River.

ACTIVITIES

■ **WILDLIFE OBSERVATION:** Selawik NWR is remote, with limited access. If you are hardy and are looking for a distant wilderness adventure—by canoe, kayak, or boat—you might consider it. The upper 168 miles of the Selawik River is a designated Wild River, although very few recreational users have ever run it. While floating the upper Selawik, you'll have the chance to parallel the invisible Arctic Circle and experience a wilderness that few people have seen. The Selawik is a peaceful, slow-moving Class 1 river, nestled beneath the Purcell and Kiliovilik mountains.

■ **PUBLICATIONS:** Refuge brochure; bird and wildlife checklists.

> **HUNTING AND FISHING**
> A short **waterfowl** season takes place in late summer/early fall, and **caribou** and **moose** are commonly hunted in the fall.
>
> Visitors can also catch **sheefish** that weigh as much as 50 pounds.

Tetlin NWR
Tok, Alaska

Marsh marigolds

Crossing the border into Alaska from Yukon Territory, you're entering pure, exhilarating space, vistas that roll on as far as the eye can see, mountains that reach for the sky, and water everywhere. The marshes, lakes, ponds, and forest speak of a land that overwhelms the imagination with its size and beauty. Tetlin NWR lies at Alaska's front door, entrance to our last great wilderness.

HISTORY

Tetlin NWR was formed in 1980 as part of the Alaska National Interest Lands Conservation Act signed by President Jimmy Carter. ANILCA set aside—for conservation—lands in Alaska that total an area larger than California. Tetlin NWR, with an area of 1,141 square miles, is the second-smallest wildlife refuge in Alaska but has the third highest visitation—160,000 visitors each year.

GETTING THERE

Tetlin is bounded on the north by the Alaska Canada Hwy. (ALCAN) and on the south by Wrangell–St. Elias National Park and Preserve. The ALCAN skirts the refuge for around 65 mi., beginning at the border crossing between Yukon Territory and Alaska. To locate Tok, follow Rte. 2 southwest from Fairbanks or Rte. 1 (452 mi.) northeast from Anchorage (483 mi.).
■ **SEASON:** Refuge open year-round.
■ **HOURS:** Refuge open 24 hours. Visitor Center, 7 miles from the Alaska-Yukon Territory boundary at Milepost 1229, open daily, 8 a.m.–4:30 p.m., Memorial Day–Labor Day. Refuge headquarters in Tok, at Milepost 1313.9, open Mon.–Fri., 7:30 a.m.–5 p.m.
■ **FEES:** None.
■ **ADDRESS:** Tetlin NWR, P.O. Box 779, Tok, AK 99780
■ **TELEPHONE:** 907/883-5312

TOURING TETLIN

■ **BY AUTOMOBILE:** The Alaska Highway, along the north border of the refuge, serves as a tour route. Interpretive cassettes can be picked up at the Visitor Center (Milepost 1229) and dropped off at the Alaska Public Information Center in Tok (Milepost 1314). The route includes seven roadside pullouts with displays explaining the wetlands, burns, and the changing landscape.

■ **BY FOOT:** There are only 2 miles of maintained trails, but visitors can walk into the refuge anywhere between the border and Milepost 1242.5 and at several other points, as long as undergrowth is not too thick. Check with refuge staff for current conditions.

Remember: Never go deeply into the Alaska forests without a topography map and compass and without notifying authorities of your itinerary.

■ **BY CANOE, KAYAK, OR BOAT:** Deadman Lake campground has a boat ramp; a small boat access is also available from the Alaska Highway at Desper Creek (Milepost 1226), the old Riverside airstrip (Milepost 1281), and at the Tanana River bridge (Milepost 1303). Canoes can be launched at Lakeview Campground.

■ **BY PLANE:** Charter plane flights to the interior of the refuge can be arranged in Tok and at an airfield at the end of Nabesna Road. Only permitted air taxis are allowed on the refuge.

WHAT TO SEE

■ **LANDSCAPE AND CLIMATE** Two great glacial rivers, the Chisana (pronounced Shoe-SAN-ah) and Nabesna flow through Tetlin to join and become the Tanana, the largest tributary of the Yukon River and one of Alaska's biggest streams. Rolling hills break the wide river valley and the intricate complex of marshland and lakes, with elevations ranging from 1,650 feet to 8,040 feet. Temperatures in the Upper Tanana Valley can sink to minus 72 degrees in January, making it one of the coldest inhabited places in North America; most of the annual precipitation of 10 to 14 inches arrives as snow, which can fall at any time. The months of mid-June to mid-August are usually pleasant, with July temperatures a comfortable 50 to 80 degrees.

THE ENERGETIC BEAVER Beavers can manipulate the landscape as easily as any wildlife biologist with a bulldozer and a water pump. Beavers need a home in the middle of 2 to 3 feet of water for safety; if the water level isn't suitable, they bring it up themselves by the quick construction of a dam from rocks, mud, and trees and branches they've cut down with their sharp teeth. The dams can reach 10 feet in height and stretch 20 feet across at the base. If a tree is felled too far from the water, the beavers will dig a ditch so that they can float the log to their building site. Once the water is at an appropriate level, the beavers construct their home, made of more felled logs and branches, wattled together with mud, with an entrance underwater. They eat the bark and leaves of trees and shrubs and the stems and roots of pond vegetation and sedges. For a winter menu, they collect edibles during the summer and stockpile them underwater near their home. If you hear the slap of a tail on water, the beaver has seen you, given warning to his fellows, and retreated to its home. Sit quietly, and it may come out again.

■ PLANT LIFE

Wetlands One difficulty of hiking near Alaskan wetlands is the unpredictability of the muskeg, which are deep layers of peat that have built up over the centuries to a density that allows them to act like a sponge, holding water. Stepping onto what looks like a solid tussock, you may find yourself sinking several feet. Calf-high rubber boots, known as Alaskan sneakers, are de rigueur when walking on this terrain.

A variety of wildflowers bloom throughout the refuge from late May through August, with June the peak month for wildflower viewing. Growing in boggy meadows, bog rosemary spreads its pleasing clusters of pink petals. Its scientific name, *andromeda polifolia,* refers to a character from Greek mythology, Andromeda, who was chained to a rock in the middle of the ocean—much as bog rosemary clings to small tussocks surrounded by wetland. A shrub growing in the marsh areas that looks similar to bog rosemary is Labrador tea, with dull green leaves bearing reddish brown hairs on the underside. The latter plant has long been used to make tea; if you want to steep the leaves for an aromatic drink, take care to distinguish Labrador tea from bog rosemary, which is toxic. Bog rosemary is *hairless* on the underside of its leaf. Also, trapper's tea and bog rosemary, both shrubs, look similar, and trapper's tea is also toxic. Look at the edge of ponds to see the arctic sweet coltsfoot, its pinkish white blossoms blooming at the top of 2-foot-tall bare stalks, and the bright yellow marsh marigold. Bog blueberries ripen in early to mid-August and may be picked.

Forest Tetlin is home to a taiga (pronounced TIE-gah) forest, a Russian term meaning "land of little sticks." Small black spruce— only 3 inches in diameter and 12 feet tall—can be 150 years old. It's common to see clusters of black spruce gather around a single tree; the lower branches of the spruce root and create a ring of small trees around the mother tree. Also growing in the boreal forest is white spruce, the most common tree of interior Alaska, distinguished from black spruce by its larger size, slightly longer cones and needles, and its preference for well-drained sandy soils along edges of lakes and rivers. To distinguish spruce from hemlock, another common Alaskan tree, grasp (carefully) the needles. Spruce will prickle; hemlock won't.

■ ANIMAL LIFE

Birds Tetlin is on the Pacific Flyway and has one of the highest densities of nesting waterfowl in Alaska; each year 35,000 to 65,000 ducklings are fledged on the refuge. Green-winged teal, mallards, American wigeons, ring-necked ducks, lesser scaup, white-winged scoters, and buffleheads are the most common species.

Spring and fall migration brings thousands of tundra and trumpeter swans through the refuge. As many as 200,000 sandhill cranes—nearly half the world's population—also migrate through the refuge. Tetlin has one of the largest concentrations of ospreys in Alaska. Altogether 143 bird species are known to breed on the refuge.

Mammals A high concentration of beaver occurs in the Scottie Desper Creek area (see sidebar). Portions of five different caribou herds winter on or near Tetlin. Other winter residents include moose, wolf, fox, lynx, and snowshoe hares—the lynx's preferred food. When snowshoe hares are plentiful on Tetlin, so are lynx. These large cats weigh 18 to 35 pounds and have been known to travel from 100 to 400 miles to find a new home when snowshoe hares become scarce. Their large feet enable them to move on top of the snow and effectively pursue their prey.

Fish Northern pike and grayling are native species in the upper Tanana Valley, and several land-locked lakes are stocked with lake and rainbow trout.

Snowshoe hare

ACTIVITIES

■ **CAMPING:** Deadman Lake Campground (Milepost 1249.3) has 16 sites, and Lakeview Campground (Milepost 1256.7) offers eight sites. Both campgrounds are open from around late May to mid-September. A handicapped-accessible fishing pier is available at Deadman Lake, and swimming is possible if you don't mind cold water, bugs, and algae. The refuge also has two public-use cabins, at Wellesley and Jatahmund lakes. Both are accessible only by plane or snowmobile (in winter) and require advance reservations. There are no fees for the cabins.

■ **WILDLIFE OBSERVATION:** Along the Alaska Highway, look for waterfowl at Milepost 1223.4, arctic loons at Milepost 1226, bank swallow nests on the north side of the highway at Milepost 1256.2, and bald eagles flying along the Tanana River. Moose, caribou (in winter), and foxes are often spotted along the highway. August is good for seeing greater white-fronted and Canada geese, September for migrating sandhill cranes, and October for migrating trumpeter and tundra swans.

> **HUNTING AND FISHING** Hunting is permitted for **moose, caribou**, waterfowl, **grouse**, and **ptarmigan**.
>
> The fishing opportunities include **arctic grayling, burbot, lake trout, northern pike**, and **whitefish**.

■ **PHOTOGRAPHY:** To photograph wildlife along the Alaska Highway, use your car as a blind. If you do get out of your car, give wildlife plenty of space, be alert to alarm signs from the animal, and leave as soon as the animal exhibits them. Cow moose are very protective of young calves and will charge and trample threatening intruders. Using panoramic cameras may you help capture a real sense of the immense space that is Alaska.

■ **HIKES AND WALKS:** The 0.25-mile Taiga Trail at Deadman Lake Campground leads to an observation deck overlooking the lake. Along the way, hikers may see bog flowers, berries, and the taiga forest with its "little sticks" black spruce trees (See "Forest," above). The 1.2-mile Hidden Lake Trail starts at Milepost 1240, passing bogs and mixed forest to the lake, which is stocked with rainbow trout.

■ **SEASONAL EVENTS:** October: National Wildlife Refuge Week

■ **PUBLICATIONS:** *Exploring Alaska-Yukon Bordercountry: Kluane National Park Reserve, Tetlin National Wildlife Refuge and Wrangell-St. Elias National Park* by Jill De La Hunt (NorthWord Press/Alaska Natural History Association, 1995).

Togiak NWR
Dillingham, Alaska

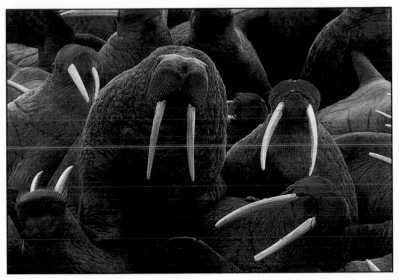

Walrus basking on beach

From sea cliffs and coastal bays to glacier-carved valleys and mountains, Togiak NWR provides many safe havens for a wide range of wildlife. At this extreme southwestern Alaska refuge, as many as a quarter-million waterfowl converge on the surrounding bays and lagoons to feed and rest during their spring and fall migrations. The coastal headlands of Cape Newenham and Cape Peirce attract millions of nesting seabirds. Along the rivers, brown bears are in abundance, feeding on salmon. Anglers visit the refuge from all over the world to fish for all five species of Pacific salmon, plus rainbow and lake trout, Dolly Varden, and grayling.

The Wood River and Ahklun mountains offer spectacular scenery. Deeply carved glacial lakes mirror snow-clad peaks, hanging valleys, and cirques. These rugged mountains form a north-south rampart shared by the refuge and Wood-Tikchik State Park to the east.

HISTORY

This 4.3-million-acre refuge was established under the 1980 Alaska National Interest Lands Conservation Act to protect its rich complex of habitats and many wildlife species. The northern half of Togiak refuge is a designated Wilderness Area. About 24,000 visitors per year use Togiak, including a good number of local residents.

Lands within Togiak NWR have been used by Alaska Native peoples for thousands of years. Today, about 4,000 residents from several communities continue to depend on fish and wildlife resources as a major source of food. Salmon has long been considered a mainstay for many Natives.

GETTING THERE

Access to the refuge is mainly by aircraft. Nonlocal visitors usually fly to Dillingham, the primary access point, or Bethel. Daily commercial flights are available from Anchorage to these communities. From Dillingham or Bethel, visitors can

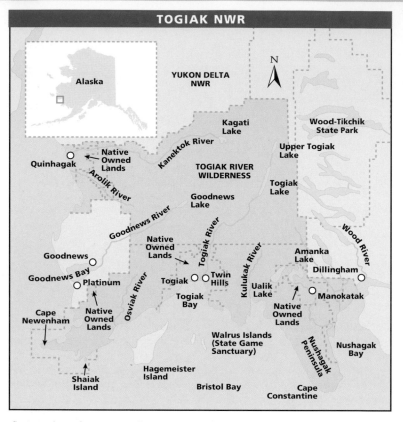

fly into the refuge on smaller commuter flights or on chartered air taxi flights. Many recreational visitors fly into the refuge from lodges in Wood-Tikchik State Park (located near Aleknagik).

Boat use is extensive on refuge rivers, especially on the Kanektok, Goodnews, and Togiak rivers. Inflatable rafts, kayaks, canoes, and motorized boats are all permissible where water depths permit. Licensed commercial guides are available for sport anglers and for river rafting trips.

■ **SEASON:** Open year-round, although the highest visitor use occurs in the summer and fall during prime fishing season.

■ **HOURS:** Refuge office, Dillingham, open Mon.–Fri., 8 a.m.–5 p.m.

■ **FEES:** None.

■ **ADDRESS:** Togiak NWR, 6 Main St., P.O. Box 270, Dillingham, AK 99576

■ **TELEPHONE:** 907/842-1063

TOURING TOGIAK

■ **BY AUTOMOBILE:** There are no roads on Togiak refuge.

■ **BY FOOT:** There are no established trails in the refuge. The best hiking opportunities are in the Wood River and Ahklun mountain regions, along the rivers and gravel bars and on the beaches.

■ **BY CANOE, BOAT, KAYAK, OR RAFT:** Several rivers are suitable for river running, particularly the Goodnews, Togiak, and Kanektok rivers. River users are asked to camp on gravel bars below the mean high water mark to avoid any trespassing on private property. Downstream of the wilderness area, most of the uplands are owned by local village corporations. Consult the refuge manager for more detailed information regarding private lands that border refuge rivers.

WHAT TO SEE

■ **LANDSCAPE AND CLIMATE** From the sculptured 1,000-foot cliffs of Cape Peirce and Cape Newenham to the glaciated 5,000-foot Wood River Mountains, Togiak NWR keeps changing its terrain and ecosystems as you move through the landscape. The southern part of the refuge is dominated by wetlands, with extensive lakes, ponds, and tidal sloughs. A haven for waterfowl, Nushagak Peninsula provides ideal nesting habitat for ducks, with densities as high as 32 ducks an acre.

In the northern wilderness area of the refuge, three major rivers flow from glacier carved headwater lakes in the scenic Ahklun and Wood River Mountains. You can expect moist, rainy conditions through much of the summer. Summer temperatures range between 45 and 73 degrees F. Snow covers the mountains by early October, and by November the lakes and rivers are sheathed in ice. Winter temperatures range from 45 degrees to minus 10 degrees, with occasional drops to 30 below.

■ **PLANT LIFE**

Wetlands Wetlands make up about 20 percent of the refuge; dominant plant species include sedges, marsh cinquefoil, and cottongrass. Extensive eelgrass beds in Chagvan and Nanvak bays, along with tidal flat wetlands, provide important staging and feeding habitat for millions of migratory waterfowl and shorebirds.

Upland habitat In the more well-drained areas, shrubs such as willow, alder, and dwarf birch dominate much of the landscape. Crowberry, alpine blueberry, and bearberry often lie beneath the shrub canopy. On the alpine tundra ridges, white mountain avens (a low-growing perennial and member of the rose family), Labrador tea, and pink alpine azalea intersperse with lichens and mosses to create a colorful mosaic in June and July. Although there are a few isolated stands of trees in the Togiak, Kanektok, and Goodnews drainages, no significant forests are present.

Horned puffin

■ **ANIMAL LIFE**

Birds Birds from the North American Pacific Flyway and several Asiatic routes congregate in Togiak refuge during spring and fall migrations. The bays and lagoons offer one of the last pit stops for migrants before they move north to their breeding grounds or south for the winter. Roughly 50 percent of the world's brant population stop to rest or feed on Nanvak and Chagvan bays. As many as 50,000 birds have been seen at one time. Tens of thousands of emperor geese and king and Steller's eiders migrate through Nanvak Bay.

In addition to the 30 species of waterfowl recorded at Togiak, 31 species of shorebirds also use the lowlands and tidal flats as a migratory staging area. Some of these, such as western and rock sandpipers, dunlins, semipalmated and black-bellied plovers, and red-necked phalaropes, also nest in the refuge in high numbers.

Nushagak Peninsula offers ideal nesting habitat for many waterfowl species, including the graceful tundra swan, lesser Canada goose, and mallard. Among ducks, the most common nesters are oldsquaw, black scoter, greater scaup, and northern pintails. The sea cliffs of Cape Peirce and Newenham also provide vital nesting habitat for several million seabirds; among them are high densities of common murres, black-legged kittiwakes, tufted and horned puffins, and three species of cormorants.

As you move inland, the refuge offers prime habitat for many nesting raptors and passerines. Bald and golden eagles are the most commonly sighted birds of prey. Expect to hear the joyful call of the Lapland longspur and the soft peeping of savannah sparrows, the two most abundant songbirds. The scrub willows are filled with the comical call of the willow ptarmigan, a common year-round resident. Along the rivers and streams you might spot the American dipper performing its characteristic knee bends in the shallow areas.

Mammals Of the 31 terrestrial mammals residing at Togiak refuge, the brown bear is one of the more common big game species. Approximately 400 brown bears roam throughout the refuge. During summer, bears feed mostly on salmon in the streams and rivers. The remainder of the year the bears' diet includes plants, berries, ground squirrels, marmots, and marine mammal carcasses that wash ashore.

Moose and caribou are also present throughout the refuge. As many as 40,000 to 50,000 caribou from three different herds may reside in the refuge during the fall and winter months. Wolverines, wolves, and red and arctic fox are the most common predators.

The Cape Newenham and Nanvak Bay coastlines offer important resting areas for a number of marine mammals: Walrus, Steller's sea lion, and two species of seal haul out on the beaches.

Several whale species migrate through the waters off capes Peirce and Newenham. From late April through early June, gray whales are the most abundant, with as many as 300 animals passing close to shore daily. Beluga whales calve near the mouth of Igushik River, and killer whales are sometimes seen.

Fish Welcome to angler's paradise. Five species of salmon, lake and rainbow trout, Dolly Varden, grayling, northern pike, and burbot all frequent the local rivers, streams, and lakes. Salmon that spawn in refuge waters are part of the world's largest salmon fishery.

In terms of commercial and subsistence harvest, sockeye salmon are the most important fish here. The commercial harvest in adjacent coastal waters averages

Sockeye salmon

430,000 fish annually. Nearly all of the sockeye salmon spawning on the refuge occurs above Togiak Lake, in late August.

The chinook (king) salmon is important for subsistence and sport fishing. Chinook salmon spawn in the Togiak, Kanektok, and Goodnews drainages. Coho (silver) salmon also spawn in these rivers and tributaries and are an important subsistence resource for local residents in surrounding villages.

ACTIVITIES

■ **CAMPING:** There are no designated campsites on the refuge. Camping on refuge lands or adjacent state-owned lands is limited to three days at one location. At the outlet of Kagati Lake, camping is limited to one day because of the area's higher number of anglers and float parties.

As you leave the Togiak wilderness area, you enter a region that is largely owned by local village corporations. Trespassing on these lands is prohibited. If you limit your camp locations to sand and gravel bars along the river, you will not be trespassing on private lands. Visitors should respect the cultural heritage and subsistence activities of local residents. Pack out everything that you take in. If you see trash others have left, pack it out as well.

■ **WILDLIFE OBSERVATION:** Brown bears are commonly seen on any of the salmon streams and rivers. As many as 10,000 walrus haul out at Cape Peirce between May and November. Only six visitors per day are allowed to explore this area, so as not to disturb the walrus. Several other sites along Cape Newenham

> **HUNTING AND FISHING Moose** and **caribou** are the predominant species hunted in fall and winter. Various species of **ducks** and **geese** can also be hunted in fall.
>
> Sportfishing is the primary recreational activity on rivers in the refuge. Most sport anglers use one of nearly 30 commercial guides permitted to operate within the refuge.

and Cape Peirce provide resting habitat for marine mammals such as the sea lion and harbor seal, thus providing good wildlife viewing opportunities.

■ **HIKES AND WALKS:** There are no established trails on the refuge. Attractive hiking opportunities exist around the headwater lakes, and along alpine tundra ridges in the Wood River and Ahklun mountain regions.

■ **FLOAT TRIPS:** A number of rivers can be floated within the refuge. The Goodnews, Kanektok, and Togiak rivers receive the heaviest recreational use because of their outstanding scenery and fishing opportunities. Most visitors access the rivers by chartering a floatplane to one of a number of headwater lakes. Float trips generally last from four to 10 days.

■ **WINTER ACTIVITIES:** Snowmobiles are the most popular means of travel during the winter. They are primarily used by local residents to access the interior of the refuge for hunting. Ice-fishing and cross-country skiing are other popular activities.

■ **SEASONAL EVENTS:** October: National Wildlife Refuge Week; Spring: community festival held in Dillingham, with arts and crafts, food, and games; July and August: Environmental Education Camp for school groups

■ **PUBLICATIONS:** Brochures and information on the refuge's Conservation Management Plan. *Alaska Fishing* by Rene Limeres and Gunnar Pedersen (Foghorn Press, San Francisco, 1995).

Yukon Delta NWR
Bethel, Alaska

Delta wetlands, Yukon Delta NWR

In early June, the light lingers and the scent of salmon fills the air along the Kuskokwim River. Follow the sloughs near Bethel, and you'll see bright reddish strips of king salmon hanging on fish racks, local residents drift-netting in powerboats, and families setting up fish camps near the shore. Salmon is the most important food staple for the Yupik Eskimos who live, widely dispersed, throughout Yukon Delta NWR.

This is a land of *greats*. Great salmon runs, several million shorebirds and waterfowl, hundreds of thousands of lakes and ponds, and two of America's greatest rivers, the Yukon and the Kuskokwim. These two huge waterways flow through the refuge and form an incredible delta comprising the largest expanse of intertidal habitat in North and South America. Bigger than the Mississippi. Bigger than the Amazon. The vast and flat wetlands of the delta stretch for hundreds of miles under the biggest sky imaginable.

HISTORY

Lands within Yukon Delta NWR were first recognized and set aside as important wildlife habitat in 1909 by President Theodore Roosevelt. Over the years the refuge has experienced three name changes and several land additions under different administrations. The boundaries of today's refuge were created by the 1980 Alaska National Interest Land Conservation Act.

In terms of federal land ownership, the 19.1-million-acre Yukon Delta NWR is the second largest refuge in the United States, slightly smaller than Arctic NWR. However, the boundaries of Yukon Delta NWR encompass more land than any other refuge in the United States, about 25 million acres, of which 6 million acres are Native-owned lands.

The refuge includes two designated Wilderness Areas: the 1.3-million-acre Andreafsky Wilderness to the north, and 600,000 acres of wilderness on Nunivak Island in the Bering Sea.

No refuge in America has so many villages within its boundaries. Approximately 20,000 people live in 43 villages scattered throughout the refuge. Most of the residents are Yupik Eskimos, whose subsistence economy and culture has traditionally depended on the wildlife resources of the region. In most of the delta's villages, fish accounts for 30 to 60 percent or more of the yearly food supply. Residents also hunt for waterfowl, caribou, and other wildlife.

Approximately 280,000 people visit Yukon Delta refuge each year. This figure largely represents the many multiple visits of local residents. Less than 5 percent of the visitors are nonresidents.

GETTING THERE

The Yukon Delta NWR is accessible only by air. Daily jet service is available from Anchorage to the town of Bethel, where the refuge headquarters is located. Lodging, restaurants, and stores are found in Bethel, the major hub for the Kuskokwim delta region. From the Bethel airport, drive 2 mi. along the only paved road in town to reach the refuge office and Visitor Center, located across from a big hospital that resembles a yellow submarine. Most nonlocal visitors travel out to the refuge from Bethel via small charter aircraft.

If you intend to visit areas along the Yukon Drainage, air service is available to the villages of St. Marys and Emmonak. To Nunivak Island, daily flights are available to the village of Mekoryuk.

A number of guides and outfitters are available for floating, fishing, hunting, and birding trips. Contact the refuge office for current information.

■ **SEASON:** Open year-round. The refuge is lightly visited by outsiders, who come mostly during the summer months.

■ **HOURS:** Open 8 a.m.–4:30 p.m.

■ **FEES:** None.

■ **ADDRESS:** Yukon Delta NWR, P.O. Box 346, Bethel, AK 99559

■ **TELEPHONE:** 907/543-3151

TOURING YUKON DELTA

There are 6 million acres of private land within the external boundaries of the

Black-legged kittiwake

YUKON DELTA NWR

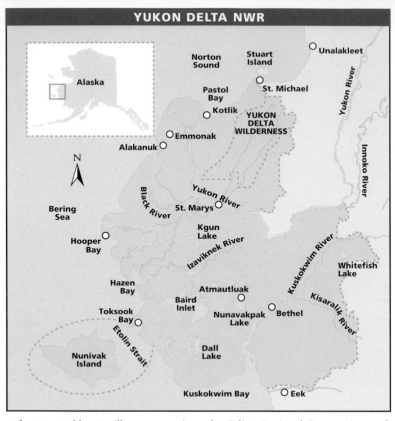

refuge, owned by 43 village corporations, the Calista Regional Corporation, and many individuals. These lands, along with hundreds of scattered fishing and hunting camps, should be respected as private property. If you are planning a trip to Yukon Delta NWR, it is important to consult with the Association of Village Presidents in Bethel regarding the location of private properties and the procedures for visiting villages. Call 907/543-7300, or write to P.O. Box 219, Bethel, AK 99559.

■ **BY FOOT:** There are no established trails in Yukon Delta NWR. Hiking conditions are relatively poor in the lowlands, because of the marshy terrain. The best walking in the refuge is in upland areas such as the Kilbuck Mountains, in the eastern portion of the refuge.

■ **BY KAYAK OR BOAT:** A relatively small number of visitors float rivers on the refuge. Most float the Yukon and Kuskokwim rivers or their tributaries. Contact the refuge manager for options.

WHAT TO SEE

■ **LANDSCAPE AND CLIMATE** Rivers, sloughs, lakes, and ponds dominate Yukon Delta NWR. About one-third of the refuge is covered with water, making it a desirable habitat for millions of waterfowl. Alaska's two largest rivers, the Yukon and the Kuskokwim, are the land's main arteries.

The refuge stretches west to east from Nunivak Island in the Bering Sea to the village of Aniak, 180 miles inland on the Kuskokwim River. Upland areas include the Nulato Hills in the northern part of the refuge and the Kilbuck

Mountains, which run along the eastern border. These gentle mountains contain peaks that rise from 2,000 to 4,000 feet.

The climate is largely influenced by Bering Sea maritime conditions. Summer temperatures average in the mid-50s, and the area receives considerable cloudiness, fog, strong winds, and light rain. The most hospitable weather occurs from mid-May to late June.

■ PLANT LIFE

Wetlands Most of the Yukon Delta NWR is treeless, with less than 10 percent of its lands covered with forest. Grasses, sedges, and dwarfed shrubs prevail in this wetlands-dominated environment.

A moist, spongy layer of tundra blankets most of the land. Beneath the tussock-studded tundra lies permafrost, a layer of permanently frozen ground. During the brief summer the tundra bursts with color. You might see the bright pink plumes of bistort or smell the fragrant white blossoms of Labrador tea. Pockets of wildflowers are interspersed with cotton grass, crowberry, and a variety of lichens and mosses.

Berries, including blueberries, cloudberries, crowberries, and cranberries are picked eagerly by most delta residents and bears.

Forest Trees grow very slowly because of harsh subarctic conditions. The inland portions of the Yukon and Kuskokwim rivers are sparsely wooded. White spruce and birch dominate well-drained soils, while the more scraggly black spruce grows in poorly drained areas. Willow and alder thickets and aspen are commonly encountered along inland rivers and valley slopes.

■ ANIMAL LIFE

Birds The Yukon-Kuskokwim Delta is America's premier bird nursery, support-

Emperor goose goslings, Yukon Delta NWR

ing 55 species of nesting waterfowl and shorebirds. Millions of birds arrive each spring from nearly every state and province in North America and from all continents that border the Pacific Ocean. The vast majority of North America's cackling Canada and emperor geese nest on the refuge, along with huge concentrations of white-fronted geese and brant.

These four species of geese, whose numbers declined drastically in the 1970s, have largely recovered, a result of a successful goose management plan negotiated by the U.S. Fish & Wildlife Service and hunter groups in 1984. In addition to half a million breeding geese, more than 1 million ducks, nearly 100,000 loons, and tens of thousands of swans return to the refuge each year to nest.

But that's not all. The delta is also the most important shorebird nesting area in the country. Several million shorebirds breed, nest, or stage in the delta region. Shorebird species include dunlin, western sandpiper, rock sandpiper, black turnstone, plovers, snipes, godwits, and the rare bristle-thighed curlew.

Coastal cliffs along Nelson and Nunivak islands support many seabird nesting colonies. You might see noisy murres swarming above the cliffs, black-legged kittiwakes, horned and tufted puffins, or parakeet auklets.

The Kisaralik River, which meanders west from the Kilbuck Mountains, has a diversity of birds of prey. Golden eagles, gyrfalcons, and rough-legged hawks are the most commonly seen.

Mammals Two caribou herds utilize the refuge on a seasonal basis. The Kilbuck caribou herd leaves the mountains and moves into the delta lowlands in the fall and winter. This small herd is expanding its range and is gradually increasing in numbers. Tens of thousands of caribou from the Mulchatna herd reside in the refuge during fall, winter, and spring months.

The refuge has a relatively low density of moose. Most of the moose here can be found along the upper Yukon and Kuskokwim rivers in the eastern portion of the refuge. Both grizzly and black bears call the Yukon Delta home. Grizzly bears, the most common bear, reside mainly in the Andreafsky hills or

Musk-ox

roam through the Kilbuck Mountains. Black bears populate the forested areas in the eastern portion of the refuge. While uncommon, polar bears are occasionally spotted on the delta coast.

Other refuge mammals include introduced herds of musk-ox and reindeer on Nunivak Island, and many furbearers. Beaver, muskrat, and mink use many parts of the refuge. Arctic fox are numerous along the coast, and red fox are common inland.

Marine mammals Along the coast you might spot a number of marine mammals. Binoculars are a must for close-up views. Bearded, harbor, ribbon, spotted, and ringed seals, Steller's sea lions, Pacific walrus, and beluga whales frequent the coastal and marine habitats of the refuge. **Fish** Five species of Pacific salmon migrate through the refuge and spawn in many of the tributary rivers and streams of the Yukon and Kuskokwim rivers. The commercial harvest of delta king salmon is also one of the largest in Alaska. Other fish in refuge waters include several whitefish species, northern pike, sheefish, burbot, grayling, Dolly Varden, and rainbow trout.

HUNTING AND FISHING Subsistence hunting and/or fishing is commonly practiced by local Native peoples here. **Musk oxen** can be hunted on Nunivak Island through a limited drawing permit system.

Visitors have the opportunity to fish for a variety of species in refuge rivers including **rainbow trout, grayling, char,** and **Dolly Varden**.

ACTIVITIES

■ **CAMPING:** There are no designated campgrounds or trails in Yukon Delta NWR. If you're planning a trip to the region, you should consult the refuge manager as well as the Association of Village Council Presidents in Bethel regarding camping possibilities and how to avoid trespassing on private lands.

■ **WILDLIFE OBSERVATION AND PHOTOGRAPHY:** A few guides offer wildlife observation and birding trips in the refuge; contact the refuge manager for current information. Serious wildlife photographers have excellent photo opportunities given the fact that the Yukon Delta NWR offers world-class habitat for millions of nesting birds. Use common sense when taking pictures. Avoid sensitive nesting areas. Respect birds and other wildlife by keeping at a safe, reasonable distance from their territories. Because this is grizzly bear country, study up on how to avoid conflicts.

■ **SEASONAL EVENTS:** October: National Wildlife Refuge Week; May: Spring bird walks in celebration of International Migratory Bird Day.

■ **PUBLICATIONS:** Refuge brochures; educational materials; bird and wildlife checklists. *The Kuskoquim River* (vol. 15, no. 4) by Alaska Geographic Society (Anchorage, 1988). *The Lower Yukon River* (vol. 17, no. 4) by Alaska Geographic Society (Anchorage, 1990).

Yukon Flats NWR
Fairbanks, Alaska

Common redpoll

As you fly over the vast Yukon Flats there is a sense of limitless space. Tens of thousands of lakes and ponds glisten in the endless sunshine. Oval and crescent-shaped green meadows reveal places once flooded with water. About halfway across the Flats, as you near the Arctic Circle, the third longest river in America comes into view. It is mighty. It is silty. The Yukon River sweeps through the Flats, making graceful turns as it meanders nearly 2,300 miles from its headwaters at Lake Laberge in the Yukon Territory, Canada, to the Bering Sea.

The Yukon River has created one of the largest inland wetland basins in the world. With approximately 40,000 lakes on the refuge, you could explore four each day for the next 27 years! For migratory ducks, swans, or geese, these lakes and the surrounding wetlands are a paradise. Yukon Flats refuge is home to more than a million breeding ducks and other species of waterbirds, shorebirds, and songbirds.

HISTORY

Established by the 1980 Alaska National Interest Lands Conservation Act, 8.6-million-acre Yukon Flats NWR is situated in the heart of Alaska, with the Yukon River its main artery. This third-largest wildlife refuge is bigger than the states of Maryland and Delaware combined. It was set aside to protect one of the greatest waterfowl breeding areas in North America.

Within the refuge boundaries are nearly 2 million acres owned by Native regional and village corporations and local residents. One Koyukon and six Gwich'in Athabascan Indian villages are inside or adjacent to the refuge. Many of these residents continue to hunt, fish, and trap as they lead a subsistence way of life. There are about 7,500 visitors to the refuge each year, largely local residents.

GETTING THERE

Located about 100 mi. north of Fairbanks, Yukon Flats NWR is primarily accessed by aircraft or boat. Regularly scheduled flights are available to Fort Yukon and to four other communities within the refuge. You can also charter aircraft to remote lakes and rivers from Fairbanks, Fort Yukon, and Circle. Due to the nature of the wetlands terrain, most users boat through the refuge during the summer months, many of them starting from the Yukon River bridge crossing on the Dalton Hwy., or from Circle, at the end of the Steese Hwy., north of Fairbanks.

- **SEASON:** Open year-round.
- **HOURS:** Office hours: 8 a.m.–4:30 p.m.; refuge open 24 hours a day.
- **FEES:** None.
- **ADDRESS:** Yukon Flats NWR (administration), 101 12th Ave., Room 264, Fairbanks, AK 99701. There is no visitor contact station on the refuge.
- **TELEPHONE:** 800/531-0676; in Alaska, 907/456-0440

TOURING YUKON FLATS

There are many private inholdings within the refuge. Navigable rivers passing through private lands are available for public use up to the ordinary high-water mark. Be respectful of local residents by not trespassing. When planning your trip, contact the refuge office regarding the current status of private lands.

- **BY AUTOMOBILE:** There are no roads within Yukon Flats refuge with the exception of roads in the vicinity of communities. The Steese Highway to Circle

BOREAL FOREST In Greek mythology, Boreas was the god of the north wind. Today, the word "boreal" refers to the natural world of our northern regions. The boreal forest makes up one-third of the earth's forests and is also known as *taiga*. The boreal forest ranges from Alaska through most of Canada, Scandinavia, Siberia, and other northern parts of Asia. In Alaska the boreal forest extends from the south slopes of Brooks Range to the Kenai Peninsula and from Canada across interior Alaska to Norton Sound. This mixed forest is largely comprised of white or black spruce, quaking aspen, paper birch, and poplar. Wildfires, permafrost, and sunlight are the driving forces that determine which species dominate the forest.

The boreal forest ecosystem provides habitat for many mammals, including caribou, moose, grizzly and black bear, lynx, snowshoe hare, wolf, red fox, marten, wolverine, and smaller creatures such as the northern flying squirrel. The raven, gray jay, black-capped and boreal chickadee, common redpoll, and the boreal owl can be spotted throughout the year. In spring, the northern forest is alive with birdsong: Approximately 50 species migrate here to breed. Robins, yellow-rumped warblers, white-crowned sparrows, Swainson's thrushes, and many other songbirds are among the migrants.

In Canada, about one-third of the boreal forest has been clearcut, and there is great concern over forest harvest levels, particularly in light of global climate change and habitat loss. Most of the boreal forest in Alaska is relatively undisturbed and ecologically intact, yet there is increasing pressure in some areas for large-scale commercial logging. Alaska's national wildlife refuges allow small-scale timber harvesting for house logs, firewood, and other local uses.

and the Dalton Highway (haul road) at the Yukon River crossing are the nearest points to the refuge accessible by automobile.

■ **BY FOOT:** Most of the Yukon Flats is truly wild. There are no designated trails. You may discover a few old campsites and man-made trails, particularly near villages. The best hiking is in upland areas such as the scenic White Mountains along the southern boundary of the refuge.

■ **BY CANOE, KAYAK, OR RAFT:** One of the more popular ways to see the refuge is by boat. Beaver Creek, Birch Creek, the Porcupine, Sheenjek, Chandalar, and Yukon rivers all offer excellent opportunities for canoeists, kayakers, and floaters. Given the vastness of the refuge, it is unlikely that you will encounter other visitors, except near villages. Ask the refuge managers for suggested itineraries.

WHAT TO SEE

■ **LANDSCAPE AND CLIMATE** The vast majority of the refuge is a wetland basin extending more than 200 miles east and west, and more than 100 miles north to south. These lowlands are dominated by water: countless lakes, ponds, sloughs, rivers, and streams, many fringed by marshy meadows and forest. The Yukon River meanders snakelike for 240 miles through the Flats. There are roughly 7,000 miles of rivers and streams that eventually feed into the Yukon.

The refuge includes the northern edge of the scenic and rugged White Mountains, so-called because of their sculptured white limestone formations. To the north, the foothills of the Brooks Range encircle the Flats.

Be prepared for a land with temperature extremes among the greatest on earth. In the winter extended periods of minus-50 degrees are common, with low temperatures in excess of minus-70 degrees. Water freezes on its way to the ground when poured out of a cup. Trees crack, ice shrieks, and sounds travel so far that

Gray jay

some people claim they can hear strange sounds produced by the northern lights. During the summer there is endless sunshine and temperatures can reach 100 degrees, the highest ever recorded north of the Arctic Circle.

■ **PLANT LIFE** Seasonal flooding of the Flats coupled with naturally occurring wildland fires produces a variety of vegetation. Duckweed, pondweed, rushes,

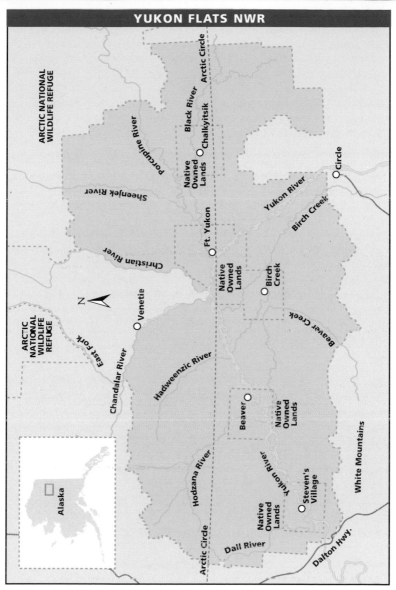

YUKON FLATS NWR

sedge, and horsetail thrive in the ponds and marshes. Mixed stands of spruce, birch, poplar, willow, and alder frame the rivers and streams. Wildland fires result in a new succession of plants and deciduous trees, offering habitat for browsing moose. On the northern and southern fringe of the refuge, hills covered with a mixed forest of white spruce, birch, and aspen extend into the lowlands.

■ ANIMAL LIFE

Birds The Yukon Flats supports one of the highest densities of nesting ducks in Alaska, with as many as 1.2 million breeding ducks here. There's a good chance that some of the ducks in your home state may have nested in the Yukon Flats. Ducks banded on the refuge have been recovered from 45 of the 50 U.S. states, 11 foreign countries, and eight Canadian provinces. Pintails, scaup, scoters, wigeons, canvasbacks, green-winged teal, and shovelers are some of the more abundant duck species. The rich wetlands also provides ideal habitat for as many as 20,000 Pacific, common, and red-throated loons, along with many other species of migratory waterbirds, including tundra and trumpeter swans.

During years of drought in the southern prairies of the United States and Canada, the Yukon Flats serves as a reliable breeding area for birds that are displaced from their traditional nesting grounds. Loss of prairie wetlands to agriculture and human settlement also increases the importance of the millions of acres of stable wetlands in Alaska.

In addition to waterfowl, Yukon Flats has desirable habitat for many migratory songbirds, such as the yellow warbler. This striking yellow bird can be seen nesting in the willow thickets near lakes and rivers. You can marvel at the fact that this delicate bird, weighing only as much as nine paperclips, migrates thousands of miles from Alaska to Central or South America.

Of the 120 species of birds using the refuge, only 13 are year-round residents. Well-adapted birds that endure the winter include ravens, gray jays, chickadees, and ptarmigan.

Mammals The wetlands and boreal forest provide excellent habitat for a number of furbearers including beaver, muskrat, marten, mink, lynx, wolf, and wolverine. Some village residents continue to trap and snare these animals. Furs are still used for clothing, such as parka ruffs and mittens, and they contribute to the economy of the region.

Moose are found throughout the refuge, along the waterways, lakes, and ponds. They are the most important game animal for local residents. The meat from one adult moose, coupled with other wild resources, can sustain an average family for a year. Moose hides are still tanned to make winter boots, moccasins, and mittens.

Caribou wander through the refuge on a very irregular basis. Both grizzly and black bears inhabit Yukon Flats. Grizzly bears are most commonly seen here in the open upland country and in mountainous areas. Along

Marten

Beaver Creek, a National Wild River, you might spot Dall sheep grazing at higher elevations in the White Mountains.

Fish The Yukon and 10 other rivers provide prime habitat for three species of salmon and 15 species of freshwater fish. Spawning salmon that travel up the Yukon River and its far-reaching tributaries have one of the longest freshwater migrations of fish on earth. Fishing is an important subsistence activity for local villagers.

ACTIVITIES

■ **CAMPING:** There are no designated camping areas or public-use cabins on the refuge. Be prepared to experience nature on its own terms, bringing with you

YUKON FLATS HUNTING AND FISHING SEASONS

Hunting
(Seasons may vary)

	Jan	Feb	Mar	Apr	May	Jun	Jul	Aug	Sep	Oct	Nov	Dec
black bear				■	■	■	■	■	■			
grizzly bear				■	■				■			
caribou								■	■			
moose								■	■			
grouse	■	■	■					■	■	■	■	■
ptarmigan	■	■	■	■	■	■	■		■	■	■	■
geese									■	■		
duck									■	■		

Fishing

	Jan	Feb	Mar	Apr	May	Jun	Jul	Aug	Sep	Oct	Nov	Dec
chinook salmon						■	■	■				
coho salmon						■	■	■				
chum salmon						■	■	■				

Residents of seven villages, mainly Gwich'in Athabascan Indians, regularly harvest fish, wildlife, and plants from the refuge. A number of large mammals may be hunted including black and grizzly bear, caribou, and moose. Hunting for grouse and ptarmigan is permitted throughout the year, except during nesting season. Along the Yukon River you may spot summer fish camps. Refuge visitors may fish for salmon during the summer, along with other species such as grayling and northern pike.

everything you need to take care of yourself. All lands beneath the ordinary high-water mark of rivers are available for public use.

■ **FLOAT TRIPS:** No permits are required for float trips. However, it's advisable to leave a float-trip plan with a friend or relative. Be prepared to be self-sufficient in this vast wilderness.

■ **WILDLIFE OBSERVATION:** The refuge offers good opportunities to see a diversity of birds and other wildlife along its many rivers, lakes, and ponds. Many bird species breed in the refuge, so it's important to avoid sensitive nesting areas. Keep a safe distance from moose and bears; both can be extremely dangerous, particularly females with their young. If you have poor visibility when walking through brushy areas, make noise to alert these animals of your presence.

■ **SEASONAL EVENTS:** October: National Wildlife Refuge Week

■ **PUBLICATIONS:** Refuge brochure; bird and wildlife checklists. *The Upper Yukon Basin* (vol. 14, no. 4) by Alaska Geographic Society (Anchorage, 1987).

Deer Flat NWR
Nampa, Idaho

Golden eagle

The manufactured western oasis has a singular appearance: The water seems flatter than flat, and there's lots of it. It's fringed by verdant margins of implanted deciduous trees—tangled willow, cottonwood, Russian olive—bearing familiar shades of green. There are ample "recreation areas"—meaning access points for powerboats and water skiing—and the whole works is situated within a parched landscape, the natural landscape of sagebrush, sun-scorched flats, and rolling hills, a world with little use for water.

The often generic qualities of such places belie their value for wildlife, and 11,430-acre Deer Flat NWR is a perfect example. On the western side of Idaho, on the inner edge of the Pacific Flyway, Deer Flat offers just what shorebirds, waterfowl, warblers—even owls—are looking for. Birds are the primary attraction here, and diversity is high year-round—tremendous, even, during migration. Another draw is the Snake River. Along a 113-mile corridor stretching west into Oregon, visitors with the right watercraft can explore numerous islands that are home to a great array of native species.

HISTORY

The story of Deer Flat is much like that of so many other regions of the west—one of bringing water to the desert. Some water was here; in the area that is today the refuge, a low swale with springs grew an abundance of grass. Elk and mule deer, fleeing harsh winters in nearby mountains, gathered in this area to feed, giving this place its name.

When President Theodore Roosevelt created the Bureau of Reclamation (BOR) in 1902, Boise landowners recognized an opportunity to convert sagebrush to cash crops. A man named J. H. Lowell was instrumental in securing a commitment from the BOR for a large-scale irrigation project. Between 1906 and 1909, a $2.5-million project ensued, with a reservoir constructed and the "New

York Canal"—named for the hometown of the investors—installed on the Boise River to divert water into the new pools. The result, a 9,000-acre lake, supplied water to irrigate 200,000 acres of croplands.

Roosevelt declared Deer Flat a wildlife refuge in 1909, though it remained unstaffed until 1937, when the Snake River Migratory Waterfowl Refuge was created. Each remained a separate refuge until they were merged in 1963. About 90,000 people visit Deer Flat each year.

GETTING THERE

Deer Flat is located in Nampa, ID, about 15 mi. west of Boise on I-84. From downtown Nampa, drive south on 12th St. to Lake Lowell Ave.; turn right and continue west 4 mi. to the refuge headquarters.

- **SEASON:** Open year-round.
- **HOURS:** Open daylight hours; refuge headquarters and Visitor Center, with interpretive exhibits and displays, are open weekdays, 7:30 a.m.–4 p.m.
- **FEES:** None.
- **ADDRESS:** 13751 Upper Embankment Rd., Nampa, ID 83686
- **TELEPHONE:** 208/467-9278

TOURING DEER FLAT

- **BY AUTOMOBILE:** The refuge offers excellent access for wildlife observation. A 29.5-mile refuge auto birding tour (the accompanying brochure is extremely useful) begins at the east end of Upper Dam. A driving tour (and accompanying brochure) of the Snake River is also available.
- **BY FOOT:** Most foot travel takes place along 10 miles of refuge roads encircling Lake Lowell. The 0.75-mile Headquarters Trail is self-guided. Foot access to islands in the Snake River Sector is prohibited between February 1 and May 31 to protect migratory birds. Cross-country skiing and ice skating are permitted in all recreation areas as conditions allow.
- **BY BICYCLE:** The refuge offers lots of potential biking opportunities. Biking is permitted year-round in all developed recreation areas and along refuge roads and maintained trails. The south side of Lake Lowell is flat; the north side features some sizable hills. The terrain is generally wide open, offering expansive views.
- **BY CANOE, KAYAK, OR BOAT:** Lake Lowell is open to powerboats and sailboats between April 15 and September 30. Water skiing, jet skiing, and sailboarding are very popular; the lake is not much of an opportunity for paddlers. The Snake River Sector, consisting of 113 river miles, with numerous islands used by nesting waterfowl and other wildlife, is accessible only by boat. Check at the Visitor Center for current conditions and launching sites on the river.

WHAT TO SEE

- **LANDSCAPE AND CLIMATE** Deer Flat refuge is located primarily in southwestern Idaho, in the Boise Valley about 15 miles east of the Oregon state line, and it includes islands in Oregon waters. The refuge and valley are part of the Snake River Plain, a semiarid to arid region of rolling hills, through which the Snake River has carved a series of deep, often spectacular canyons. Prior to settlement, this region featured unbroken expanses of sagebrush steppe, stretching east to the Boise Front, where Idaho's share of the Rockies rises abruptly from the plain, and to the southwest, into the desolate slopes and canyons of the Owyhee Mountains. The refuge lies at an elevation of about 2,500 feet.

The climate here features dry, cloudless summers, with high temperatures in

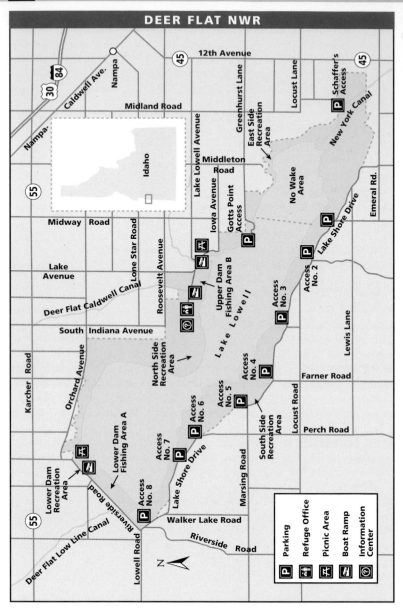

DEER FLAT NWR

the 90s. Compared with the adjacent mountains, winters are cool and mild, and most snow that falls doesn't stick around long. Most precipitation accumulates during the winter or in spring, but all told the area receives a scant 11 inches (average) annually.

The dominant feature of the refuge is Lake Lowell, one of the largest "off-river" impoundments in the West; without the Boise River to replenish it, however, it would not exit. Maximum lake depth is about 45 feet, though in most areas it is closer to 20 feet. This warm-water fishery is popular with anglers.

Deer Flat's other refuge unit is the Snake River Sector, a reasonably good place to see this powerful western river as it emerges from canyons to the east and flows across open plains. Beginning at the Canyon/Ada county line, the refuge corridor extends 113 miles to Farewell Bend, in Oregon. Some 94 islands (there are many more) are within refuge boundaries, ranging in size from 1 to 58 acres.

■ PLANT LIFE AND HABITATS

Wetlands The Boise Valley has always been an important wintering area for waterfowl on the Pacific Flyway; the creation of Lake Lowell added a substantial piece of habitat for their needs. The lake fills with spring snowmelt, then diminishes through the summer as water is utilized for irrigation. This yearly "draw down" creates expansive shallows where aquatic vegetation, especially smartweed, grows in abundance. Mudflats, too, are created, supporting a rich array of invertebrate life that attracts shorebirds.

Arid lands A small portion of Deer Flat includes uplands of native sagebrush steppe, with greasewood, big sagebrush, and rabbit brush varieties; grasses include Great Basin wild rye and exotic species, including cheatgrass, an introduced grass that regrows quickly after a fire. A similar plant community exists on many of the islands in the Snake River Sector.

Forests Thickets of riparian woodlands—primarily willows, mature stands of cottonwood, and Russian olive—occupy exposed fingers of land and shoreline surrounding Lake Lowell; the north side of the lake features the heaviest concentrations. Many of the islands in the lower portion of the Snake River Sector feature tangled woodlands of willow, box elder, maple, and cottonwood.

■ ANIMAL LIFE

Birds Birding is special at Deer Flat, particularly during spring and fall migration, and refuge staff have a wealth of information on where and when the many uncommon species show up. The highlights that follow here focus primarily on the unusual or notable migrants; many other birds are readily seen year-round.

When the mudflats appear on Lake Lowell, shorebirds materialize. White-faced ibis, American golden plover, stilt sandpiper, short-billed dowitcher, and the parasitic jaeger (a gull-like bird) have all been seen. The Pacific loon, Bonaparte's and Sabine's gulls, along with bald eagles, pass through.

Owls are diverse: The burrowing, long-eared, short-eared, northern saw-whet,

Short-eared owl

western screech, barn, and great horned all nest on-site, though are more readily spotted in winter. The northern pygmy owl is sighted rarely, as is the snowy owl in winter. You have a good chance of seeing and hearing several songbird species during migration. They include a wealth of warblers—the Nashville, palm, and Townsend's, among many others—along with white-throated sparrow, least fly-catcher, evening grosbeak, Vaux's swift, and Say's phoebe. Raptors cruising high in the skies during migration include northern goshawk, golden eagle, gyrfalcon (an Arctic falcon that is the largest of the falcons), and Cooper's hawk.

Mammals Though birds are by far the primary attraction here, a number of mammals are present, and a few notable species may be seen in areas that receive less recreational use or during periods of the day and year when things are quiet.

This is kangaroo rat country, and Deer Flat supports a thriving population of the Ord's kangaroo rat. Look in upland areas for burrow entrances, about 3 inches in diameter, on slopes and around shrubs. A tap at the entrance just might trigger a drumming from inside, as the Ord's thumps its large hind feet to signal danger. When sitting or moving slowly, its lengthy tail leaves a very clear drag mark on the ground.

Another readily seen mammal is the mule deer, present year-round. The Nuttall's cottontail, red fox, coyote, beaver, muskrat, and mink are abundant. Less often seen here are the pygmy rabbit, raccoon, white-tailed jackrabbit, and badger. River otters (deep brown on top, shiny silver below) are present year-round but less easy to encounter. You might look for their slides worn into riverbanks.

Ord's kangaroo rat

Reptiles and amphibians The gopher snake and garter snake are common and may be seen spring through fall; also present is one species of horned lizard.

Fish Lake Lowell supports a fishery of largemouth and smallmouth bass, bluegill, catfish, crappie, and yellow perch.

ACTIVITIES

■ **CAMPING:** Camping is not permitted on the refuge; camping is available at Eagle Island and Veterans Memorial state parks, east and north of the refuge along ID 55.

■ **SWIMMING:** Swimming is permitted in designated areas at Upper and Lower Embankments in Lake Lowell. Swimming is not permitted in the canal.

■ **WILDLIFE OBSERVATION:** April and May are prime months for the spring songbird migration at Deer Flat, and a good time to see many other species as well. Access to much of the refuge is closed between October 1 and

DEER FLAT HUNTING AND FISHING SEASONS

Hunting (Seasons may vary)

	Jan	Feb	Mar	Apr	May	Jun	Jul	Aug	Sep	Oct	Nov	Dec
upland birds									■			
duck	■									■	■	■
coot	■									■	■	■
chukar	■									■	■	■
mule deer										■	■	

Fishing

	Jan	Feb	Mar	Apr	May	Jun	Jul	Aug	Sep	Oct	Nov	Dec
largemouth bass	■	■	■	■	■	■	■	■	■	■	■	■
bullhead	■	■	■	■	■	■	■	■	■	■	■	■
crappie	■	■	■	■	■	■	■	■	■	■	■	■
trout	■	■	■	■	■	■	■	■	■	■	■	■
perch	■	■	■	■	■	■	■	■	■	■	■	■
bluegill	■	■	■	■	■	■	■	■	■	■	■	■
smallmouth bass	■	■	■	■	■	■	■	■	■	■	■	■
channel catfish	■	■	■	■	■	■	■	■	■	■	■	■

Hunting is permitted for ducks and coot from Oct. through mid-Jan. Fishing is permitted year-round on Lake Lowell and Snake River Island Sector.

April 14, but areas around refuge headquarters are very productive, and refuge staff will gladly suggest other places to try.

■ **PHOTOGRAPHY:** There are fine opportunities to photograph vast flocks of waterfowl and concentrations of shorebirds around Lake Lowell. During quiet times, upland wildlife such as mule deer and small mammals may be captured on film. Photographers with the appropriate boat will find the Snake River Sector outstanding for landscape images; islands offer other great opportunities.

■ **HIKES AND WALKS:** Drive to the Teal Lane parking area to Headquarters Trail, and take a very pleasant stroll through some of Deer Flat's most extensive mature woodlands—enough to qualify as "timber." This is a prime area for songbirds and owls.

■ **SEASONAL EVENTS:** The refuge celebrated its 90th birthday on October 16, 1999, with tours, displays, and featured speakers. Call the refuge for information on future seasonal events.

■ **PUBLICATIONS:** Refuge brochure; checklists of birds and mammals; maps of refuge units.

Hart Mountain National Antelope Refuge

Lakeview, Oregon

Pronghorn antelope

Hart Mountain is a place of immense wildness, born out of a volcano's repeated eruptions and the shifting of a great block of the earth some 2,500 feet above the valley it once was. Pronghorn antelope race free here across a vast, barren landscape, and the silence is enormous.

HISTORY

By the 1930s, the near extinction of pronghorn antelope by overhunting caused local residents near Hart Mountain to push for the creation of a refuge to protect the remaining pronghorns. In response, President Franklin Roosevelt, in 1936, established both the Hart Mountain National Antelope Refuge and Sheldon National Wildlife Refuge (24 miles south in Nevada), the winter home of the pronghorns. Although Hart Mountain is 65 miles from the nearest sizable town, the 270,000-acre national antelope refuge still draws around 12,500 visitors annually.

GETTING THERE

From Klamath Falls drive east on OR 140 to Lakeview. Follow OR 140 north for 5 mi., then east 15 mi. Drive north 19 mi. to Plush and continue 25 mi. farther to Hart Mountain.

From Reno drive north on US 395 to Lakeview, then follow instructions above. Note: There is no auto-repair service, food, gas, or phone on the refuge. Plush has water, phone, food, and gas. The nearest auto repair is in Lakeview. Refuge headquarters is about 4 mi. inside the refuge entrance.

■ **SEASON:** Refuge open year-round.

■ **HOURS:** Visitor room at refuge headquarters open 24 hours (not staffed on a

PRONGHORN ANTELOPE Pronghorns are North America's fastest mammals. If these animals frequented freeways with a 55-mile-per-hour speed limit, they might find themselves ticketed by the highway patrol. They've been clocked at speeds up to 60 miles an hour and can easily run for long distances at 40 miles per hour. Pronghorns are a biological family unto themselves and are commonly referred to also as "pronghorn antelope," but true antelopes they are not.

Before North America was settled by Europeans, there were an estimated 30 to 40 million pronghorns on the continent. By the early 1900s, hunting had nearly wiped them out, with only 13,000 or so remaining in the United States;. A count taken in 1937, a year after the Hart Mountain refuge was established, showed around 2,400 pronghorns on the refuge. The numbers continued to decline, remaining very low through the 1950s and '60s, but by 1999 the numbers had rebounded to around 1,900.

Pronghorns are curious animals and will stand attentively watching approaching strangers, then bound gracefully away, their white rumps marking their presence long after they've blended into the mottled browns and grays of the high desert. It is worth a trip to Hart Mountain, Sheldon (in Nevada), or Modoc (in California) refuges just to see these beautiful animals race across the desert.

regular basis). Administrative office, Hart Mountain and Sheldon refuges, in Lakeview (third floor, U.S. Post Office), open Mon.–Fri., 8 a.m.–4 p.m.
■ **ADDRESS:** Hart Mountain National Antelope Refuge, P.O. Box 111, Lakeview, OR 97630
■ **TELEPHONE:** 541/947-3315

TOURING HART MOUNTAIN

■ **BY AUTOMOBILE:** There are no paved roads on the refuge, but 27 miles of main (dirt) roads are graded. One, accessed from Plush, cuts through the refuge to headquarters and continues north to the east exit toward Frenchglen. It is not passable after major snowstorms. The other graded road turns south from headquarters to Blue Sky with a branch leading to the Hot Spring campground. All spur roads off Blue Sky Road are closed from December 1 to June 14.

Approximately another 56 miles of refuge roads are rough jeep trails, requiring 4WD and high-clearance vehicles. Pick up a map at headquarters.

The Bureau of Land Management's Lakeview to Steens Backcountry Byway crosses the refuge on the gravel road to Frenchglen. The byway, 40 miles of paved and 50 miles of gravel roads, passes the Warner Wetlands Area of Critical Environmental Concern, where cranes, egrets, ducks, herons, and swans can be seen during spring and fall migration. When the byway ends at OR 205, visitors can continue on the Steens Mountain Backcountry Byway.

■ **BY FOOT:** The wilderness of Hart Mountain has no hiking trails or campgrounds, but visitors may walk anywhere they wish—except in areas temporarily closed for wildlife sanctuary. The terrain, however, can be quite rough, making it difficult to venture far from the refuge roads.

■ **BY BICYCLE:** Mountain bikes are allowed on refuge roads.

■ **BY HORSEBACK:** Off-road horseback riding is permitted throughout the refuge.

HART MOUNTAIN NATIONAL ANTELOPE REFUGE

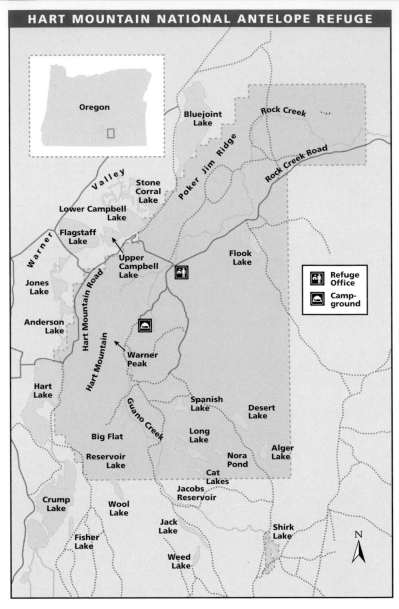

WHAT TO SEE

■ **LANDSCAPE AND CLIMATE** Hart Mountain is a massive upthrust fault block—12 miles long and 4 miles wide—that towers 1,500 to 2,500 feet over the Warner Valley to the west. Steep escarpments cut by canyons, rugged cliffs, and knife-edge ridges present a forbidding face. To the east, much of the refuge is over-laid with a lava cap that slopes gently downward toward Guano and Catlow val-leys. To the north Poker Jim Ridge rises steeply on the west and slopes gently away to the east. To the south minor faulting has created low rimrock escarpments. Hart Mountain, at 8,060 feet, is the high point in the refuge; the low point lies at 4,400 feet in the Warner Valley. The refuge tablelands, ranging between 6,000 and

6,500 feet, are dotted with playas, dry lake beds, and small drainages, often near the rimrock. In this dry land, only 6 to 8 inches of rain falls along the west escarpment, increasing to 12 to 18 inches on the mountain. Much of the precipitation falls as snow. Winters are cold, averaging 15 to 32 degrees, and summers bring extremes, with daytime highs in the 90s while nights dip as low as 25 degrees.

■ PLANT LIFE

Arid lands The sagebrush covering some of Hart Mountain's eastern slopes is not the sage used to flavor Thanksgiving turkey stuffing—a fact that can be confusing, since both smell similar, even though they're entirely different plants. The cooking herb is a salvia, while the big sage of the mountainous west is a wormwood that would prove intensely bitter if you tried to cook with it.

Sagebrush

Big sage, the most common plant seen in the high desert, extends a taproot as far as 10 feet down and often grows near low sage, a smaller relative. All the sages can be recognized by their pungent odor.

Growing at higher elevations in the refuge is the snowbrush, sometimes called cinnamon brush or mountain balm. It can also be identified by its spicy and sweet smell, most noticeable after a rain or when its leaves are crushed. Growing in thickets up to 9 feet in height, the shrub (a type of ceanothus), blooms with myriad white flowers. Its seeds remain viable for up to 200 years, lying in wait for a fire to trigger germination.

Other plants sharing the dry slopes are the wild gooseberry and chokecherry, a shrub or small tree with dark purple or black cherries and flowers that are also white but grow in clusters 2 to 5 inches long. In the same plant community, groves of aspen, their leaves quaking in the slightest breath of wind, make a beautiful golden landscape during fall foliage.

■ ANIMAL LIFE

Birds More than 260 bird species have visited Hart Mountain, including the sage grouse, waterfowl, and songbirds. The best season for viewing the most birds runs from May to October.

The golden eagle, bird of legend and majesty, lives all year at Hart Mountain. The eagles frequent tundra and grasslands to prey on rabbits and mice but nest on inaccessible cliffs in remote locations. Their vast homelands circle the globe. Tartars used the feathers to fletch their arrows, believing it made the arrows

Mule deer

invincible; the Romans used the golden eagle as an emblem for their imperial standard and believed its majestic soaring put it in contact with the gods, making it Jove's favorite messenger. Native Americans used its feathers to dress their war bonnets and as a sacred decoration for peace pipes. Similar in size to the bald eagle, the golden can be distinguished in flight by its lack of white head and tail.

Also common to Hart Mountain is the northern flicker, a member of the wood-pecker family. The flicker nests in tree cavities; and if it can't find a ready-made cavity, it will make one by chipping away at a tree trunk with its sturdy beak.

Mammals Hart Mountain's wild and inaccessible cliffs are home to a herd of bighorn sheep. Weighing as much as 300 pounds and standing about 4 feet high at the shoulder, bighorn have unsurpassed skills for climbing and jumping and will leap to safety from ledge to ledge if threatened. The massive curled horns of the ram make it one of the most distinctive hoofed mammals found in the West.

Mule deer, the West's most abundant hoofed mammal, can also be seen at Hart Mountain. The common name comes from its scientific designation—*hemionus*. The Greek prefix *hemi* means half, and *onus* means an ass—thus mule deer. Lighter than the bighorn, the deer weighs 100 to 200 pounds, and its coats are made of hollow, tubular hairs so buoyant that the skins have been used as life pre-servers. Both male and female deer have metatarsal glands near the heels of their hind legs, and mothers and fawns recognize each other by sniffing these glands.

Fish The Catlow redband trout and the Alvord and Sheldon tui clubs are natives to the area. Introduced fish include cutthroat and rainbow trout, largemouth bass, white crappie, bluegill, and yellow perch.

Reptiles and amphibians This refuge is too cold and dry to support a large number of amphibians. The three found at Hart Mountain are the Great Basin spadefoot, Pacific treefrog, and the introduced bullfrog. All live around the numer-ous springs, ponds, and reservoirs on the refuge and along the stream courses.

The rocky canyons, outcroppings, and bluffs are home to a number of snakes, including the rubber boa, striped whipsnake, and gopher snake. Warning: Watch for the poisonous western rattlesnake, found throughout the refuge, and for the night snake, also poisonous but usually active only at night. The desert night snake is gray or beige with dark gray or brown spots.

ACTIVITIES

■ **CAMPING:** Hot Springs campground, located 4 miles south of refuge headquarters and open all year, is primitive, with no water and pit toilets. The unroofed Hot Springs bathhouse (at the campground), open for day use only, is a popular attraction on the refuge, with 99-degree water flowing into it year-round from a nearby spring. A new, primitive campground for horse campers has opened at Post Meadows.

■ **WILDLIFE OBSERVATION:** Three locations offer the best chance for seeing pronghorns. Look for them in early morning or late afternoon. Around headquarters, look for pronghorns while driving Frenchglen and Petroglyph Lake roads. The largest herds on the refuge may be seen summer through fall in the lakebed and plateau country south of Blue Sky Road. Also look for pronghorns in Spanish Flat about 2 miles from South Boundary Road. For birdwatching the small ponderosa pine forest at Blue Sky and the riparian area around Hot Springs campground are good choices.

■ **PHOTOGRAPHY:** The changing play of light and shadow in the canyons creates a good chance for scenic photos. It's unlikely you'll get close enough to the pronghorns or bighorn sheep for photography without a powerful zoom lens.

■ **HIKES AND WALKS:** A short trail with five interpretive signs at the Warner Valley Overlook offers a spectacular view that seems to stretch forever; on a clear day you can see for 100 miles. Get directions from the refuge staff on taking short walks to see lava formations. The elusive bighorn sheep are best seen by getting off the roads and hiking. Day hikes go into DeGarmo and Arsenic canyons; during summer and early fall there's a chance of viewing rams there. A self service backpacker's permit is available at the refuge office for overnight hikes.

■ **ROCKHOUNDING:** Visitors are allowed to collect 7 pounds of rocks daily. Lucky visitors may find opals, blue agates, or jasper.

HART MOUNTAIN HUNTING AND FISHING SEASONS

Hunting (Seasons may vary)	Jan	Feb	Mar	Apr	May	Jun	Jul	Aug	Sep	Oct	Nov	Dec
partridge	■									■	■	■
pronghorn antelope								■	■			
deer									■	■		
bighorn sheep									■			

Fishing	Jan	Feb	Mar	Apr	May	Jun	Jul	Aug	Sep	Oct	Nov	Dec
rainbow trout	■	■	■	■	■	■	■	■	■	■	■	■
lahontan cutthroat trout	■	■	■	■	■	■	■	■	■	■	■	■
redband trout	■	■	■	■	■	■	■	■	■	■	■	■

Upland game-bird hunting is limited to an area along the western refuge boundary from the northern boundary south to Upper Campbell Lake and from Hart Lake south to the southern boundary. Fishing is permitted year-round along the Rock and Guano creek drainages.

Klamath Basin NWR Complex

Bear Valley NWR, Clear Lake NWR,
Klamath Marsh NWR, Lower Klamath NWR,
Tule Lake NWR, Upper Klamath NWR
Tulelake, California

Sunrise over Lower Klamath refuge

Their wings rattling the air across a vast expanse of sky, a thousand tundra swans settle on Tule Lake. Several miles away, two thousand ducks flutter into the sky, then drop back to bob on the rippling waters of Lower Klamath Refuge. Klamath Basin, a crossroads on the Pacific Flyway, is a rest stop for some 80 percent of the birds migrating on the West Coast. To explore the six refuges in the basin, along the California-Oregon border, is to be awed by the vitality and resilience of the 2 million birds flying through here each year. Each bird has persisted, despite what is seen by many as a concerted effort to destroy the wetlands it needs for survival.

HISTORY

Once a huge, ancient lake filled Klamath Basin. By the time white settlers arrived in the late 1800s, the lake was long gone, leaving its ghostly imprint in a vast wetland of shallow lakes and freshwater marshes filling 289 square miles of the basin. These wetlands, home to 6 to 7 million migrating and nesting birds, were known as the western Everglades and were considered the greatest waterfowl nursery in the United States (Alaska wasn't yet a state).

All that changed forever when the U.S. Bureau of Reclamation began the Klamath Reclamation Project in 1905, draining wetlands for farming. Today two-thirds of the bird populations that used to come to Klamath Basin have disappeared, and only 25 percent of the wetlands remain. (This as a whole is a better record than that of California, which has lost 90 percent of its wetlands.)

To protect what is left, six wildlife refuges were established in the basin, along

AVIAN CHOLERA Bald eagles, smart about conserving energy, avoid the effort of necessary hunting and may even prefer to eat birds something else has killed. That's why they're found in sizable numbers in the Klamath Basin, December through March. A deadly disease called avian cholera struck flocks of wild ducks and geese for the first time In 1944. Although the cholera is not harmful to humans and rarely attacks eagles, it kills ducks and geese within 6 to 12 hours of exposure. It strikes Klamath Basin in October or November with the arrival of the first great flocks of snow geese, which carry the bacteria. The cholera appears to spread when the tule fog hangs low and the birds sleep closer together. (Tule fog is the name given a dense, ground-hugging fog that is responsible each year for chain pileups on the freeways. The fog is formed when cold air is trapped in low spots.) From year to year, the dieoffs, which continue through spring, can be large or small. Whatever is there is meat on the table for eagles and other raptors that inhabit the basin for its easy pickings.

with a preserve administered by The Nature Conservancy and lands under control of the state of Oregon. The Bureau of Reclamation, however, still controls water rights in the basin (the refuges overlie reclamation land); and as elsewhere in the arid west, *water* is what will determine the future of the remaining Klamath wetlands.

GETTING THERE

Begin your visit to the six refuges with a stop at the Visitor Center at Tule Lake refuge on Hill Rd. From Klamath Falls, drive east on OR 140, then south on OR 39. One mi. before reaching Merrill, turn south on Merrill Pit Rd. (at NWR sign). At the end of Merrill Pit Rd. turn left on OR 161 (also known as Stateline Rd.) for 4 mi., then turn left on Hill Rd. to the Visitor Center. (The trip from Klamath Falls is about 22 mi.) From California, drive north on I-5 to Weed, then take CA 97 about 43 mi. north to CA 161 (also known as Stateline Rd.). Turn east on CA 161, which takes you through Lower Klamath NWR. Drive 18 mi., then turn south on Hill Rd. to the Visitor Center.

■ **SEASON:** Open year-round.

■ **HOURS:** Refuge open sunrise to sunset. Visitor Center open, Mon.–Fri., 8 a.m.–4:30 p.m.; weekends and holidays, 10 a.m.–4 p.m. Closed Christmas and New Year's Day.

■ **FEES:** Tule Lake and Lower Klamath auto-tour routes, $3 per car or $12 season pass. Hunting and photo blinds, $5 per day; consecutive 3-day pass, $10; consecutive 10-day pass, $10. Season pass, $50; family season pass, $75. Passes also valid at Humboldt Bay NWR and Modoc NWR.

■ **ADDRESS:** Klamath Basin National Wildlife Refuges, Rte. 1, Box 74, Tulelake, CA 96134; web site: http//www/klamath nwr.org

■ **TELEPHONE:** 530/667-2231

TOURING KLAMATH BASIN

■ **BY AUTOMOBILE:** Thirty-three miles of gravel auto-tour roads are available: Klamath Marsh (10 miles), Tule Lake (9.6 miles), and Upper Klamath (13.5 miles). US 97 skirts the east side of Upper Klamath, and CA 161 cuts across Lower Klamath.

■ **BY FOOT:** Hiking trails near the headquarters and at Klamath Marsh total 10.33 miles.

■ **BY BICYCLE:** Auto-tour routes and the hiking trail at Klamath Marsh are open to bicyclists.

■ **BY CANOE, KAYAK, OR BOAT:** Only by taking to a boat can you see these immense expanses of water from a floating bird's-eye view, and the Klamath Basin refuges have designed their canoe trails to give you a special perspective into this watery world. Three canoe trails—at Tule Lake (2 miles), Upper Klamath (8.5 miles), and Klamath Marsh (no designated length)—are open July 1 to September 30 unless a marsh has dried out, been drawn down for maintenance, or closed temporarily to protect wildlife. The 8.5-mile Upper Klamath canoe trail is open year-round and is by far the most popular of the three trails. Canoes, kayaks, and boats can be rented at Rocky Point Resort, at the northern tip of Upper Klamath Lake (reservations: 541/356-2287).

WHAT TO SEE

■ **LANDSCAPE AND CLIMATE** The tranquil pastoral beauty of the Klamath Basin contrasts with its violent formation. Lying in the eastern Cascade Mountains directly in the great volcanic belt that includes Crater Lake to the north and the Lava Beds to the south, Klamath Basin's volcanic origin is hidden beneath its marshes and lakes. An occasional cliff face, pocked with cavities formed by cooling lava, reminds visitors that this was once a rocky wasteland. January temperatures in the basin range between 4 and 54 degrees. In July temperatures increase, from around 37 to 90 degrees. About 10 inches of rain fall each year—most of it in December through March—with snowfall around 28 inches. Elevation in the refuges ranges from 4,060 feet to 6,595 feet, accounting for the cool temperatures.

■ **PLANT LIFE** The basin is heavily farmed—around half of Tule Lake refuge is leased to farmers—and visitors will see crops of potatoes, sugar beets, onions,

Forest, Klamath Marsh NWR

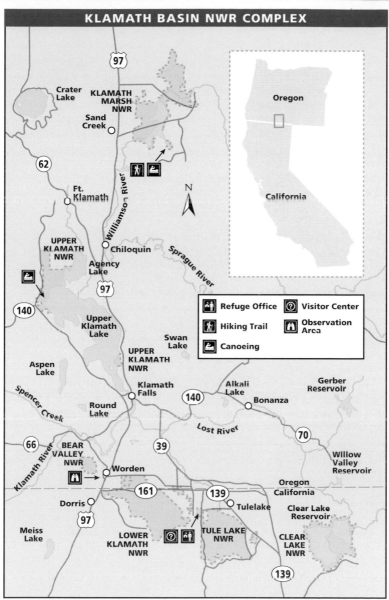

KLAMATH BASIN NWR COMPLEX

Legend:
- Refuge Office
- Visitor Center
- Hiking Trail
- Observation Area
- Canoeing

grain, and deep green alfalfa growing near the natural plant communities found in the marshes.

Wetlands Tules and cattails (see sidebar on tules, Tule Lake refuge) grow thick in the marshes and wetlands of Klamath Basin. Cattails—their familiar female flowers resembling fuzzy, oversized brown hot dogs—are natural water filters that help clean the marsh of contaminants. In summer, look for the bright yellow flowers of the wocus, or yellow water lily, blooming from mid-June through August. Out of sight underwater, but vitally important as a food source for waterfowl, are sago pondweed (a spindly plant with narrow, flat leaves) and coontail, a bushy, free-floating plant used in aquariums and one of the few vascular plants without roots.

Forest The land around Tule Lake is generally devoid of trees, testament to both the arid climate and the fact that most of the refuge is former lakebed; but at Klamath Marsh, a successional growth of alder and conifers—primarily lodgepole and ponderosa pine—reminds visitors that the basin is surrounded by parts of five national forests (Winema, Rogue River, Fremont, Klamath, and Modoc), which shelter a wide array of animals, including deer, pronghorn, elk, and bear.

Arid lands The high desert's sagebrush and bunchgrass give way to a flourishing juniper forest on the rocky uplands around Clear Lake. The lake's shoreline of tule marsh disappeared when water levels rose after the lake was dammed in 1911. Hidden among the sagebrush are dainty summer wildflowers (look for the orange flowers of Indian paintbrush), appearing much too fragile to survive in the harsh environment.

■ ANIMAL LIFE

Birds Even in the depth of winter, the basin is alive with birds. More than a thousand bald eagles winter here from December through February, the largest gathering of bald eagles in the Lower 48. Thousands of tundra swans herald the approach of spring as they arrive in February and March, sitting like puffy white balls on the frozen lakes.

The northern migration reaches its peak in March or early April when from one to two million waterfowl—including greater white-fronted geese, northern pintails, and green-winged teal—pass through. March also sees the return of white pelicans to their three breeding colonies in the basin. Spring shorebird migration peaks in April and May.

May and June mark the birth of ducklings as white-faced ibis breed in the marshes. In July northern orioles nest in trees around the refuge Visitor Center; the fall migration of shorebirds also begins in July.

In August and September white-fronted geese arrive, along with double-

Northern pintail

crested cormorants, herons, gulls, and grebes, all on their fall migration. Sandhill cranes stage in September and October while snow geese fly in during October and November. Fall migration, at its peak in mid-November, ends here in December when the lakes and marshes freeze over and most migrants fly south, completing the cycle of the seasons.

Mule deer

Mammals　The basin is home to 78 mammals—big ones such as elk, pronghorn, and black bear—and little ones like the Pacific water shrew, silver-haired bat, and least chipmunk. Your chances of seeing a number of these are good. Mule deer regularly visit the bird feeding station at the Visitor Center to eat the birdseed, and coyotes (pronounced KIGH-oats in these parts) are out early in the morning hunting breakfast. River otter and an occasional long-tailed weasel can be spotted in the marshes; and if you don't actually see a beaver, you can at least observe their industrious efforts as loggers.

Reptiles and amphibians　Three species of frog—spotted, western, and Pacific—live in the basin along with seven harmless reptiles (rubber boa, gopher, and common garter snakes among them), but keep an eye out for the eighth, the poisonous western rattlesnake, always recognized by the rattles at the end of its tail.

Fish　Fish at Klamath Basin occupy the unfortunate position of serving as dinner for many of the birds and mammals living here. Kokanee salmon and trout (rainbow, brown, and brook) are a main course for bald eagles. Other fish include the Klamath Lake sculpin and the Pit-Klamath lamprey. Two endangered species, the lost river and shortnose suckers, also swim in these waters.

Invertebrates　Human visitors are a potential meal for the millions of mosquitoes buzzing here June through September. Take mosquito repellent, wear long pants, a long-sleeved shirt, and a hat to protect your head; and, if you're particularly attractive to mosquitoes, wear a mosquito net over the hat.

ACTIVITIES

See individual refuges for wildlife observation, hikes and walks, and boating information.

■ **CAMPING:** No camping is allowed on the refuges. Best bet for camping is about 18 miles south of Tule Lake refuge at Lava Beds National Monument; this 43-site campground is rarely full. The refuge Visitor Center has a list of accommodations throughout the area. A primitive camp (around 5 sites) is available at Rocky Point canoe launch, Upper Klamath refuge.

■ **PHOTOGRAPHY:** Bald eagles and hawks use the only tree in sight around Tule Lake for a perch, and one of the basin's eight photo blinds is strategically

HUNTING AND FISHING Since the Klamath Basin refuges spread over both California and Oregon, pick up hunting regulations for both states, and be sure to check with refuge headquarters before planning a hunting or fishing trip, as regulations can change annually. Contact headquarters for specific information on the species of wildlife and fish that may be hunted at each location.

At Tule Lake, Lower Klamath, Bear Valley, and Clear Lake, hunting is permitted, but no fishing is allowed.

At Upper Klamath and Klamath Marsh, both hunting and fishing are permitted.

placed near the tree. The Visitor Center has a list of the blinds, including the wildlife you're likely to see, how to reserve a blind, and suggestions on the best equipment to use in order to take home a spectacular photograph from Klamath Basin. Be prepared to get up early. Most of the blinds are situated for morning photography, and several require you to be there before 7:30 a.m.

■ **SEASONAL EVENTS:** February: Bald Eagle Conference, on President's Day weekend, in Klamath Falls. Intended for families, it offers crafts classes for kids and adults, tours to refuge highlights and nearby attractions, birding in the basin, and, for all ages, bathouse building.

■ **PUBLICATIONS:** *A Birder's Guide to the Klamath Basin* by Steven Summers (Klamath Basin Audubon Society, 1993). *Klamath Basin National Wildlife Refuges* (Klamath Basin Wildlife Association, 1997).

Bald eagle

Bear Valley NWR
Tulelake, California

The name isn't right, and it's closed to the public, but Bear Valley NWR maintains an aura of fascination for visitors to Klamath Basin. The refuge is the winter roosting site for 300 to 500 bald eagles—the largest gathering of our national bird outside Alaska. The eagles, arriving in mid-November and leaving by mid-March, roost in the great conifers of Bear Valley's old-growth forest, then fly out at dawn to the basin's other refuges to eat waterfowl, rodents, and fish. The flyout is Bear Valley's big attraction, and you can witness it from the road outside the refuge.

HISTORY

The name is a bit misleading. Bear Valley is a 6.5-square-mile, 4,200-acre forested hillside of old-growth conifers with an elevation range of 4,090 to 6,595 feet. Established in 1978, its popularity is not vast, but its champions are enthusiastic: About 1,400 visitors watched the flyout in 1997.

GETTING THERE

Drive around 13 mi. south of Klamath Falls on US 97. Just south of Worden, turn west onto the Keno-Worden Rd. Cross the railroad tracks and turn left onto a gravel road. Continue about 0.5 mi. and park along the shoulder to watch the flyout.

WHAT TO SEE

Rouse yourself before daybreak to watch a hundred bald eagles, their massive wings spreading to seven and a half feet, flying silently overhead as dawn breaks. Look west toward Hammaker Mountain for eagles flying east along the ridges and directly overhead. The biggest concentration of eagles during the flyout, starting about a half-hour before sunrise, occurs in the first hour. Remember: This is January and February, and you should dress warmly. Don't forget your binoculars. If a dawn rendezvous isn't your style, you can watch the eagles later catching their breakfast on nearby Lower Klamath refuge.

Clear Lake NWR
Tulelake, California

Wind whips across the harsh, desolate high-desert landscape surrounding Clear Lake Reservoir, so remote that only 1,235 visitors found their way there in 1997. In summer, heat soaks into the earth, and all is still. A visit to this bleak land of sagebrush and juniper trees is a chance to see California in all its untamed wildness and marvel at the number of birds and mammals that call it home.

HISTORY

Clear Lake Reservoir, covering half the refuge, supplies water to farmers in the

American white pelicans

eastern half of Klamath Basin. Established in 1911, the 52-square-mile refuge (33,440 acres) is closed to the public; but Clear Lake can be seen from Forest Road 136, skirting the southern boundary of the reservoir.

GETTING THERE

About 20 mi. south of Tulelake on CA 139, turn east (left) on the signed, gravel forest road (Clear Lake Reservoir Rd). If you reach the right turn to Lava Beds National Monument, you've gone too far. On the gravel road, stay left at first Y, then continue to the northeast. Caution: Heavy rains can turn the refuge road into a quagmire, requiring 4-wheel-drive. The road is not cleared of snow.

WHAT TO SEE

Thrusting its long yellow bill into Clear Lake, the white pelican scoops up a short-nose sucker (an endangered species) and stores the fish in its capacious pouch, to be digested at leisure. Unlike brown pelicans, white pelicans do not fish by flying and diving into the water. Floating high on the water, they simply dip their beaks to catch an unsuspecting passing fish. The lake's rocky islands hold one of the West's few nesting colonies of white pelicans, and some 1,000 of them fledge there each summer. Look for huge white birds, their wingtips extending to 9 feet, flapping their wings for liftoff, then gliding in formation high in the sky. Fellow nesters on the lake's islands include double-crested cormorants, an estimated 5,800 ring-billed gulls, and 3,500 California gulls

Rock cliff with petroglyphs

On land, a herd of 40 to 50 pronghorns may be seen at any time of year; and flitting about the bushy juniper trees, small mountain bluebirds dine on juniper berries, their blue plumage startling against the snowy landscape of winter. Temperatures in the coldest months drop to 20 to 40 degrees, and a foot or more of snow may cover the rock-encrusted desert. In summer, temperatures soar into the 90s. (Hot days and cold nights are typical of this high desert, where the refuge elevation ranges from 4,523 to 4,600 feet.) Carrying water is a necessity when exploring Klamath Basin's semidesert uplands, formed thousands of years ago by the repeated eruptions of nearby Medicine Lake volcano.

This broad, rounded volcano (known as a shield volcano) erupted sporadically over a period of more than 500,000 years and is the largest volcano in the Cascade Mountains. (Don't miss a side trip to nearby Lava Beds National Monument, where more than 380 lava tube caves are open for exploration. The tubes formed when hot fluid lava erupted. As the lava flowed down slope it began to cool and solidify on the sides and top while the molten lava inside the shell continued to flow, draining out and leaving behind a hollow tube.) A short turnoff to the right on the entry road to Clear Lake leads to a lava face called Petroglyph Point, where barn owls, cliff swallows, and prairie falcons roost in myriad holes on the face, formed when a cinder cone erupted from ancient Tule Lake and made an island. No one knows which ancient native tribe carved the petroglyphs. A steep trail leads to the top of the face for an expansive view of the plateau. Caution: Watch for rattlesnakes.

Black-crowned night heron

Klamath Marsh NWR
Chiloquin, Oregon

A lush field of pond lilies, their bright yellow blossoms reflecting on the rippling water, creates a textured green and yellow carpet spread across Klamath Marsh NWR (formerly Klamath Forest NWR), the northernmost of the marshes in Klamath Basin. Meadows dotted with summertime wildflowers offer expansive views beyond the marsh, and a pine forest snuggled along the marsh's eastern edge shelters Rocky Mountain elk and secretive great gray owls.

HISTORY

Historic home of the Klamath Indian tribes, Klamath Marsh was established as a refuge in 1958 when the first 16,400 acres were purchased from the Klamath Indian tribe with federal Duck Stamp funds. Wet meadows and a natural marsh make up almost 90 percent of the present 63-square-mile refuge, with pine forest covering the remaining acreage, all at an elevation of about 4,500 feet. Annually, around 6,500 visitors explore Klamath Marsh refuge.

GETTING THERE

Drive north on US 97 about 45 mi. from Klamath Falls. Turn east (right) onto

WOCUS WATER LILIES Even the beaver's appetite for the rhizomes of the Wocas, or yellow pond lily, can't prevent its vigorous growth habits. Once rooted, this perennial spreads thickly, floating on the water's surface, often crowding out other plants. The delicate appearance of the glossy leaves and fragile flowers gives no indication of the plant's enormous rhizome growing underwater, sometimes 16 feet long and 6 inches in diameter.

The Wocus (from the Native *wok,* meaning "seed pods of the wocus") was a major food staple for the Klamath Indians, who gathered the seed pods, which are shaped like acorns matured with a conical head. The head would then be parched over a fire; after the fruit and seeds were separated out, the seeds were pounded and cooked again, then eaten.

Blooming from June through mid-August, the Wocus is now a food for wildfowl and deer, who consume its flowers, leaves, and stems.

Silver Lake Rd. and go approximately 9.5 mi. to just past where the marsh and forest meet. Take the first right onto gravel Forest Service Rd. 690.

TOURING KLAMATH MARSH

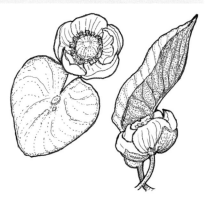

Yellow pond lily

■ **BY AUTOMOBILE:** A short auto route of l0.5 miles and an extended route of 13.5 miles are passable in summer. A high-clearance vehicle is recommended, but 4-wheel-drive isn't necessary. Caution: The road is slick after heavy rains and is not plowed clear of the abundant winter snows.

■ **BY FOOT:** A 5-mile (one-way) recreational trail is open to hikers, who may also walk the entire auto loop.

■ **BY BICYCLE:** Mountain bikers can follow the gravel auto-loop route.

■ **BY CANOE, KAYAK, OR BOAT:** Wocus Bay, at the southern tip of the marsh, is open for canoeing or kayaking from July 1 to September 30. No motorized boats are allowed. Check with refuge headquarters before planning a trip, because water levels may be too low for boating in a dry summer—and the canoeing area can be closed at any time to protect wildlife. The canoe launch is approximately 4 miles south on Forest Servicc Road 690 from its intersection with Silver Lake Road. To rent canoes or kayaks, call Rocky Point Resort (541/356-2287).

■ **BY SKIS OR SNOWSHOES:** In heavy snow years, the 10 miles of Forest Service Road 690 become an ungroomed cross-country ski trail.

WHAT TO SEE

■ **LANDSCAPE AND CLIMATE** Ringed by forest, this natural marsh is unquestionably the prettiest in the six-refuge Klamath complex. Because it lies some 500 feet higher than the other marshes in the basin, Klamath Marsh experiences temperatures about five degrees lower—averaging -1 to 49 degrees in January; in July, the range is around 32 to 85.

ACTIVITIES

■ **CAMPING:** Camping is not allowed on the refuge, but it is allowed on adjacent national forest land. An overnight camping trip in Winema National Forest is an excellent way to observe wildlife. Klamath Marsh is the only refuge in the basin where you can camp out in the national forest and have a ringside seat to observe wildlife in the refuge across the road. Carry water and bring mosquito repellent. In winter, when the trail is open for cross-country skiing, there is opportunity for snow camping and viewing of a completely different group of birds. You won't see many mammals at this time, however: Many of them are hibernating through the winter months.

■ **WILDLIFE OBSERVATION:** The marsh is famous for its 60 pairs of sandhill cranes. Other inhabitants you're likely to see are white-headed woodpeckers (the only woodpecker found in the West with a white head), yellow-headed blackbirds, Steller's jays, and ruddy ducks.

Canoeing or kayaking is a great way to take in the lush scenery in and around the marsh, which shelters 42 species of animals and birds. Take suntan lotion, sunglasses, and a hat to explore the 700 acres of open water and tule and cattail marsh, where you may see pied-billed grebes, cinnamon teal, and black-crowned night-herons. Look for the short-necked heron standing patiently in the water, waiting for a fish or frog to swim by.

■ **HIKES AND WALKS:** The 5-mile recreation trail (serving also as Forest Service Road 690 and the route to the canoe launch) meanders along the east side of the marsh, in and out of the refuge and adjoining Winema National Forest. Here it is particularly interesting to observe the two biomes—marsh and forest. Songbirds keep to their forest home while waterfowl inhabit the marsh.

Lower Klamath NWR
Tukelake, California

As great billowing masses of birds fly into the Klamath marshes during the spring and fall migrations, the noise is overwhelming: The cackling of thousands of geese combines with the quacks, whistles, and cries of ducks numbering in the hundreds

Tundra swans

RUDDY DUCKS The ruddy duck struts through the water with its head thrown back as if reaching for its erect tail feathers. Known in various parts of the country as sleepy duck, paddy-whack, stub-and-twist, booby coot, and dumb bird, the ruddy duck lacks the large wing area of geese or swans. It will never soar over the marsh. Because its wings are even smaller than usual for a duck, the ruddy has to work harder at flying than most other ducks. The ruddy's feet are set so far back on the body that it can only take a few steps before it falls over awkwardly on its breast. Functioning like twin outboards, the ruddy's feet make the duck a great swimmer, but a terrible walker.

As the ruddy flies through a freezing fog, its wings gather frost, ice up, and no longer support flight, and the ruddy falls ignominiously out of the sky. Not being able to run, it can't take off even if it deices. The duck needs water. So if you discover a ruddy on your lawn one winter morning, put it into a box and launch it into a lake, river, or pond. The duck will be just fine.

Leo Smothers, Klamath Basin refuges volunteer

of thousands to create a phantas-magoria of motion, color, and noise. Anyone witnessing this astonishing aerial panorama will understand why Lower Klamath is often named one of the 10 top refuges in the United States.

HISTORY

Encouraged by members of the National Audubon Society, who observed the startling decline in birds near the turn of the century, President Theodore

Ruddy duck

Roosevelt established Lower Klamath in 1908 as the nation's first waterfowl refuge. Its 53,598 acres are divided into marsh (56 percent), croplands (28 percent), and uplands (16 percent), all between 4,000 and 4,500 feet in elevation. Lower Klamath and Tule Lake are the basin's most visited refuges. Almost 220,000 people tour Lower Klamath each year.

GETTING THERE

From the Klamath Basin NWR Visitor Center on Hill Rd. in Tule Lake, drive north to CA 161, along the Oregon–California border. Turn west on CA 161 and follow it through the Lower Klamath refuge.

TOURING LOWER KLAMATH NWR

■ **BY AUTOMOBILE:** The auto-tour route has two entrances off CA 161. Both entrances link to a loop encircling one of the refuge's marshes. Along the route, interpretive panels describe the habitats—seasonal wetlands, permanent marshes, and dry uplands.

■ **BY BICYCLE:** The auto-tour route is open to bicycles.

ACTIVITIES

■ **WILDLIFE OBSERVATION:** Among the tules, groups of small, chunky brown ducks feed on smartweed. With its erect tail, the ruddy duck is easy to spot. Nibbling at the seeds of smartweed, the ruddy is feeding on one of the food staples in the refuge. Smartweed, recognized by its large lance-shaped leaves (up to 6 inches long), was earlier known as "arsmart," for its tendency to inflame the hindquarters of persons who used it there. To see the male ruddy in its full glory, visit during spring mating season when its plumage turns bright chestnut brown and its beak turns blue.

Tule Lake NWR
Tulelake, California

It's only when you drive the square corners of the Tule Lake auto route that you realize this crown of the refuges along the Pacific Flyway, once one of the biggest marshlands west of the Mississippi, is actually two man-made sumps created by dikes, receiving drain water from Klamath Basin's agricultural fields. Toxicity levels present in the water from agricultural pesticides and fertilizers are not enough to deter the migratory birds. By November a million ducks, geese, and swans have arrived at Tule Lake and nearby Lower Klamath refuges—tens of thousands of snow geese from Siberia, sandhill cranes, tundra swans from the Arctic, Canada geese, Ross's geese, mallards, wigeons, and the swift-flying green-winged teals.

HISTORY

Like a sea tide, Tule Lake once flowed over the surrounding marshlands when the wet years came and receded during the dry years. Fluctuating water levels created a productive marsh, but it dried up by 1905 after the Reclamation Act of 1902 had put in motion the Klamath Reclamation Project, draining the basin's wetlands for agricultural use. Although Tule Lake was designated a wildlife refuge in 1928, draining continued; and by 1960 Tule Lake was only 13 percent of its original size.

Tule Lake, Tule Lake NWR

TULES The vast beds of hardstem and softstem bulrushes seen in most of the West's marshes got their local name—tule (TWO-lee)—from the Aztecs. Spaniards, moving north from Mexico into California, dropped the "n" from the Aztec "tollin" (a rush) to describe the slender stalks that grow from 3 to 9 feet tall in marshes and muddy ground around lakes and streams. The dense clumps of tules, sprouting from a rhizome, offer cover for river otters, muskrats and raccoons. Marsh wrens, water-fowl, and yellow-headed blackbirds nest in tules, and both Canada geese and white-fronted geese—as well as muskrats—eat the stems and rhizomes. Small tufts of brownish flowers bloom in summer, maturing into nut-shaped fruits that are a staple for marsh birds, ducks, and shorebirds.

Native Americans also ate the rhizomes, grinding them into flour; and they wove baskets from tule stems. Tule sleeping mats helped insulate against the cold ground because of the loose, spongy interiors of the stems.

Caution: If you're driving to the California and southern Oregon refuges in winter, watch out for tule fog. It hangs on the ground, so dense you can't see four feet in front of your nose, and is responsible for any number of fender benders and freeway pileups.

An attempt to restore marshland can be seen at Hovey Point (marker number 5 on the auto-tour route), a new seasonal marsh that will be drained periodically, and, at times, left as a permanent marsh. Birds have flocked to Hovey Point in both spring and fall, indicating their approval. Wildlife biologists hope the creation of more seasonal marshes will someday see many more birds using Tule Lake.

The refuge—of which more than half is farmland—totals 61 square miles, all between 4,056 feet and 4,600 feet. Tule Lake is the most visited of the Klamath Basin's six refuges, welcoming almost 223,000 annually in recent years.

GETTING THERE

Drive 5 mi. south on Hill Rd. from the Klamath Basin Visitor Center in Tule Lake, CA, and turn left onto the auto-tour route.

TOURING TULE LAKE

■ **BY AUTOMOBILE:** An auto-tour route (9.6 miles one-way) follows dikes along the edges of the north and south sumps.

■ **BY FOOT:** A short but very steep trail (.33 mile round-trip) ascends Sheepy Ridge behind the Visitor Center. Directly south of the Visitor Center and on the opposite side of Hill Road, a 0.5-mile trail loops through a demonstration wetland known as Discovery Marsh.

■ **BY BICYCLE:** Bicyclists may use the unpaved auto-tour route. For those in good physical shape, it's possible to ride an approximate 38-mile loop around the refuge, with the southern leg following the boundary of Lava Beds National Monument.

■ **BY CANOE, KAYAK, OR BOAT:** A marked canoe trail follows some 2 miles of quiet channels through a 2,500-acre tule and cattail marsh. The trail is open daylight hours, July 1 to September 30, but can be shut at any time because of low water or potential disturbance to wildlife. Check at the Visitor Center.

ACTIVITIES

■ **WILDLIFE OBSERVATION:** Get up early in the morning to see one of the great sights at Tule Lake. On the farm field south of the Visitor Center, as many as 13 coyotes will be busy catching voles in the field, gulping them down in one swallow and trotting along to find the next breakfast tidbit.

Don't miss Hotel Rock en route to the auto-tour route. The rock is a lava face on the west side of Hill Road, pockmarked with cavities created when the lava cooled. Before turning into the tour route, park off the highway and walk north 75 feet. The wildlife service has marked an angled line on the road. Set up a spotting scope (or use binoculars) in line with the marking and scan the cliff face. You'll find a barn owl that makes its home in one of the cavities of the lava face. In summer, cliff swallows nest on the face along with other hotel residents such as prairie falcons and a great horned owl.

California gull

Visitors come from all over the world to see the birds at Tule Lake. Drive slowly along the auto route, stay in the car, and you'll see whatever birds are in residence. In June through September, look for ruddy ducks, eared grebes, the ubiquitous great blue heron, Brewer's blackbird, and the California gull. Note the fields of cereal grain and alfalfa on your right—a feast for the birds. The great blue heron, an ashy blue gray, eats fish, grasshoppers, mice, and baby birds. You may spot it standing on one leg in a marsh waiting for a fish to swim by or in the sky, distinguished from the sandhill crane because it flies with its neck folded.

■ **CANOEING AND KAYAKING:** To find the launch site for the Tule Lake canoe trail, drive north 0.5 mile from the Visitor Center and turn east on East-West Road, driving another 3.2 miles. Just after crossing Lost River, turn right onto a gravel road and continue .25 mile to the junction at the twin pumps. Turn right again and continue .4 mile to the launch site on the right. Early morning and late afternoon offer best chances for viewing ring-necked pheasant bustling through the uplands, redhead ducks among the tules, plus ravens, mule deer, and a host of marsh birds.

■ **HIKES AND WALKS:** The trail up Sheepy Ridge behind the Visitor Center may seem straight up, but the view from the top can't be beat. The ridge separates Tule Lake and Lower Klamath refuges. A free guide, available at the trailhead, is keyed to numbered posts along the trail, where you may see yellow-bellied marmots, gopher snakes, cliff swallows, and American kestrels. Also known as a sparrow hawk, the American kestrel, about the size of a jay, can sometimes be seen hovering in the air while searching for prey or perched on a pole as it looks for lizards and mice. Look for a rusty back and tail.

Beaver

Upper Klamath NWR
Tulelake, California

Klamath Lake is a vacation destination for Oregonians, offering resorts, fishing, and boats; but launch your canoe into the great marsh at the northern end of the lake and you're in a different world. The rustle of tules breaks the deep hush of this water world as your canoe slides through the cattails and bulrushes. The slap of a beaver's tail startles a belted kingfisher into flight, then silence falls again. Floating the sinuous twists of Crystal Creek is entrée into a secret world of animals and birds hidden in this embracing marsh.

HISTORY

Both Upper Klamath and Tule Lake refuges were added to the NWR system in 1928. Located in the center of the basin's six refuges, Upper Klamath sits at about 4,200 feet and includes 23 square miles of territory; all but 30 acres are freshwater marsh and open water. Around 3,000 visitors explore the Upper Klamath refuge annually.

GETTING THERE

From the Klamath Basin refuge headquarters in Tule Lake, CA, drive north on Hill Rd., then west on CA 161, viewing Lower Klamath Marsh on your left. Turn north on US 97, then west on OR 140. Swing north (right) on either Rocky Point Rd. or West Side Rd. to one of the two boat landings. The drive is around 30 mi.

TOURING UPPER KLAMATH NWR

■ **CANOE, KAYAK, OR BOAT:** Exploring Upper Klamath refuge requires a boat, and the four segments of the Upper Klamath Canoe Trail allow you to see as much or as little as you wish. Planning your trip, figure that two physically fit persons can paddle 2 miles per hour. Here are the options: Launch at Malone Springs boat launch (5.5 miles north of OR 140) to paddle the 2 miles (one-way) of Crystal Creek. Launch at Rock Point boat launch and paddle north to make a

5.1-mile loop around Recreation Creek, Wocus Cut, Crystal Creek, and Pelican Bay. With two cars, you can put in at Malone Springs and take out at Rocky Point (3 miles one-way; no portage necessary). Note: Wocus Cut may be dry by late August. Since the Rocky Point launch has access to Klamath Lake, you're likely to encounter motorized boats on Pelican Bay, the southern loop of the trail.

WHAT TO SEE

The aspen, cottonwood, and willow along the lake's edge offer shelter to flycatchers and warblers. Most birds in the basin stop by Upper Klamath sometime during the year; look for pintails, mallards, gadwalls, and canvasbacks. Other commonly observed species include white pelicans (found nesting in the marsh), Canada geese, bald eagles, and osprey. The secretive yellow rail sometimes winters in the marsh. Difficult to see, the rail stays hidden rather than flying when flushed; it is most active at night.

Gadwall

Malheur NWR
Princeton, Oregon

Arid uplands, Malheur NWR

Everything about Malheur NWR is big—from the vast sweep of the high desert to the miles of lush open water amid arid land to the infinite blue of the sky arching over the great block of Steens Mountain in the background. Birds come here in numbers not often equaled elsewhere, making the refuge a major destination for birders. In the past, however, the area was not always appreciated. Less concerned about the magnificent scenery than his own misery, a French trapper named this place *Malheur* (Mall-ure, as in lure), which means "misfortune" in French.

HISTORY

As the United States high-stepped toward the 20th century amid the opulence of the Gilded Age, the rage in ladies' fashion were hats strikingly decorated with a long, plumed feather, preferably from an egret. By 1898, plume hunters plundering Malheur had decimated the egret population. President Theodore Roosevelt was persuaded in 1908 to protect Malheur Lake and its surrounding marshes as a bird sanctuary. In 1935 President Franklin Roosevelt oversaw the purchase of French's P-Ranch and the Blitzen River Valley, assuring the refuge's water supply. The sanctuary officially became Malheur NWR in 1940, at a size of 291 square miles These days, about 64,500 visitors enjoy the property annually.

GETTING THERE

Malheur NWR is in east-central Oregon, about 32 mi. southeast of Burns. From Burns take OR 78 east out of town about 2 mi., then turn south on OR 205 and continue for 24 mi. At the refuge sign, turn east and go 6 mi. on Harney County Rd. 405, which becomes Princeton Rd. Turn left at top of hill to headquarters.
- **SEASON:** Open year-round.
- **HOURS:** The refuge is open dawn to dusk. Visitor Center and office are open

Mon.–Thurs., 7 a.m.–4:30 p.m.; Fri. to 3:30 p.m. Volunteers open the Visitor Center on weekends, mid-April–early October.
- **ADDRESS:** Malheur NWR, HC 72 Box 245, Princeton, OR 97721
- **TELEPHONE:** 541/493-2612

TOURING MALHEUR

- **BY AUTOMOBILE:** The 41-mile gravel auto-tour route runs north to south through the heart of the refuge, passing wetlands, riparian and upland habitats, and the six best sites at Malheur for viewing wildlife. Automobiles and ATVs are allowed only on roads shown in refuge brochure.
- **BY FOOT:** There are a couple of short walking paths and a loop trail following various bodies of water. Generally, hiking is limited to roads open to vehicular traffic and to stream and canal banks in the public fishing area.
- **BY BICYCLE:** Bicyclists can use any roads open to motorized vehicles.
- **BY CANOE, KAYAK, OR BOAT:** Canoes or boats with electric motors are allowed on Krumbo Reservoir during fishing season and on Malheur Lake during hunting season. All other refuge waters are closed to boating.
- **BY HORSEBACK:** Horseback riding is allowed on refuge roads open to cars.

WHAT TO SEE

- **LANDSCAPE AND CLIMATE** Water flows freely into this arid, high-desert basin (elevation around 4,100 feet), creating 32 miles of river floodplain, marshes, ponds, and lakes. At the refuge's northern end, in wet years, wide-spreading, sweet-water Malheur Lake overflows to join with Mud Lake and the alkali Harney Lake into one massive sweep of water. Tucked into the base of Steens Mountain, (a 30-mile-long fault block, the largest in the northern Great Basin), Malheur refuge is fed by three rivers flowing into the flatlands. Blitzen River, rising in the snow-covered reaches of Steens Mountain in the southeast, got its name in 1864 when Captain George B. Currey crossed the river during a thunderstorm while chasing Indians. Captain Currey called it "Donner und Blitzen," German for "thunder and lightning." Silver Creek flows from springs around Harney Lake; the Silvies River rises in the northern mountains. Snow can cover the refuge in winter, with January temperatures averaging 20 to 40 degrees. Summers are hot; July temperatures can rise to about 90. Around 10 inches of rain fall here each year.

- **PLANT LIFE**
Wetlands Rushes and cattails grow thickly in Malheur's marshes—redhead ducks nest among the cattails, spike rush, Baltic rush, and bur reed. Baltic rush spreads by rhizomes and grows in a line of stalks emerging from its extended rhizome. It

Redhead duck

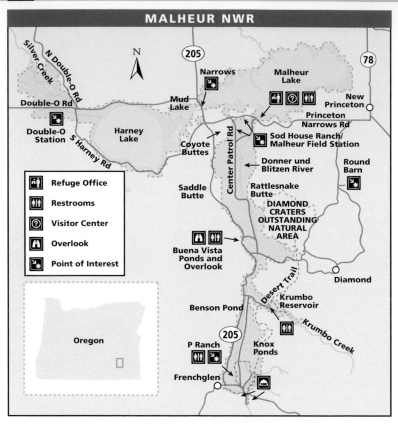

MALHEUR NWR

sprouts a cluster of tiny white flowers growing from one side of the stem. Spike rush can be recognized by a narrow tapered tuft of 50 to 100 tiny flowers enclosed by brownish bracts at the top of the tall green stem. Bur reed's stems often float atop or under the water. Its name derives from the small green globular burrlike fruits.

Willows growing in riparian areas along the river and stream banks serve as shelter for the numerous songbirds found at Malheur.

Arid lands Three upland plants serve as food for pronghorns and deer and as nesting sites for sage thrashers, pheasants, quail, and ducks. The chokecherry (also called capulin) grows to 8 feet tall; in spring its small white flowers, blooming at the end of its branches, are visible from a distance. Its astringent raw fruit puckers the mouth but makes good jam and syrup.

Greasewood (or chamise), a member of the rose family, has needlelike leaves grouped in clusters and tiny white flowers (blooming in spring), also in clusters up to 4 inches long. Growing 4 to 8 feet tall, greasewood is extremely flammable and contributes to the rapid spread of brush fires.

Sagebrush, icon of western lore, likes the hot dry reaches of Malheur and grows here in abundance. A member of the sunflower family (and not our seasoning "sage," which belongs to the mint family), sagebrush was once used for sweat baths and saunas. The dampened branches were placed on hot rocks heating the sauna, and in due time the pungent scent of sage permeated the atmosphere. If beekeepers are nearby, you'll find bees collecting nectar that eventually

SAGE GROUSE One of the more amazing mating rites practiced by birds can be observed on Malheur refuge in April when the sage grouse, America's largest grouse, gather on their traditional parading grounds, known as leks. The male grouse, about the size of a small turkey, fans its tails and struts around the lek, inflating its white chest sacs until two yellow skin patches are exposed, looking much like a couple of fried eggs, sunny side up. The sacs collapse, making a popping sound, accompanied by cooing and a bubbling sound from the grouse. The females, in the center of the lek, check out the males, waiting for the one who gains dominance. The dominant male will then copulate with all the females. Following mating, the females depart to build nests and raise their chicks alone.

The sage grouse get their name from their dietary preference—sagebrush leaves—and they live only where sagebrush can be found.

becomes fragrant sage honey. Great Basin wild rye, a short-lived perennial, serves as forage for refuge mammals.

■ ANIMAL LIFE

Birds The overwhelming number of bird species seen at Malheur—more than 320—has made the refuge a prime destination for birders. More than 200 pairs of sandhill cranes nest on Malheur each year. The cranes walk sedately, unlike the jerky steps of the heron, and fly with slow, graceful strokes, gliding on wind current, necks extended. During their spring mating ritual, done either in pairs or in groups, the cranes bow to one another and hop and skip or jump into the air, great wings extended and legs dangling. By September the cranes have been joined by other sandhill cranes

Sage grouse.

that summer in the north; they gather in the grain fields near the refuge headquarters to feed before all depart for the flight to California, where they winter in California's Central Valley.

Late March usually sees the peak number of species in the refuge as birds stop to feed and rest during their spring migration. Among the many birds are long-billed curlews, double-crested cormorants, tundra swans, white-fronted, snow, Ross' and Canada geese, and numerous ducks.

Unusual species of interest to birders are the marbled godwit, ruddy turnstone, and solitary, pectoral, and Baird's sandpipers.

Warblers, vireos, tanagers, and buntings fly through in April, with numbers peaking in mid-May.

Badger

Mammals Malheur is home to numerous mammals, some 58 species in all, including mule deer, coyotes, raccoons, long-tailed weasels, mink, and badgers. Fourteen species of bats live on the refuge; the most common are the little brown and Yuma myotis and the big brown and hoary bats. Malheur's rodents include the least chipmunk, Belding's ground squirrel, the Great Basin pocket mouse, and Ord's kangaroo rat. Beavers make their home in Malheur's extensive ponds.

Fish Redband trout, a desert subspecies of the rainbow trout, are found here.

Reptiles and amphibians The refuge is home to garter snakes, western rattlesnakes, and the Oregon spotted frog.

Invertebrates Deerflies, horseflies, and no-see-ums annoy visitors, and it's said you can't walk on the refuge in May without sucking in mosquitoes.

ACTIVITIES

■ **CAMPING:** There is no camping on the refuge, but the BLM's Page Springs primitive campground is located just off the beginning of the Steens Mountain loop road at the south end of Malheur. The campground's water is turned off in winter and is turned on again the first of May. For information about other BLM campgrounds in the area, call 541/573-4400. Steens Mountain Resort has full hookups.

■ **WILDLIFE OBSERVATION:** In March, geese, swans, cranes, and ducks can be found feeding in flooded meadows near the town of Burns or on the Double-O unit at Malheur. The Blitzen Valley is out of the major migration corridors but is the best place to see trumpeter swans and greater sandhill cranes. To view migrating songbirds, look around refuge headquarters, Benson Pond, and P-Ranch. Highest numbers are present in mid-May.

As summer begins to dry out the lakes, southbound shorebirds can be seen feeding on the mudflats at the Double-O Unit and Harney, Mud, and Malheur lakes. Least and western sandpipers and both greater and lesser yellowlegs are common. Look for warblers, sparrows, and other songbirds at refuge headquarters, P-Ranch, and Page Springs from mid-August through late September.

■ **PHOTOGRAPHY:** The sage grouse mating dance is a popular photo subject.

MALHEUR HUNTING AND FISHING SEASONS

Hunting (Seasons may vary)	Jan	Feb	Mar	Apr	May	Jun	Jul	Aug	Sep	Oct	Nov	Dec
geese	■									■	■	■
duck	■									■	■	■
coot	■									■	■	■
chukar	■									■	■	■
Hungarian partridge	■									■	■	■
pheasant										■	■	■
quail										■	■	
dove									■			
pigeon									■			
pronghorn antelope								≡				
deer										■		
Fishing												
black bass				■	■	■	■	■	■	■		
rainbow trout				■	■	■	■	■	■	■		
redband trout				■	■	■	■	■	■	■		

During hunting season, boats with electric motors are allowed on Malheur Lake hunt areas. Water levels at the lake vary widely from year to year, sometimes making access difficult. During fishing season (late April though Oct.), motorless boats and boats with electric motors are permitted only on Krumbo Reservoir.

Visit the lek at dawn and be prepared to film in low light. The refuge has no blinds, but photographers may bring their own portable blinds.

■ **HIKES AND WALKS:** Songbirds—willow flycatchers, yellow warblers, vireos, and tanagers—stop off in Malheur during the spring migration (peaking in mid-May), and a good place to see them is on the 13-mile fishing trail loop along the banks of the Blitzen River. Access to the trail is at P Ranch.

Two short .25-mile paths lead to overlooks at headquarters and Buena Vista ponds on the tour route south of headquarters.

A loop trail used during fishing season follows the banks of East Canal, Bridge Creek, and the Blitzen River. Hiking is also permitted along the banks of Krumbo Reservoir and on the Barnes Springs footpath near Frenchglen.

A portion of Desert Trail, part of the proposed National Scenic Desert Trail, enters the refuge near Page Springs on Steens Mountain. For maps and information, call the Bureau of Land Management, 541/573-4300.

■ **SEASONAL EVENTS:** April: Tours to the sage grouse lek and the wildhorse corrals are among the more than 15 events offered during the annual three-day John Scharff Migratory Bird Festival & Art Show. Held in Burns the first weekend of the month (the second weekend if there's a conflict with Easter), the festival highlights spring migration in the refuge and Harney Basin. (Scharff was the first manager of Malheur NWR.) For information, call the Harney County Chamber of Commerce, 541/573-2636.

■ **PUBLICATIONS:** *Birds of Malheur National Wildlife Refuge, Oregon,* by Carroll D. Littllefield (Oregon State University Press, Corvallis, 1990).

Mid-Columbia River NWR Complex

Umatilla NWR, Toppenish NWR, McNary NWR,
McKay Creek NWR, Cold Springs NWR
Umatilla, Oregon

Refuge wetlands, Umatilla NWR

The great Columbia flows 1,240 miles from British Columbia through Washington to the Pacific. As it turns west, it cuts 300 miles to the Pacific, forming all but 120 miles of the state line between Washington and Oregon. Little is left of the wild Columbia and the extensive marshes that once surrounded it, its power harnessed over the years by dams for hydroelectric power and irrigation water. A group of five national wildlife refuges that span the Columbia in northeast Oregon and south-central Washington preserve some of the remaining wetlands and re-create some of what has been lost. Within an easy drive of one another, sharing the diverse habitats surrounding the river, and attracting similar wildlife, the refuges demonstrate the changes that occur when a wild river is dammed.

■ **ADDRESS:** For Umatilla, Toppenish, McNary, McKay Creek and Cold Springs refuges: c/o Mid-Columbia River NWR Complex, P.O. Box 700, 830 Sixth St., Umatilla, OR 97882

■ **TELEPHONE:** 509/545-8588

Umatilla NWR
Umatilla, Oregon

HISTORY

The construction of the John Day Lock and Dam caused the Columbia River to rise 25 feet and replaced the wild river with a broad, sluggish reservoir, Lake Umatilla, drowning the area's wetlands. The 37-square-mile Umatilla NWR was established in 1969 to mitigate the loss of wildlife habitat caused by the new dam completed that same year.

Each year about 65,000 wildlife enthusiasts and hunters visit the refuge; 30 percent of them come by boat.

GETTING THERE

Umatilla refuge has units in both Oregon and Washington. From Portland, OR, drive east 148-mi. on I-84. Turn north 16-mi. on US 730 to Umatilla, where refuge headquarters is located at 830 Sixth St. To go directly to the Washington units of Umatilla, cross the Columbia on US 94 by turning north 102-mi. east of Portland at Biggs. Drive east on WA 14 about 57-mi. Washington units of the refuge (Whitcomb, Ridge and Patterson) can be seen from the highway. To visit Oregon units (McCormack and Boardman), drive west from Umatilla on US 730. To reach McCormack Unit, turn north on Paterson Ferry Rd. to. To reach Boardman Unit, continue west on US 730 to I-84. Drive west on I-84 and exit north at Boardman.

■ **SEASON:** Refuge open year-round.

■ **HOURS:** Refuge open daily, dawn to dusk. Headquarters open Mon.–Fri., 8 a.m.–4 p.m.

TOURING UMATILLA

■ **BY AUTOMOBILE:** A 5-mile auto-tour route provides a good look at the McCormack Unit by passing through irrigated croplands where farmers grow corn, weat and alfalfa, and by Mccormack Slough.

■ **BY BICYCLE:** Bicyclists may ride on any refuge roads open to automobiles.

■ **BY CANOE, KAYAK, OR BOAT:** Five launch sites are available. In Washington, turn south off WA 14, following WA 221 less than a mile to the river. A second launch is available at Crow Butte State Park, adjacent to the west end of the refuge. On the Oregon side, drive west from Umatilla on US 730. Turn north at Irrigon to the river. To find the fourth boat ramp, continue west on US 730 and turn north on Paterson Ferry Road to the river. A fifth launch site is available at Boardman. Drive north at the Boardman exit from I-84 to the railroad tracks. Turn left to the boat ramp.

■ **BY HORSEBACK:** All vehicle roads are open to horseback riding.

WHAT TO SEE

■ **LANDSCAPE AND CLIMATE** Sprawling along the Columbia in Washington and Oregon's eastern desert, Umatilla is a mix of still backwaters, river islands, reservoirs, creeks, and shrub-steppe uplands, all spread across the hot, dry desert where only 8 inches of rain falls annually and temperatures veer between 43 and 108 degrees in July. Chilly January temperatures range from 7 to 54 degrees. Crow Butte, half of an island (the other half is a state park) at the downriver end of the refuge, marks the refuge's western boundary, while Paterson Slough lies along the north side of Lake Umatilla, indicating the eastern end of the 20-mile-long refuge.

PLANT LIFE

Wetlands The wetlands of Umatilla are heavily managed, with undesirable species bulldozed and the areas replanted with grasses such as Sandberg's bluegrass, Great Basin wild rye, and several wheatgrasses—streambank, tall, and thickspike. Cattail and hardstem bulrush grow naturally in the emergent marshes. Other plantings include chokecherry and coyote willow.

UMATILLA NWR

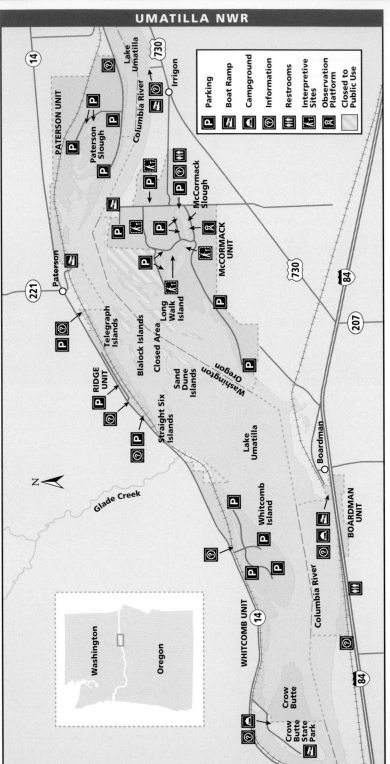

Cottonwood, ubiquitous throughout the West, grows along creek banks and dry washes—wherever there's enough water to satisfy its thirst. Cottonwoods are the biggest broadleaf tree in the northwest, growing to 100 feet in 35 years. When the tree's seeds, encased in fluffy, cottony white balls, float to the ground in June, it looks as if snowflakes are drifting through a blue sky. Warning: Don't park your car under a cottonwood. It sheds a sticky resin that takes a great deal of elbow grease to remove.

Grasslands Around 1,400 acres of the Whitcomb and McCormack units on the refuge are planted in crops that include wheat, buckwheat, tall fescue, alfalfa, peas, and corn. In exchange for use of the leased land, farmers leave part of the crop—about 25 percent—on the ground for wildlife to eat.

Arid lands The restoration of Umatilla's former pasturelands includes the planting of several native shrubs—big sagebrush, rubber rabbit brush, Rocky Mountain juniper, and Antelope bitterbrush. The bitterbrush is an important browse plant (shoots and twigs). It has three-lobed leaves and cream-yellow flowers. Rabbitbrush's bright golden-yellow flowers form a distinctive and rather showy flat head, and the plant is often sparsely leafed when blooming.

■ ANIMAL LIFE

Birds Most species of ducks found in the West—except for sea ducks—visit Umatilla. Huge numbers of ducks can be seen on the refuge in December—the count varies considerably from year to year (85,000 to 458,000).

A series of islands in the Columbia serves as nesting sites for Canada geese. The peak time to view the approximatly 90,000 wintering geese at Umatilla is December and January. Great blue herons and black-crowned night-herons nest at Umatilla along with long-billed curlews, whose beaks are almost as long as their bodies. The curlews' spectacular mating ritual occurs in March. The males present an impressive aerial display, winnowing (fanning) their wings as they hang in the air and then diving, with the whirring sound of their wings filling the air.

Long-billed curlews

Mammals A large herd of some 200 to 250 mule deer feeds on the McCormack Unit. Other mammals commonly seen include coyotes and raccoons.

ACTIVITIES

■ **CAMPING:** Camping is not permitted on the refuge. Camping in Washington is available at Crow Butte State Park at the west end of the refuge. Oregon campers can stop at Boardman Marina or at Hat Rock State Park, east of Umatilla.

■ **WILDLIFE OBSERVATION:** In March, Parking lot A off Patterson Ferry Road on the McCormack Unit is a good place to observe long-billed curlew courtship displays every 15 to 20 minutes. Wildflowers are in full bloom in spring and make colorful displays throughout the refuge. At dusk in summertime look for long-eared and burrowing owls hunting for mice in the fields. Remember that all refuge islands, except for Whitcomb, are closed to the public year-round.

■ **PHOTOGRAPHY:** Use fast film and a telephoto lens to capture the midair courtship display of the long-billed curlews.

■ **SEASONAL EVENTS:** March: Curlew Day, late in the month, with walking tours to see curlew courtship behavior, and a slide presentation on the bird's natural history.

HUNTING AND FISHING Hunting for a variety of waterfowl, including **Canadian geese, duck, coot,** and **snipe,** is permitted at Umatilla. **Upland game birds** such as **valley quail** and **pheasant** may be hunted from Oct. through Dec. Mule deer may also be hunted in Sept. Fishing for smallmouth bass and walleye is permitted on the refuge year-round.

Prairie falcon

Toppenish NWR
Toppenish, Washington

Great flocks of ducks rise in a whir of wings, so many that they blur the view of Mt. Adams in the distance. Winter brings geese, trumpeter swans, and some

50,000 ducks to fill the vast marshes and ponds of Toppenish refuge. Located in a serene farming valley, this little-known refuge is a place to wander in solitude and view some of the more than 250 bird species that use the area as home or a migratory stopover.

HISTORY

Toppenish refuge was established in 1964 to protect waterfowl and other migratory birds. The smallest of the five refuges in the Mid-Columbia complex, Toppenish is tiny (1,978 acres) and attracts visitors in modest numbers, around 3,500 annually.

GETTING THERE

From Seattle, drive southeast on I-90, then south on I-82 to Toppenish (160 mi. total). Drive south about 10 mi. on US 97 to the refuge entrance on the west side of the highway at Pumphouse Rd. From Portland drive 102 mi. east on I-84 and turn north on US 97 about 48 mi. to the refuge entrance. From Spokane, drive west on I-90, south on I-82 to

Sage thrasher

Toppenish (233 mi. total). Follow instructions above.

■ **SEASON:** Refuge open year-round.

■ **HOURS:** Refuge open daily, 5 a.m.–1 hour after sunset. Headquarters on the refuge staffed periodically in early morning and late afternoon hours.

WHAT TO SEE

■ **LANDSCAPE AND CLIMATE** The refuge, used chiefly by hunters, lies at the southern end of the Yakima Valley in the heart of the Yakima Indian Reservation. Rattlesnake Hills to the north and Toppenish Ridge and Horse Heaven Hills to the south are backdrops to the refuge's broad, flat marshlands. Extending 27 miles within the floodplain of Toppenish Creek, the refuge is divided into six separated parcels whose elevation varies by only 10 feet—730 to 740 feet. Little rain falls in this parched land—8 to 10 inches a year—where temperatures rise to 100 degrees in the summer (nights are a cool 60 degrees), but winters are a cold 10 to 50 degrees. A short trail leads from US 97 (the trailhead north of Pumphouse Road) by an orientation and viewing kiosk. The trail continues to refuge headquarters, offering views of the riparian habitat along Toppenish Creek.

■ **ANIMAL LIFE** Although Toppenish is known for the spectacular flights of ducks and Canada geese during spring and fall migrations, a number of other interesting bird species can be seen on the refuge. In the shrub-steppe flatlands, the sage thrasher is a common sight in spring and summer. Recognized by its straight, slender bill, white-spotted tail, and streaked breast, the thrasher, when courting, flies in a zigzag pattern low over the sage, then lights and flutters his upraised wings.

TOPPENISH HUNTING SEASONS

Hunting (Seasons may vary)	Jan	Feb	Mar	Apr	May	Jun	Jul	Aug	Sep	Oct	Nov	Dec
geese	■									■	■	■
duck	■									■	■	■
coot	■									■	■	■
snipe	■									■	■	■
pheasant										■	■	■
quail										■	■	■

Varied areas within the refuge are open to hunting different days of the week, so be sure to check with headquarters before planning a hunting trip. Fishing is not permitted.

Another inhabitant of the shrub-steppe is the sage sparrow, a small, wary bird that scurries from one bush to the next when feeding. Perched atop a sage bush, it jerks its tail. Look for the sparrow, which nests here, in spring and summer.

Arriving to dine on geese and ducks, bald eagles and prairie falcons join other raptors on the refuge—including northern harriers, red-tailed hawks, and American kestrels.

A stroll along the 1-mile loop trail running beside Toppenish Creek leads through a riparian area and by wetlands where it is possible to observe black-capped chickadees, western wood pewees, and the willow flycatcher. River otters, mink, and the rare black bear also use the area.

McNary NWR

Burbank, Washington

River guides will tell you, only half seriously, that power spots exist where rivers meet. If that's true, McNary NWR is one of the country's more powerful refuges.

Pond, McNary NWR

It lies in the cup of the confluence of two of the West's great rivers, the Columbia and the Snake. Backwaters from the lake formed behind McNary Dam, 30 miles downstream, have filled the refuge lowlands, creating ponds and the extended, U-shaped oxbow, now called Burbank Slough, that form the refuge's McNary Division, located at the northern edge of the small town of Burbank.

Only a quarter-mile wide at points, McNary's marsh is bounded by housing development, a highway, and the traffic noise typical of an urban refuge.

A string of islands in the Snake River above the confluence make up the Strawberry Islands division of the refuge; the Hanford Islands division is on the Columbia River.

HISTORY

McNary was established in 1956 as mitigation for wildlife habitats lost when McNary Dam filled. The 3,631-acre refuge welcomes around 10,400 visitors annually.

GETTING THERE

From Yakima, drive south on I-82 to Pasco, then south 1 mi. on US 395. Turn east on Maple St. to refuge headquarters.

■ **SEASON:** Refuge open year-round.

■ **HOURS:** Refuge open 5 a.m.–1 hour after sunset. McNary Environmental Education Center, staffed by volunteers, open Tues.–Sat., 9 a.m.–1 p.m. The center offers environmental education activities to local schoolchildren.

WHAT TO SEE

■ **LANDSCAPE AND CLIMATE** Lying at 340 to 380 feet, McNary bakes in dry heat, with summer temperatures ranging from 60 all the way up to 117 degrees. Only 6.75 inches of rain fall annually, mostly in winter, when January temperatures can range from minus 18 to 58 degrees. Vegetation is typical of wetlands and dry shrub-steppe environments—hardstem bulrush, willows, box alder, cottonwood, antelope bitterbrush, rabbit brush, and sagebrush.

■ **ANIMAL LIFE** The low, resonant cooing of the mourning dove alerts visitors to the presence of this spring and summer resident at McNary. Walking, the mourning doves trip daintily along, scarcely lifting their feet off the ground; in flight, during mating season, the male flies 40 to 50 feet into the air, then glides down, swaying in one direction and then the other. Alighting, the dove checks its momentum by spreading its tail feathers so that the white band tipped with a bar of black is prominent, distinguishing it from the rock dove, the ubiquitous urban pigeon that is also a common resident at McNary throughout the year. Note: The peregrine falcon, released in cities and nesting on the ledges of tall office buildings, dines on rock doves; but its unerring hunt-

Mourning dove

MCNARY HUNTING AND FISHING SEASONS

Hunting
(Seasons may vary)

	Jan	Feb	Mar	Apr	May	Jun	Jul	Aug	Sep	Oct	Nov	Dec
geese	■									■	■	■
duck	■									■	■	■
coot	■									■	■	■
snipe	■									■	■	■
pheasant										■	■	■

Fishing

	Jan	Feb	Mar	Apr	May	Jun	Jul	Aug	Sep	Oct	Nov	Dec
bass				■	■	■	■	■	■	■		
crappie				■	■	■	■	■	■	■		

Pheasant hunting is open Wed., Sat., and Sun. Bank fishing for bass and crappie Feb. 1–Sept. 30; no boats or other floating devices are allowed. On the Strawberry Island/Hanford Island Division, shoreline fishing is open July 1–Sept. 30.

ing instincts have done little to reduce the population of these prolific pigeons, which are suspected of carrying human diseases.

To see the myriad ducks (100,000 mallards) and geese that winter at McNary and breed in the spring, drive the 2-mile all-weather gravel access road along the reservoir's west side. It passes 10 parking lots and two boat ramps. On McNary's east side, a county road has access to four parking lots, one with a boat launch (car-top boats only).

Stop off at McNary Enviromental Education Center for a closeup look at mounted birds that inhabit the refuge, then walk the 1-mile hiking loop and nature trail. The center is staffed by local members of the National Audubon Society. The trail passes a good-size observation and photography blind at water's edge, where visitors may see tundra swans and ring-billed gulls (in winter). McNary is a small refuge with a large concentration of birds, many of them almost habituated to visitors; the chance of seeing them up close is good. Look for beavers, otters, and badgers around the wetlands; coyotes are abundant.

ACTIVITIES

■ **CAMPING:** No camping is allowed on the refuge, but the Army Corps of Engineers' Hood Park is nearby on the Snake River.

McKay Creek NWR
Pendleton, Oregon

When the July sun blasts down and temperatures of 105 degrees prevail over Oregon's eastern desert, the McKay Reservoir offers a cool respite from the heat. Visited by as many as 300 persons a day during hot summer weekends, McKay Creek NWR is shared by people and wildlife until the month of February, when the refuge is closed to public use and a sanctuary is created for wintering waterfowl, pheasant, and eagles. Public use begins again a month later in March.

Like Cold Springs NWR, McKay Creek presents a changing image, depending on when you visit. An irrigation reservoir lying in the arid desert plain of northeastern Oregon, McKay—when it's full, usually by May—covers 2 square miles of open water, offering a welcome expanse of cool water reflecting the lush groves of

McKay Reservoir, McKay Creek NWR

cottonwoods and willows around it. By late August, the water fills only 250 acres, and the reservoir is reduced to desolate mud-encrusted banks surrounding small pools of water.

HISTORY

McKay (Mick-EYE) Creek NWR was established in 1927 as a breeding ground and refuge for birds. Managed by both the U.S. Fish & Wildlife Service and the Bureau of Reclamation, the 3-square-mile refuge welcomes around 38,000 visitors annually.

GETTING THERE

From Portland, drive 189 mi. east on I-84. Turn south on US 395 at Pendleton toward Pilot Rock. The refuge entrance is approximately 8 mi. from Pendleton.
■ **SEASON:** Refuge open almost year-round—closed from first Monday after state waterfowl hunting season begins in Jan. through Feb. 28.
■ **HOURS:** Refuge open 5 a.m.–1 hour after sunset.

WHAT TO SEE

■ **ANIMAL LIFE** The refuge, lying at an elevation of 1,300 to 1,400 feet, once attracted more than 150,000 ducks and some 30,000 geese each winter. Those figures have dropped to fewer than 6,000 ducks and around 1,000 geese. The bird population has shifted west to Umatilla NWR, where the fields of corn and grain grown on the refuge provide a ready supply of food.

Small numbers of great blue herons, pied-billed grebes, and black-crowned night-herons can be seen at McKay along with shorebirds such as northern phalaropes, killdeer, and spotted sandpipers.

A number of raptors frequent the refuge seasonally, including four species of owls (barn, short- and long-eared, and great horned) and three species of hawks (Cooper's, rough-legged and red-tailed). The most common hawk seen in the West is the red-tailed, which can often be spotted perching on a telephone pole or sweeping near the ground in search of prey. It nests on rim rocks or in large trees

MCKAY CREEK HUNTING AND FISHING SEASONS

Hunting (Seasons may vary)	Jan	Feb	Mar	Apr	May	Jun	Jul	Aug	Sep	Oct	Nov	Dec
geese	■	▪	▪	▪	▪	▪	▪	▪	▪	■	■	■
duck	■	▪	▪	▪	▪	▪	▪	▪	▪	■	■	■
chukar	■	▪	▪	▪	▪	▪	▪	▪	▪	■	■	■
quail	▪	▪	▪	▪	▪	▪	▪	▪	▪	■	■	■
pheasant	▪	▪	▪	▪	▪	▪	▪	▪	▪	■	■	■
Hungarian partridge	▪	▪	▪	▪	▪	▪	▪	▪	▪	■	■	■
Fishing												
bass	▪	▪	■	■	■	■	■	■	■	▪	▪	▪
crappie	▪	▪	■	■	■	■	■	■	■	▪	▪	▪
bullhead	▪	▪	■	■	■	■	■	■	■	▪	▪	▪

Visitors travel to McKay Creek NWR from as far away as Portland to fish, the refuge's most popular activity. Upland bird hunting and waterfowl hunting is permitted on Tues., Thurs., and Sat.

and will carry off a farmyard chicken if prey is not available in the wild. Mule deer, bobcats, and coyotes are also residents of the refuge.

ACTIVITIES

■ **SWIMMING:** Swimming, usually near the boat launches, is allowed during open season, March through September.

■ **BOATING:** A 2-mile all-weather gravel access road along the reservoir's west side passes 10 parking lots and two boat ramps. On McKay's east side, a county road passes four parking lots, one with a car-top boat launch. The entire reservoir is open for boating, water skiing, and jet skiing March through September but shuts down completely October through February to give the birds sanctuary.

Cold Springs NWR
Hermiston, Oregon

Pretty little Cold Springs NWR offers a textbook example of an "overlay refuge." These refuges sit atop a body of water that is controlled by

Great horned owl

California quail

another agency—in this case, the U.S. Bureau of Reclamation. The U.S. Fish & Wildlife Service manages the land surrounding the water but does not control the water. Visit Cold Springs in the winter and you'll see a pretty tree-lined reservoir, an island of wildlife surrounded by agricultural fields. Visit Cold Springs in late summer and you'll see dry, cracked mud edging a receding pond whose water has been used to irrigate the area's agricultural holdings. The pond's surface covers only 200 acres, down from 1,550 acres at full pool.

HISTORY

Cold Springs Reservation was established by President Theodore Roosevelt in 1909 as the fifth wildlife preserve and breeding ground for native birds on the West Coast. President William Taft enlarged it in 1922, and President Franklin Roosevelt changed its name to Cold Springs NWR in 1940. The 4.9-square-mile (3,117-acre) refuge is the primary water source for agriculture in the Hermiston area and is explored by approximately 35,000 visitors each year.

GETTING THERE

From US 395 in Hermiston, take Highland Hills Rd. east, which turns into Loop Rd. The refuge is about 6 mi. from Hermiston.
■ **SEASON:** Refuge open year-round.
■ **HOURS:** Refuge open daily from 5 a.m.–1 hour after sunset when the entrance gate closes automatically.

WHAT TO SEE

■ **LANDSCAPE AND CLIMATE** The refuge terrain is flat. Only 8 inches of rain fall each year on earth parched by July temperatures reaching occasional highs of 108 degrees (summer nights can drop to a cool 43 degrees). January temperatures range from 7 to 54 degrees.

■ **ANIMAL LIFE** More than 6,000 migrating ducks and around 900 geese visit

COLD SPRINGS HUNTING AND FISHING SEASONS

Hunting
(Seasons may vary)

	Jan	Feb	Mar	Apr	May	Jun	Jul	Aug	Sep	Oct	Nov	Dec
geese	■									■	■	■
duck	■									■	■	■
quail	■									■	■	■
pheasant	■									■	■	■

Fishing

	Jan	Feb	Mar	Apr	May	Jun	Jul	Aug	Sep	Oct	Nov	Dec
bass			■	■	■	■	■	■	■			
crappie			■	■	■	■	■	■	■			

Hunting for ducks, geese, and upland birds is allowed on the south side of the reservoir on Tues., Thurs., and Sat. Fishing, both from boats and the bank, is a popular activity March 1–Sept. 30—only bank fishing is allowed the remainder of the year.

the refuge from October through February. Your best bet for viewing large groups of migrants is to park at the refuge's east end. The capacious stick nests of great blue herons can be seen in winter in cottonwood trees on the northwest side of Memorial Marsh; a second colony of great blue herons and double-crested cormorants nests on the main stem of Cold Springs Creek.

Five species of sandpipers—lesser, western, spotted, solitary and semipalmated—use Memorial Marsh during September along with greater and lesser yellowlegs, black-necked stilts, and long-billed dowitchers.

Bitterbrush and big sagebrush in the upland shrub-steppe habitat provide cover for coyotes, bobcats, and California quail. A herd of migrant elk can be seen on the refuge at various times during the year, and mule deer browse in the riparian area, thick with willow and cottonwoods, around the reservoir. Look for tree stumps with scooped-out teeth marks in the gnawed areas— evidence of beaver, also in the riparian area.

ACTIVITIES

■ **BOATING:** A gravel access road along the southern edge of the reservoir leads to five parking lots and two boat ramps. Both nonmotorized boats and boats with electric motors are allowed on the reservoir from March 1 to September 30; the northern three-quarters of the reservoir is closed October 1 through February 28 to create a sanctuary for migrating birds.

■ **HIKES AND WALKS:** Areas south of West Inlet Canal are open for hiking.

■ **CYCLING AND HORSEBACK RIDING:** Both horseback riders and bicyclists may used roads open to cars.

Oregon Coastal Refuges Complex

Oregon Islands NWR, Bandon Marsh NWR, Cape Meares NWR
Newport, Oregon

Oregon Islands NWR

US 101 clings to the Oregon coast from California to Washington, passing, among other things, some 80 state parks, six wildlife refuges, and 1,400 offshore reefs, rocks, and islands that are home to more than 1 million birds—all this besides traversing some of the West Coast's most exquisite scenery. Windy, rocky, drenched with spray from crashing waves, the Oregon coastal island refuges belong to the birds. Both the Oregon Islands and Three Arch Rocks NWRs, the two offshore refuges, are off-limits to humans, who can only gaze at them from ship or shore and marvel at their beauty.

HISTORY

The California Gold Rush nearly cleaned out the West Coast's seabird colonies nesting on the rocks and islands off the coast of Oregon and California. Millions of eggs were gathered to supply restaurants in San Francisco and Sacramento, and the birds were wantonly killed for target practice and sport. Before the bird populations were totally decimated, a naturalist and photographer named William Finley and his partner Herman Bolhman arrived on the Oregon coast and began photographing the devastation. Through his photographs and written correspondence, Finley convinced President Theodore Roosevelt to establish Three Arch Rocks (1907), the first national wildlife refuge west of the Mississippi River. (See William L. Finley NWR in the Willamette Valley NWR group.) Five more Oregon coastal refuges have been established, including Oregon Islands (1935), Cape Meares (1938), Bandon Marsh (1983), and Siletz Bay and Nestucca Bay, both in 1991.

HOW SAND MOVES Many a beachgoer has arrived at a favorite ocean-side beach after a lapse of time only to discover that the beach isn't the same beach at all; it's changed shape. The sand that makes up the beach began its journey high in the mountains as rocks or pebbles washed down river in swift currents to the ocean, where it is dispersed along the shore-line. How that sand is deposited on the beach—or removed, as the case may be—depends on ocean currents, wave action, and the size of the sand particles. Large grains of sand make steeper beaches; small grains are often found in wide, flat beaches.

Just where a river's sand is eventually deposited, after the ocean currents pick it up, depends on the angle of the current passing the river's mouth. If the waves arrive perpendicularly to the shore, the sand spreads out around the mouth of the river; but if the waves arrive at an oblique angle, they pick up the sand and carry it with them, dropping it only when they crash into an obstruction such as a man-made jetty or breakwater or when they finally hit shore. This oblique movement of water is known as a littoral current. On a windless day, if you toss a beach ball into the surf and watch which way it drifts, you will know in which direction the littoral current is moving. Once the sand has created a beach, the changing size of the beach depends on another type of wave action. Waves are formed by wind blowing across the ocean hundreds of miles from shore, forming ripples. As the wind continues to blow, the ripples turn into a series of swells of equal height and equal distance (or period) between them. The strength of the wind, how long it blows, and how far from land determines the size of the swells. Heavy winds close to shore generate the biggest waves. These waves begin to break when the water depth is less than half the distance between the crests of neighboring swells.

In winter, storms are often closer to shore and generate steep waves that come in quick succession (a shorter period), tearing up the beach and removing sand. In summer, calmer seas return the sand, and the beach is once again broad and flat.

GETTING THERE

Oregon Islands NWR stretches along the entire 368-mi. Oregon coast. Seeing it involves either a boat trip or a drive along US 101 with stopoffs at numerous viewpoints where the rugged rocks and islands—home during breeding season to more than a million birds and marine mammals—can be viewed. Along the way, the four land-based national wildlife refuges preserve an array of wetlands, headlands, and some of the most gorgeous scenery in the West. We present here an overview of the wildlife and plant life along the coast, followed by a detailed "drive" south to north, stopping at each of the Oregon Coastal refuges.

■ **SEASON:** Viewpoints are open all year, but both offshore refuges (Oregon Islands and Three Arch Rocks NWRs) and two of the four land-based refuges (Siletz Bay and Nestucca Bay NWRs) are closed to the public. Visitors are welcome at Bandon Marsh and Cape Meares NWRs.

■ **HOURS:** Most viewpoints open 24 hours.

■ **ADDRESS:** Oregon Coastal Refuges, 2127 SE OSU Dr., Newport, OR 97365-5258

■ **TELEPHONE:** 541/867-4550

TOURING THE OREGON COASTAL REFUGES

■ **BY AUTOMOBILE:** US 101 is in effect the "auto-tour route" for the six Oregon Coastal refuges. You will find some sections of this justly famous highway busy with urban traffic or recreational travelers, but some beautiful stretches are relatively quiet and calm, including areas with viewpoints over beaches and islands in the Oregon Coastal refuge complex.

■ **BY FOOT:** The Coquille Point unit of Oregon Islands NWR and Cape Meares NWR have trails totaling about 1 mile. The Oregon Coast hiking trail winds 2 miles through Cape Meares, linking Cape Meares State Park with the refuge and descending to the beach. Bandon Marsh can be accessed from a primitive trail off Riverside Drive, one mile south of its intersection with US 101.

■ **BY BICYCLE:** All of the Oregon coastal refuges are closed to bicycles. However, the 368-mile Oregon Coast bike route utilizes US 101 except for a short stretch between Bandon and Coos Bay. The route is signed and passes 15 campgrounds with sites specifically for bikers and hikers. Plan six to eight days for the trip and a north-to-south route to take advantage of prevailing summer winds. Information and map: Oregon Dept. of Transportation, Transportation Bldg., Salem OR 97310.

■ **BY CANOE, KAYAK, OR BOAT:** Boat tours (to see gray whales and the offshore refuge islands) and sea kayak tours are offered in several locations. All boats, both commercial and private, must stay at least 500 feet from the islands to avoid disturbing birds and mammals. Kayak tours of the Coquille River estuary, including Bandon Marsh, are available in Bandon. Call Adventure Kayak (541/347-3480) for information on tours.

WHAT TO SEE

■ **LANDSCAPE AND CLIMATE** The Oregon coast is one of the great scenic tours in the West—rocky shorelines broken by more than a dozen rivers, vast mudflats teeming with wildlife, and 40 miles of sand dunes in the Oregon Dunes National Recreation Area, located between North Bend and Florence. A carefully

Pigeon guillemots

preserved and dense treeline of Douglas fir, hemlock, and Sitka spruce along the highway conceals the clear-cutting and slash left behind by lumbering operations, but visitors can see a grove of easily accessible old-growth forest at Cape Meares NWR.

This is a wet and windy coast. Rainfall varies from 72 inches annually at Newport to 59 inches at Bandon, most falling from November through March. The coastline is hilly, with refuge elevations ranging from sea level to around 630 feet. Although brisk to strong winds blow fairly steadily, the coast has a mild climate, varying little from north to south—35 to 55 degrees in January, 50 to 72 degrees in July. The offshore islands, rocky and bare, rise sharply out of the Pacific; their pockmarked cliffs provide sites for the thousands of birds that nest on them.

■ PLANT LIFE

Wetlands A type of softstem rush, Baltic rush grows in salt marshes and tidal flats. Slough sedge, with leaves about one-half-inch wide, can also be found in the upper parts of the tidal marshes. The Makah Indians use the sedge for basketmaking by splitting and flattening the firm inner leaves and then drying them. Some coastal freshwater wetlands occur in low-lying areas behind sand dunes. These areas, called "deflation plains," are carved out by the wind when the adjacent sand dunes become stabilized by vegetation.

Forest The Oregon coast is heavily forested, with species that include Sitka spruce, western hemlock, and Douglas fir. Thickets of red alder can be seen at forest's edge where the sunlight needed by the alder is available. Part of the Siuslaw National Forest hugs US 101 along the coast between Beachside State Park and Hecata Beach.

Common murres

■ ANIMAL LIFE

Birds Tufted puffins nest at Three Arch Rocks NWR, sharing the rocks with a vast colony of common murres. On the Oregon islands alone more than 1.1 million seabirds nest—a total that exceeds the number of seabirds in California and Washington combined.

Common murres about the size of a crow (around 17 inches) are the most abundant and most easily observed seabirds nesting on the Oregon coast. From a distance, they look a little like penguins. Nesting in large colonies, the female murres each lay a single, large pear-shaped egg (that won't roll away) right on the rock surface. The parents take turns incubating the egg by holding it on top of their webbed feet and nestling it into their breast feathers. Common murres can live for more than 26 years and can dive to depths of 600 feet in search of small fish, their principal food source.

Puffins are difficult to see along the coast because they nest underground in

Tufted puffin

vegetated areas amid offshore rocks. If you do see one, they're easily recognized by their comical colored bills and long yellow head tufts. Puffins (also known as sea parrots) nest in a 3- to 6-foot-long burrow dug by both the male and female. They use their large bills and the sharp claws on the toes of their webbed feet to dig the burrows. The birds come to land only to nest, spending most of the year at sea in the north Pacific Ocean. Puffins have a difficult time getting into the air. At sea they run along the water's surface for a considerable distance before being able to lift off from the water; on land they dive off cliffs to work up enough speed for flying. Underwater, where they fish, they are very agile, propelling themselves with their wings and using their large, webbed feet as rudders.

Both western and glaucous-winged gulls nest on the offshore rocks and islands along with rhinoceros auklets, pigeon guillemots, and Brandt's, pelagic, and double-crested cormorants.

Mammals The offshore islands are a prime haulout site for seals and sea lions. The largest of the *eared* seals, Steller's sea lions have rear flippers that they can turn under themselves, enabling them to walk on land. The thick, coarse hair that looks like a mane around their oversize necks and shoulders gave the sea lions their name. An adult male Steller's sea lion, averaging more than 1,200 pounds, defends his territory during the mating season, around mid-May through mid-July, and mates with a number of females. Sea lion skins were used by Native Americans to make clothing, boat coverings, boots, and gloves; the tough whiskers of the sea lions were once used by the Chinese to clean their opium pipes.

Hair seals (harbor, spotted, and bearded) can't bend their hind flippers—on land they hump and slide along, propelling themselves with their front flippers.

Awkward on land, harbor seals are sleek and graceful in water. They can dive to more than 600 feet and can stay under water for more than 20 minutes. Seal

OREGON ISLANDS NWR

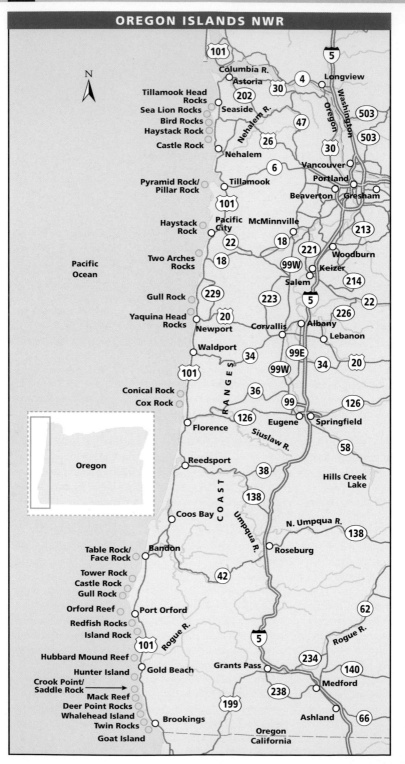

N

Columbia R.
Astoria
101
Longview
4
5
Washington
30
Oregon
202
Tillamook Head Rocks
Sea Lion Rocks
Seaside
503
Bird Rocks
Haystack Rock
503
47
Castle Rock
26
Nehalem R.
30
Nehalem
Vancouver
6
Portland
Pyramid Rock/
Pillar Rock
Tillamook
Beaverton
Gresham
Haystack Rock
Pacific City
McMinnville
213
Pacific Ocean
22
18
221
Woodburn
Two Arches Rocks
18
99W
Keizer
214
Gull Rock
229
223
Salem
22
20
5
226
Yaquina Head Rocks
Newport
Corvallis
Albany
Lebanon
Waldport
34
99E
34
20
101
99W
R
A
N
G
E
S
Conical Rock
Cox Rock
36
99
Florence
126
Eugene
Springfield
126
Siuslaw R.
58
Reedsport
38
Hills Creek Lake
138
Coos Bay
C
O
A
S
T
Umpqua R.
N. Umpqua R.
138
Table Rock/
Face Rock
Bandon
Roseburg
Tower Rock
Castle Rock
Gull Rock
42
Orford Reef
Port Orford
62
Redfish Rocks
Island Rock
Rogue R.
Hubbard Mound Reef
101
Grants Pass
Rogue R.
Hunter Island
Gold Beach
234
140
Crook Point/
Saddle Rock
Mack Reef
Medford
Deer Point Rocks
Whalehead Island
199
Ashland
66
Twin Rocks
Brookings
Goat Island
Oregon
California

Oregon

Elephant seals

pups can swim almost immediately after birth and remain with their mothers only around a month, when half their body weight is still fat, tiding them over until they learn to hunt the fish that are their chief diet.

The Shell Island/Simpson Reef Unit of Oregon Islands NWR, viewable from Cape Arago, is the world's northernmost pupping site for northern elephant seals. California sea lions also haul out on the Oregon islands.

■ **PUBLICATIONS:** *Oregon Wildlife Viewing Guide,* by James A. Yuskavitch (Falcon Publishing, Helena, Mont., 1994).

Oregon Islands NWR
Newport, Oregon

This 762-acre refuge stretches from the California border to Tillamook Head; you can see the refuge's 1,400 offshore rocks, reefs, and islands from at least 32 view-points along the coastline. If your itinerary is such that you have time for only one stop, choose Coquille Point, a tiny headland with interpretive trails on the coast near Bandon that is the only shore-based segment of the Oregon Islands refuge, originally called Goat Island Reservation. The refuge was renamed Oregon Islands NWR in 1940. Around 388,000 visitors view the Oregon Islands refuge every year.

Raked by wind, both winter and summer, Coquille Point overlooks spectacular scenery—wind- and wave-carved rocks and a great surf rolling in with massive waves, spraying foam 50 feet into the air—overwhelming in intensity and beauty. Seabirds wheel and cry over the islands, gray whales pass in season (December through January and March through May), and numerous Steller's sea lions, harbor seals, and elephant seals sun on the islands' shores. From April to August, look for common murres, pigeon guillemots, Brandt's and pelagic cormorants, black oystercatchers, tufted puffins, and western gulls. Brown pelicans arrive in June through October, and in March to early April, Aleutian Canada geese use Table Rock, just north of Coquille Point. A .25-mile staircase trail descends from the headland to the beach, where it's possible to search for agates.

To Coquille Point: In Bandon, from US 101, turn west on 11th St. which ends at Coquille Point.

Other viewpoints from which the Oregon Islands refuge may be seen are located in a series of state parks along the coast. South to north between the California border and Bandon, they are: Harris Beach, Boardman, Cape Sebastian, Battle Rock (with interpretive panels), and Cape Blanco.

Bandon Marsh NWR
Bandon, Oregon

Immediately north of Bandon between the Coquille River and US 101, Bandon Marsh NWR protects an extensive salt marsh within the Coquille River estuary. To explore by canoe or kayak, launch west of US 101 on the Coquille River or at the Bandon waterfront, where canoe and kayak rentals are available. Riverside Drive, between US 101 and downtown Bandon, provides foot access to the marsh; at low tide at this small refuge (303 acres), a short, primitive hiking trail is accessible. Bandon Marsh refuge welcomes around 5,000 visitors annually. A 600-acre upstream addition to Bandon Marsh was anticipated in 2000.

Bandon Marsh is one of the Oregon coast's best birding areas, where thousands of shorebirds stop to feed during spring and fall migration. There are chances of seeing rare Asiatic species, including the ruff, bar-tailed godwit, bristle-thighed curlew, great knot, and Mongolian plover. More common shorebirds include least and western sandpipers; black-bellied, semipalmated, and lesser golden plovers; sanderlings, whimbrels, and marbled godwits. Coho and chinook salmon and steelhead and cutthroat trout use the estuary. Fishing, hunting, and clamming are allowed on the refuge.

GRAY WHALES A West Coast tradition brings thousands to the coast each year to watch passing gray whales. Swimming a roundtrip of some 12,000 miles a year at the sedate rate of 3 to 5 miles an hour, the whales migrate between Baja California, where they breed and give birth, and the nutrient-rich Bering and Chukchi seas off the northwest coast of Alaska. To feed their enormous bulk (they grow to 50 feet in length during their 50-year life span and weigh about 50 tons), gray whales eat about 2,600 pounds of small crustaceans a day, foraging at the bottom of the sea. These whales are toothless. They use their baleen—140 to 170 plates of long, fingernail-like material suspended from their upper jaws—to trap the tiny invertebrates they eat. They gulp a mouthful of water, then expel it, trapping the invertebrates in the baleen as the water rushes in and out.

Gray whales are the most conspicuous of the Pacific whales, not only because they migrate only a half-mile or so offshore but also because, while land mammals exchange only around 10 to 20 percent of the air in their lungs each time they breathe, gray whales expel around 80 percent. The exhaled air, which looks like a water spout, is usually warmer than the surrounding atmosphere and condenses rapidly, creating a jet of "steam," often the first indication to onshore sightseers that one of these ancient mammals is passing.

More than 11,000 gray whales follow the migratory path along the West Coast, so your chances of seeing them are good. Numerous whale-watching excursions leave from towns along the coast.

Sleeping western sandpiper

■ North of Bandon

Eight miles north of Bandon, turn west off US 101 to Cape Arago and Shore Acres state parks for views of California and Steller's sea lions and harbor, northern fur, and northern elephant seals hauled out on Simpson Reef and Shell Island, part of the Oregon Islands NWR.

Thirteen miles north of Florence, Devil's Elbow State Park is a small, charming cove with excellent views of the offshore Devil's Elbow (Oregon Islands NWR). A trail links the cove with Heceta Head Lighthouse, an excellent viewpoint from which to spot passing gray whales. Continuing north, another good viewpoint is Yaquina Head Outstanding Natural Area, providing views of sea mammals, birds, and whales. The Yaquina lighthouse is open in summer for tours. Yaquina Head is a day-use fee area with a $5-per-car entry fee.

> **HUNTING AND FISHING**
> Hunting and fishing are permitted only at Bandon Marsh among the Oregon Coastal Refuges Complex.

Cape Meares NWR
Tillamook, Oregon

Break out your sense of wonder as you stroll through a fragment of old-growth forest preserved at Cape Meares National Wildlife Refuge. Great hemlock and Sitka spruce trees, some 200 feet high and hundreds of years old, stand amid a lush forest floor rich with a carpet of decaying logs, seedlings, and shrubs. Shafts of sunlight penetrate where fallen trees create an opening in the high canopy, and seedlings that will be the next hundred years' trees get their start in the damp moss clinging to the broad surface of nurse logs, fallen giants that provide nutrients as they decay.

Don't miss the Octopus Tree, a Sitka spruce with six thick branches that grow out in a 30-foot ring around the trunk perpendicular to the ground, then turn up, much like a candelabra. A short trail leads to the tree from the picnic area, both in the state park.

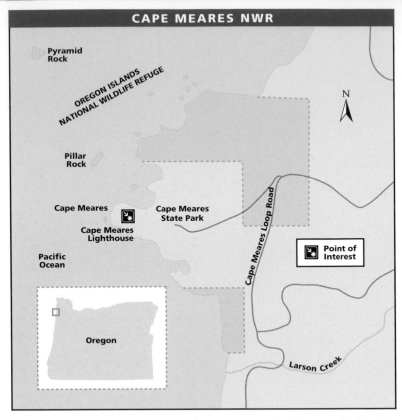

CAPE MEARES NWR

Pyramid Rock

OREGON ISLANDS NATIONAL WILDLIFE REFUGE

N

Pillar Rock

Cape Meares

Cape Meares Lighthouse

Cape Meares State Park

Cape Meares Loop Road

Point of Interest

Pacific Ocean

Oregon

Larson Creek

The marbled murrelet, one resident at Cape Meares, builds its nest high in the crowns of the great trees of the old-growth forest, the nests so hidden away that for years no one knew where these small seabirds went when they left the ocean each night, flying toward land.

Although this is the second smallest of the Oregon coastal refuges—only 139 acres—Capes Meares attracts more visitors (501,000 annually) than any other wildlife refuge in states on the Pacific. Wrapping around two sides of Cape Meares State Park, the refuge and park have interconnecting trails leading through the old-growth forest. Two miles of the Oregon Coast Trail wind through the forest and descend to the beach. Three Arch Rocks can be viewed from the headland clifftops, along with migrating gray whales, nesting seabirds, and one pair of nesting peregrine falcons. Bald eagles and northern spotted owls inhabit the forest. The Cape Meares Lighthouse is open May through September, 11 a.m. to 4 p.m., and weekends, March, April, and October, 11 a.m. to 4 p.m.

To Cape Meares: Follow Three Capes Scenic Route northward from Oceanside State Park. To skip Three Arch Rocks, turn onto Three Capes Scenic Route at Tillamook, but drive north for 9 miles on the loop rather than south.

OTHER OREGON COASTAL REFUGES

The following refuges are closed to the public but may offer some wildlife viewing from passing roads or waters.

■ **Siletz Bay NWR** Lincoln City, Oregon

The Siletz River and Drift Creek flow into Siletz Bay estuary, south of Lincoln

Three Arch Rocks NWR

City. As the tide flows out, broad mudflats are exposed. Siletz Bay NWR protects 519 acres of coastal wetlands (and some uplands). Bald eagles, grebes, and loons can be see in winter from viewpoints along US 101, which cuts across the refuge (which is otherwise not visitable). In summer, kingfishers, whimbrels, brown pelicans, and herons are common here. Look for Roosevelt elk, black-tailed deer (known as mule deer east of the Cascades), river otters, and harbor seals, as well as coho and chinook salmon and cutthroat and steelhead trout. The refuge, which is expected to grow to about 1,900 acres when completed, currently has no public-use facilities.

■ **Nestucca Bay NWR** Pacific City, Oregon

Nestucca Bay refuge provides habitat for dusky and Aleutian Canada geese. The 476 acre refuge supports about 5 percent of the world's population of duskies and 100 percent of a subpopulation of Aleutian Canada geese. Uplands on the refuge (where a hiking trail is planned) rise to 455 feet.

■ **Three Arch Rocks NWR** Oceanside, Oregon

Three Arch Rocks refuge protects nesting habitat for more than 200,000 common murres, the largest common murre colony south of Alaska. Some 2,000 to 4,000 tufted puffins also nest at Three Arch Rocks, along with Brandt's and pelagic cormorants, pigeon guillemots, and Leach's storm-petrels. Steller's sea lions haul out on the rocks throughout the year, and females pup here. The 15-acre refuge includes three large rocks and six smaller rocks off the Oregon coast .5 mile west of Oceanside. To view it from Oceanside State Park, turn west off US 101 at Tillamook, then turn south onto Three Capes Scenic Route loop, leading to the park. The refuge can also be seen by looking south from Cape Meares State Park. Waters 500 feet around Three Arch Rocks are closed to all watercraft from May through September to protect marine mammals and nesting seabirds.

Sheldon NWR
Northwestern Nevada

Pronghorn antelope, Sheldon NWR

These are the high semidesert lands of the northern Great Basin, where only a century ago cattle and sheep grazed by the thousands on sprawling ranches. Sheldon NWR has seven historic ranching sites from those days, including Last Chance Ranch and Kinney Camp. Encompassing almost 575,000 acres, Sheldon has scant annual visitation of only 15,000—which works out to 38 acres per person, plenty of room for you and the wildlife to roam.

HISTORY

Evidence of humanity on the refuge extends back at least 12,000 years, and petroglyphs as old as 7,000 years have been found. About 1,500 years ago, ancestors of today's Northern Paiute and Shoshone Indians occupied the area. In the early 1800s white trappers and explorers blazed through, followed by wagon trains of settlers. Vast cattle and sheep ranches were established, but overgrazing eventually contributed to their collapse.

The refuge was founded in 1931 by the Boone and Crockett Club and the National Audubon Society, and it is named after Charles Sheldon—avid sportsman, explorer, and conservationist. In 1976 the property transferred to the U.S. Fish & Wildlife Service.

GETTING THERE

The refuge lies in northwestern Nevada, bordering the Oregon line. From Lakeview, OR, head north 5 mi. to OR 140, turn east (right), and proceed 65 mi. southeast to Sheldon's northern entrance.

From Winnemucca, NV, take US 95 north 31 mi. to NV 140, turn west (left), and proceed 68 mi. to Denio Junction. Go west (left) on NV 140 for another 17 mi. to the refuge's eastern boundary. NV 140 cuts across the refuge's northeastern corner, into Oregon. Pick up a refuge brochure, available another 12 mi. along this road.

You can also enter the refuge on long, graded dirt roads from the west and south, but 4-wheel-drive/high-clearance vehicles are strongly advised.

■ **SEASON:** Open year-round, but refuge roads (other than NV 140) are not maintained in winter.

■ **HOURS:** Refuge open 24 hours daily.

■ **FEES:** Free entry.

■ **ADDRESS:** P.O. Box 111, Lakeview, OR 97630

■ **TELEPHONE:** 541/947-3315

■ **VISITOR CENTER:** No visitor facilities or services of any kind on the refuge, except primitive campgrounds. Emergency phone available at field office, when open. Refuge brochures and maps (including campground locations) are available at north entrance and Virgin Valley Campground.

TOURING SHELDON

■ **BY AUTOMOBILE:** NV 140 slices across Sheldon's northeast corner. The refuge also maintains about 100 miles of graded dirt roads and comparable miles of jeep trails. Graded roads are passable for ordinary vehicles in dry weather.

■ **BY FOOT:** All parts of the refuge are open to hiking, but there are no established, maintained trails. Closed roads are used for hiking.

■ **BY BICYCLE:** Mountain biking is allowed on all open refuge roads.

WHAT TO SEE

■ **LANDSCAPE AND CLIMATE** Flat, open tablelands and rolling hills are cut by narrow canyons and by wider valleys with borders of precipitous rocky rims. Each major canyon contains a creek, and many drain into Virgin Creek, which over the years has carved a deep, vertical walled canyon called Thousand Creek Gorge. Several mountains poke above the tablelands and canyons. Elevations run from 4,100 to 7,200 feet.

Precipitation is sparse, averaging 14 to 17 inches a year. Temperatures vary radically, season to season and day to night, with lows of -30 degrees and highs exceeding 100. Winters are harsh, with drifting snow and high winds. Sheldon is best visited from late spring through mid-fall.

■ **PLANT LIFE**

Wetlands A variety of emergent plants, such as cattails, roundstem bulrush, black rush, and various sedges, grow around the refuge marshes, alkaline lakes, wet meadows, ponds, and fresh lakes.

Shrublands Sagebrush is a signature plant of the Great Basin, particularly its colder northern half. Sagebrush ecosystems cover the largest area of any plant community in the nation, more than half the acreage of the 11 western states. Big

Sagebrush plant, flower, and seed

sagebrush grows 2 to 7 feet high and has silvery blue-green ever-present leaves and dark gray bark. Low sagebrush features a darker leaf, grows to less than 18 inches, and prefers higher elevations. Sagebrush is the food of choice for pronghorn antelope, contributing up to 90 percent of their diet in fall and winter.

Mountainous areas Common to hillsides above 6,000 feet is the deciduous bush mountain mahogany, a slow-growing plant (to 10 feet) with small dark green leaves. Close by is bitterbrush (2 to 6 feet), a favorite browse of mule deer. Stands of juniper populate Sheldon's western edge.

■ ANIMAL LIFE

Birds Some 192 bird species are seen on the refuge. Spring and fall are good times to observe birds here, with both migrating waterfowl and neotropicals, but summer also finds many birds nesting at Sheldon, including at least 10 species of waterfowl—among them Canada geese, mallards, teal, redheads, and ruddy ducks. When water levels fall in the lakes and ponds, shorebirds move in to feed on the exposed shorelines.

The increasingly rare sage grouse, a large chickenlike bird that prefers mixed big and low sagebrush habitat, also favors Sheldon refuge.

Mammals Sheldon was set up initially to protect pronghorn antelope. They remain important residents, with their numbers peaking in winter. But California bighorn sheep also enjoy life on the refuge. Native to the area, they were extirpated in the 1930s but reintroduced in 1968. Some 150 reside here today. You will see abundant mule deer as well as some pesky squatters: wild burros and horses, fast-producing nonnatives whose overgrazing threatens the balance of the native ecosystem.

Note: A fire in the summer of 1999 burned some 42,000 acres of the refuge. This fire is expected to have a significant effect on the habitats of the mule deer and sage grouse.

Fish The refuge shelters Lahontan cutthroat trout (a threatened species), as well as native Alvord chub and Sheldon tui chub.

Reptiles and amphibians Look for the native Pacific treefrog or Great Basin spadefoot toad at almost any Sheldon body of water; these compete against the introduced and rapacious bullfrog. Found throughout the refuge is its only poisonous viper, the western rattlesnake.

ACTIVITIES

■ **CAMPING:** Fourteen primitive campgrounds, including six with handicapped-accessible restrooms. A private campground nearby has RV hookups. Refuge maps contain campground locations.

■ **SWIMMING:** No designated swimming areas, but explore the hot springs pool at Virgin Valley Campground.

■ **WILDLIFE OBSERVATION:** Swan Lake and the area known as Little Sheldon provide good pronghorn viewing. These sites can usually be reached by ordinary vehicles, but call ahead to check road conditions. Of the refuge's 15 reptiles, 12 are found in the Virgin Valley, Bog Hot, or Jackass Flats areas. Deer normally summer on Bald Mountain.

■ **PUBLICATIONS:** Refuge brochure; all-animals species brochure.

HUNTING AND FISHING Fishing at the five Duferrena ponds, Big Springs Reservoir, and Catnip Reservoir is good to excellent. The Nevada state records for **bluegill** and **yellow perch** came out of the Duferrena ponds. Also taken are **Lahontan cutthroat trout, rainbow trout, cutbows, white crappie,** and **largemouth bass.** The hunting of **pronghorn antelope, mule deer, bighorn sheep, California quail,** and **chukar** is allowed. Some areas are subject to closure.

Tualatin River NWR
Sherwood, Oregon

Red-legged frog

The remnants of a rich riparian plant community remain along the banks of the Tualatin River. Oregon ash, big-leaf maple, red alder, and black cottonwood are reminders of the lush old-growth forest that once rimmed the oxbows and meanders of the river. Tualatin, an urban refuge 15 miles from downtown Portland, preserves some of the remaining riparian habitat along the river, preventing it from being swallowed up by the ever-expanding metropolitan area.

HISTORY

Established in 1992, this urban refuge protects several parcels of land along the Tualatin River within the greater metropolitan area of Portland, which is expected to grow by at least 500,000 residents during the next two decades. The 837-acre refuge (in four separate pieces) welcomes around 465 visitors annually. Tualatin is expected to grow to about 3,000 acres, and will include such diverse environments as forested, seasonal, and permanent wetlands, riparian areas, grasslands, shrublands, and forested uplands.

GETTING THERE

From Portland drive south on I-5. Take Exit 294 and drive west on US 99W. The refuge can be viewed from US 99W between Tigard and Sherwood. The refuge is about 15 mi. from downtown Portland.

■ **SEASON:** Refuge lands are closed to the public but can be seen throughout the year from county roads that cross the properties and in summer from canoes on the river.

■ **ADDRESS:** Tualatin NWR, 16340 SW Beef Bend Rd., Sherwood, OR 97140-8306. For refuge map and bird list: visit City Hall, 90 NW Park, Tualatin, or call 503/625-5522.

■ **TELEPHONE:** 530/590-5811

WHAT TO SEE

The great flood that scoured areas of eastern Washington (see Columbia NWR) also impacted the Tonquin Scablands between Sherwood and Tualatin. Scoured bedrock knolls and channel walls can be seen along Rock Creek.

Few pristine areas remain here for wildlife that has traditionally used these lands. Although visitor facilities are not yet in place, the public is invited to join activities on the refuge—canoeing (a two- to three-hour trip on the Tualatin through the refuge is held once a year in September); birdwatching; and revegetation projects. Launch at Cook Park in Tigard or Tualatin Park in Tualatin to canoe on your own through the refuge on the Tualatin.

Western tanager

Viewing points along area roads include Hwy. 99W (elk, raptors, geese, and many species of ducks) and Scholls Ferry Rd. (OR 210), where thousands of Canada geese (including duskies and cacklers) and northern pintails have been seen. Tundra swans often feed in fields near Schamberg Bridge, just east of Elsner Road. Spring migration brings neotropical migratory birds such as the ruby-crowned kinglet, western tanager, and chipping sparrow to the refuge, where they stay to breed. Wood ducks and hooded mergansers—along with a few cinnamon teals, mallards, and Canada geese—also nest on the refuge.

The northern red-legged frog, a long-legged jumper colored red on the underside of its hind legs and on its lower abdomen, is one of the 16 frogs native to North America, and it is the largest native frog in the West. A pond frog, this one likes marshes, reservoirs, and slow-moving creeks. Listen for a continuing low clucking when Tualatin's red-legged frogs are in chorus together.

Western Oregon NWR Complex

William L. Finley NWR, Ankeny NWR, Baskett Slough NWR
Corvallis, Oregon

Cabell Marsh, William L. Finley NWR

"All is change," wrote Heracleitus, around 422 B.C., "all yields its place and goes." If the ancient Greek philosopher were a contemporary American, he might say the same thing about animal and plant species that have been eradicated from the United States since the Pilgrims landed at Plymouth Rock in 1620—more than 500 species extant then are now extinct. Today, counting plants and animals that live only in the states washed by the Pacific Ocean, there are another 538 officially "threatened" or "endangered" species. The story of the attempt to save one type of goose that isn't even yet close enough to extinction to appear on the federal endangered species list is telling. It illuminates the bonds that link our Pacific Coast NWRs in their common work and offers a glimpse of the interrelatedness of all things. The story's setting is three refuges in the Willamette Valley near Corvallis, Oregon—William L. Finley NWR, Ankeny NWR, and Baskett Slough NWR.

HISTORY

Its headwaters flowing from Copper Lake near the glacial fields of Wrangell–Saint Elias National Park in Southeast Alaska, the Copper River cuts a wide arc as it swings south to flow into the Gulf of Alaska some 225 miles east of Anchorage. Its massive delta of marshes, mudflats, islands, and sandbars is the primary nesting area for dusky Canada geese. This century's old home to thousands of generations of geese was changed when the strongest earthquake ever recorded in the United States (magnitude 8.4) rocked Anchorage on Good Friday, March 26, 1964. The earthquake's impact was so extensive that it lifted the central part of the country

3 inches, deforming altogether 100,000 square miles, more of the earth's surface than any other quake in recorded history. The Copper River Delta rose by 2 to 6 feet, turning sedge meadows and sloughs into upland easily visited by the predators who stalk the dusky geese.

The duskies, creatures of habit, leave the Copper River Delta each fall and fly south to Oregon's Willamette Valle and to a few stretches along the lower Columbia River and coastal Oregon and Washington. The Willamette Valley is one of the chief places they choose to spend their winters. But the once vast seasonal marshes of the valley, rich with meandering streams and wetlands, have disappeared as farmers drained land to create arable fields. In the early 1960s the duskies were concentrated on a private hunting club. U.S Fish & Wildlife's plan to set aside new refuges in Willamette Valley and one along the lower Columbia reflected an effort to entice the duskies to public lands and so to alleviate some of the heavy hunting pressure.

The refuges are William L. Finley, Ankeny, and Baskett Slough, within 38 miles of each other in the Willamette Valley, and Ridgefield (see Ridgefield NWR in Washington), near the confluence of the Willamette and Columbia rivers. Establishment of these safe homes for half the year and implementation of hunting

Dusky Canada goose

restrictions throughout the dusky range have arrested their decline.

GETTING THERE

Headquarters for the three refuges is at William L. Finley. To get there, from Corvallis drive south 8.5 mi. on US 99W. Watch for refuge signs on the west side of the highway. Turn west onto a gravel country road and drive 2 mi. to headquarters, a large white turn-of-the-century farmhouse on the south side of the road.

■ **SEASON:** Refuges open year-round with seasonal closures of certain areas.

■ **HOURS:** Open during daylight hours.

■ **ADDRESS:** William L. Finley, Ankeny or Baskett Slough refuges: Write Western Oregon NWR Complex, 26208 Finley Refuge Rd., Corvallis, OR 97333

■ **TELEPHONE:** 541/757-7236

TOURING WESTERN OREGON NWR COMPLEX

■ **BY AUTOMOBILE:** There are 15 miles of county roads crossing the refuges and one 3.5-mile tour route through William L. Finley refuge. Another 9.5 miles of roads parallel or cut across the refuge boundaries; several information kiosks along these roads overlook the refuges.

■ **BY FOOT:** The three refuges have a total of 15.25 miles of hiking trails, all generally available, but check at refuge headquarters at William F. Finley for temporary closure dates.

■ **BY BICYCLE:** Bicycles are allowed only on county roads crossing the refuges

HOW BIRDS MIGRATE As the silhouettes of the V-shaped formation of a flock of Canada geese cross in front of the moon, a bird biologist (or ornithologist) may be watching them through a telescope, taking count. The mystery of how birds migrate long distances—some Swainson's hawks make a round-rip migration each year of around 7,400 miles—arriving precisely at their summer or winter homes, has long fascinated birdwatchers. Although there is no complete understanding of how birds migrate, a series of classic experiments has led to these tentative conclusions:

■ First-time migrants are born with an innate program that tells them how far to migrate and in which direction to head.

■ Birds have an inner compass and may be able to "see" magnetic fields. Birds migrating at night begin their flight at sunset when the sun's rays become polarized. (Unlike ordinary light, which vibrates freely in all directions, polarized light vibrates in a single plane.) Birds may be able to see this plane of polarized light and use it to calibrate their inner compass to the earth's magnetic field.

■ Birds can also orient themselves by the stars, the daytime sun, wind, topography, and a sense of smell. None of the scientific explanations changes our wonder at a bird such as the six-ounce golden plover, which flies nonstop from Hawaii to Alaska, more than 2,400 miles, or the ruddy turnstone, flying 3,500 miles from the Pribiloff Islands in the Bering Sea to the Marshall and Caroline islands in the South Pacific.

and on the 3.5-mile tour road open to vehicles at William L. Finley refuge from May to October.

WHAT TO SEE

■ **LANDSCAPE AND CLIMATE** Sweeping north to south from Portland to Eugene, Oregon, a distance of 109 miles, the Willamette (Will-LAM-et) Valley is checkerboarded with a broad expanse of farm fields extending outward to low, rolling hills. The Willamette's environment was managed long before white settlers arrived. Kalapuya Indians burned it frequently to enhance hunting and food-gathering opportunities. Settlers arriving in the 1840s discovered vast grasslands created by the repeated burnings. Climate in the valley is mild and wet — 60 inches of rain a year, falling mostly November through March. January temperatures run from 27 to 57 degrees; in July the range goes from 49 to103 degrees.

■ **PLANT LIFE**

Wetlands Common wetland plants throughout the valley include bulrush, sedge, spike rush, smartweed, and cattail. Millet, a wetland plant that serves as food for wildlife, also grows in the refuges.

Grasslands Remnants of native prairie can be found at the William L. Finley and Baskett Slough refuges. Refuge lands are also leased to farmers for growing high-protein forage for the waterfowl—annual ryegrass, perennial ryegrass, and fescue. In spring, widlflower bloom brushes the wet prairie with blue (camas lilies, lupines, and delphiniums).

Forests Groves of stately hardwood trees grow throughout the valley and on the adjoining hillside slopes. Big-leaf maple is scattered through the valley bottoms and along the hills, often in conjunction with Douglas fir. The maple is noted for its massive burls and the size of its leaves, which have been recorded growing to 22 inches across. Its seeds have wings like tiny helicopter blades that can float considerable distances before landing, thus extending the maple groves.

Old-growth Oregon white oaks can be found on hillsides in oak savannas where the trees escaped the Kalapuya's seasonal burnings and later settlers' fires that kept their fields clear of weeds and seedling oaks. The white oak grows slowly to 80 feet, its leathery leaves spaced along heavy limbs.

■ ANIMAL LIFE

Birds Although the refuges are managed primarily for Canada geese, a total of 246 bird species has been seen in the refuges. Your chances are good for viewing wood ducks, red-tailed hawks, American kestrels, purple finches, savannah sparrows, Bewick's and winter wrens, and downy woodpeckers. The great-horned owl hunts on the refuge throughout the year, and great blue herons are also present year-round.

Mammals As the Pacific jumping mouse hops along, balancing on its long, strong tail, it brings to mind a kangaroo reduced in size to about 9.5 inches. Unlike the deer mouse, which scurries along on four feet, the jumping mouse gets around on its two long hind legs, making short hops unless a barn owl happens to be chasing it. Then the mouse attempts an escape by leaping six feet in one jump. The sound of drumming on dry leaves is probably a jumping mouse vibrating its tail.

The jumping mouse needs those big leaps—it is a food source for the coyote, fox, bobcat, short-tailed and long-tailed weasels, mink, western spotted skunk, various snakes, and several species of owls, all fellow residents of the Willamette Valley.

Reptiles and amphibians Seven species of snakes—rubber boa, northwestern and common garter, ringneck, racer, gopher, and sharp-tailed snake—live in the refuges, all of them nonpoisonous. (Rattlesnakes live in the Willamette Valley but have not been seen on the refuges.)

Wood duck

Roosevelt elk with full rack

William L. Finley NWR
Corvallis, Oregon

A thicket of trees lines both sides of the meandering west-side road leading into William L. Finley, creating a shifting play of light and shadow. The showpiece of the three Willamette Valley refuges, William L. Finley is small enough to convey a sense of intimacy but packs in more trails than refuges three times its size. It also contains some of the prettiest scenery in this part of Oregon.

HISTORY

Besides being the winter home to thousands of Canada geese, William L. Finley is the site of a historic home listed on the National Register of Historic Places. John Fiechter (pronounced FEAST-er) was a German immigrant who traveled overland to Oregon in 1846. He married Cynthia Newton in 1850, and the two acquired 640 acres (some of which is now the refuge) under the Oregon Donation Land Claim Act. By 1857 they had built Fiechter House. Tours of the home are conducted by Benton County Historical Society, June through August, Sundays, from noon to 4 p.m.

The property changed hands several times, eventually becoming a seasonal hunting estate. In 1964 Henry and Margaret Cabell sold the property to the U.S. Fish & Wildlife Service, and it became the Muddy Creek Division of Willamette NWR, later renamed William L. Finley NWR in honor of the naturalist and wildlife photographer. Finley wanted to protect Oregon's great marshes and stop sport shooting of seabirds nesting on the state's coastal islands. Because of his advocacy, some of the first refuges in the West were established—Malheur, Klamath, and Three Arch Rocks. The 5,325-acre William L. Finley refuge nowadays welcomes about 75,500 visitors annually.

GETTING THERE

The refuge has two entrances. From Portland, drive south on I-5. South of Albany turn west on US 34 to Corvallis. For the east entrance, drive south 8.5 mi. on US 99W. Watch for refuge signs on west side of the highway. Turn west onto a gravel

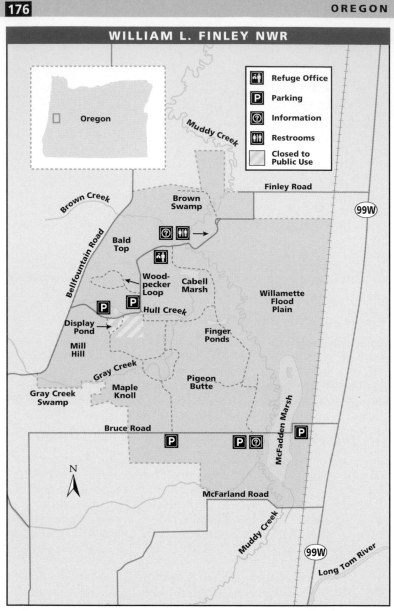

WILLIAM L. FINLEY NWR

Refuge Office

Parking

Information

Restrooms

Closed to Public Use

Oregon

Muddy Creek

Finley Road

99W

Brown Creek

Brown Swamp

Bellfountain Road

Bald Top

Wood-pecker Loop

Cabell Marsh

Willamette Flood Plain

Hull Creek

Display Pond

Mill Hill

Finger Ponds

Gray Creek

Maple Knoll

Pigeon Butte

Gray Creek Swamp

McFadden Marsh

Bruce Road

N

McFarland Road

Muddy Creek

99W

Long Tom River

country road and drive 2 mi. to headquarters, a large white turn-of-the-century farmhouse on the south side of the road. For the west entrance, from Corvallis drive southwest on US 20/34 to 53rd St., then south on 53rd to Bellfountain Rd. Continue on Bellfountain Rd. uphill to the entrance on the east side of the road. Drive east to refuge headquarters, where information may be obtained. Mileage from Portland to the refuge is approximately 93 miles.

■ **SEASON:** Refuge open May 1-Oct. 31. Auto-tour route, Woodpecker Loop Trail and Mill Hill Trail open year-round.

■ **HOURS:** Refuge open sunrise to sunset. In summer, hours are extended to a half-hour before sunrise to a half-hour after sunset. Headquarters open Mon.–Fri., 7:30 a.m.–4 p.m.

■ **ADDRESS:** William L. Finley NWR, 26208 Finley Refuge Rd., Corvallis, OR 97333-9533
■ **TELEPHONE:** 541/757-7236

TOURING WILLIAM L. FINLEY

■ **BY AUTOMOBILE:** An excellent auto tour of about 14 miles uses county roads that cross the refuge or parallel it. To make a counterclockwise tour, take US 99W south from Corvallis. Turn west into the refuge at the east entrance sign and continue to an information kiosk, restrooms, and headquarters. The route continues to the west refuge entrance. Turn south on Bellfountain Road, then make a sharp left turn and continue north on Bruce Road. Follow Bruce Road. as it turns east through the refuge. Stop at McFadden Marsh and another information kiosk. Complete the loop by driving north on US 99W.

■ **BY FOOT:** Five trails lead through William L. Finley's diverse environments (the refuge's elevation ranges from 260 to 550 feet).

■ **BY BICYCLE:** Bicycles are allowed only on refuge roads open for auto travel, and all bicycling is prohibited from November 1 to April 30.

ACTIVITIES

■ **WILDLIFE OBSERVATION:** A year-round smorgasbord of wildlife can be viewed at William L. Finley. Migrating raptors begin to arrive in September, geese in late September, and rough-legged hawks in October. Geese by the thousands graze on refuge fields throughout the winter and mix with ducks and swans in the

Rough-legged hawk

shallow wetlands. Shorebirds come through in April, and songbird migrations peak in early May. Summertime nesting ducks and their broods paddle on refuge ponds, and turtles bask on logs. Roosevelt elk, bugling in the fall, may be seen silhouetted against the sky at ridge tops, and black-tailed deer and their fawns graze in meadows. Roosevelt elk are larger and slightly darker and have more massive antlers than the Rocky Mountain elk found east of the Cascade Mountains.

HUNTING AND FISHING
Dove hunting is permitted on William L. Finley NWR in September. Bow-and-arrow hunting of **deer** is permitted in September, while hunting deer with guns is permitted in October.

Shore access is difficult due to heavy brush, so fishing is discouraged.

■ **PHOTOGRAPHY:** Using your car as a blind, try for photos of geese or elk during the winter. An overview of the Willamette Valley from the top of Woodpecker Loop Trail makes a good shot.

■ **HIKES AND WALKS:** If you have time for only one walk, hike the 1.1-mile Woodpecker Loop Trail, where five species of woodpeckers enjoy varied plant communities. Pick up the trail brochure at the trailhead, on the refuge auto route, south of headquarters. Warning: This trail used to be known as the Poison Oak Trail. Avoid poison oak, which grows in clusters of three

USING YOUR HEAD In the old cliche, people may bang their heads in frustration (being careful not to hit too hard), but woodpeckers are a more versatile sort. They use their heads and beaks as a veritable tool box, substituting them for hammers, chisels, drills, tweezers—and musical instruments.

The pileated woodpecker uses its beak to drum on a resonant piece of dead tree, announcing its availability to mate or that it's about to roost for the night. The red-breasted sapsucker drills holes in tree trunks with its beak, but instead of stuffing the holes with acorns as does its relative the acorn woodpecker, it drinks the sap as it drips out. The tiny downy woodpecker (about the size of a sparrow) hammers away at the bark on trees, searching for grubs. The northern flicker (considered a member of the woodpecker family) may be the most energetic carpenter among these handsome birds. It uses its bill to excavate a nest that may have an opening of 8 inches and extend to a depth of 15 inches.

Seven species of these colorful woodpeckers inhabit William L. Finley, and the Woodpecker Loop Trail is the best place to listen for their steady drumming or perhaps to catch a glimpse of these interesting inhabitants.

shiny, rich green leaves (reddish in fall, less shiny when mature) in the form of a single stalk, a large bush, or a vine clambering up any available tree. Poison oak may cause an oozing, itching rash even in winter, when it appears as a series of bare stalks. Stay on the maintained trail and you will avoid the poison oak.

The 2.4-mile Mill Hill Loop Trail passes Gray Creek, partially dammed by beavers. Mill Hill and Woodpecker loop trails are open year-round. The following three trails are open May 1 through October 31. The trailhead for the Beaver Pond/Cattail Pond trails is off the parking lot on Bruce Road, offering good views of spring wildflowers and migrating birds. The 1.5-mile Muddy Creek Trail is excellent for viewing wetlands and looking for animal tracks. Pigeon Butte Trail, 1.5 miles, leads to the

Woodpecker (red-shafted flicker, female)

highest point on the refuge and offers a great view of the Willamette Valley.

A good 2.8-mile hike on a refuge service road leads by Cabell Marsh and the Finger Ponds. Open May 1 through October 31, the road can be accessed near headquarters or at the information kiosk on Bruce Road. It's a good choice if several people want to hike and others prefer driving—hikers can be picked up at the opposite end of the hike at Bruce Road.

Ankeny NWR
Jefferson, Oregon

Much of the pleasure of visiting Ankeny refuge is in seeing an almost forgotten corner of the Willamette Valley as the valley must have appeared before expanding development transformed pastoral landscapes into urban centers.

Only a mile from heavy interstate traffic along I-5, Ankeny (pronounced ANN-ken-ee) is tucked away in a hidden corner of rural Oregon near the confluence of the Willamette and Santiam rivers. It's a small refuge, at 2,796 acres, with lowlands lying at 180 feet and uplands rising only to 290 feet. Ankeny attracts about 7,000 visitors annually.

HISTORY

Ankeny was established in 1965 to provide winter habitat for the dusky Canada goose.

GETTING THERE

From Portland drive south on I-5 to 13 mi. south of Salem. Go west at Exit 243 (Ankeny Hill) and drive .25 mi. Turn right and drive .2 mi. on Ankeny Hill Rd. to information kiosk. There is a restroom at the information kiosk on Ankeny Hill Rd., although the refuge does not have an information center or office.

■ **SEASON:** Refuge open May 1 to Sept.30. Information kiosk and county roads passing through Ankeny refuge are open year-round.

■ **HOURS:** Open daylight hours.

■ **ADDRESS:** Ankeny NWR, 2301 Wintel Road South, Jefferson, OR 97352-9758

■ **TELEPHONE:** 503/623-2749

TOURING ANKENY

■ **BY AUTOMOBILE:** There is no loop tour road within Ankeny refuge itself, but an excellent 11.5-mile loop can be made by using county roads (two of which cut through the refuge) and by stopping at the nine turnouts where you can enjoy extensive views of wetlands and wildlife. To plan your tour, write to the refuge for a map.

■ **BY FOOT:** There are two short footpaths leading to a variety of habitats.

WHAT TO SEE

Former marshes that had been drained and planted with crops have been restored to wetlands by bulldozing the fields to make them lower, building dikes around them, and installing water controls. The restored marshes offer migrating birds a place to stop, rest, and feed.

Almost 60 percent (2,200 acres) of the refuge is planted in cropland—corn, sudan, fescue, and perennial and annual ryegrass. From the observation kiosk you will overlook a large area of permanent open water surrounded by seasonal marsh, providing excellent views of the waterfowl during the winter, plus bald eagles and thousands of shorebirds.

More than 200 species of birds have been seen on the refuge, including falcons, swans, and a variety of songbirds. One of the refuge's smallest inhabitants is the Pacific tree frog, a tiny (2-inch) frog with long legs and the ability to leap three feet. Usually green, the tree frog takes only minutes to change its color to match its surroundings. It is one of the commonest frogs found in the Pacific states and occupies the borders of freshwater habitat—ponds and marshes—from sea level

Black-headed grosbeak

to more than 11,000 feet. The western pond turtle likes to loaf in the sun and can be seen resting on a fallen log partly submerged in a pond. The turtle eats insects and aquatic plants and any dead fish or animals it can find. On land, look for black-tailed deer and coyotes.

ACTIVITIES

■ **HIKES AND WALKS:** Two foot trails lead visitors by Ankeny's ponds. A 2-mile loop trail includes a boardwalk through a riparian forest and by an observation blind overlooking newly restored wetlands. Portions of the trail will be open year-round. The trailhead is by a parking lot off the south side of Wintel Road.

A short (0.5-mile) wheelchair-accessible loop trail leads by a blind overlooking a newly restored wetland. Look for the trailhead off the north side of Wintel Road.

> **HUNTING AND FISHING**
> **Dove** hunting is permitted through the month of September.
> Fishing is not allowed.

Baskett Slough NWR
Dallas, Oregon

For those who like to combine the rather sedate avocation of birdwatching with some real exercise, Baskett Slough NWR is the place to be. It's wide open, with expansive vistas. Baskett Slough is home to some 50,000 geese and ducks during the winter. It also offers a fine 3-mile trail that meanders uphill through an oak woodland interrupted by open ground, then heads farther uphill to the top of Mt. Baldy, where the views are splendid.

HISTORY

Baskett Slough, named after pioneer George Baskett, was established in 1965, one of four refuges intended to provide habitat for the dusky Canada goose.

GETTING THERE

From Portland drive south on I-5. In Salem turn west onto OR 22. Continue through Rickreall 1.7 mi. to the refuge, then continue another 2 mi. and watch for the information kiosk and parking area on the north side of the road. To visit the north side of the refuge, drive north from Rickreall 1.8 mi. on US 99W. Turn west on Coville Rd. and drive 1.5 mi. to the trailhead parking area. The refuge has no Visitor Center or other visitor facilities except for its viewing kiosk.

■ **SEASON:** Refuge open May 1–Sept. 30. Baskett Butte Trail open year-round.
■ **HOURS:** Open during daylight hours.
■ **ADDRESS:** Baskett Slough NWR, 10995 Highway 22, Dallas, OR 97338-9343
■ **TELEPHONE:** 503/623-2749

Dusky Canada geese

WHAT TO SEE

Baskett Slough, the smallest of the Willamette Valley refuges (2,492 acres), seems bigger because of the expansive space it occupies in open farmland near the foothills of the Coast Range to the west with panoramic views of the Cascades and Mount Jefferson to the east.

In the viewing kiosk on OR 22, a free spotting scope offers closeup views of geese and ducks on refuge ponds.

In the emergent marsh during summer drawdown, millet, smartweed, and nut sedge can be found. Baskett Slough, originally a ditch dug to drain agricultural fields, has been dammed to create a 500-acre wet-

> **HUNTING AND FISHING**
> Hunting and fishing are not permitted on the refuge.

land. White oaks dot the native prairie, creating an oak savannah, a spacious field with oak trees growing in it. Baskett Slough is notable for its colorful spring wild-flowers. The 1-inch pink flowers of the wild hollyhock blend with blue delphinium and lupine, dotting fields and roadsides.

ACTIVITIES

■ **HIKES AND WALKS:** During open season in the summer, a 4.5-mile trail stretches between Smithfield and Colville roads, with a turnoff to the oak woodland loop and Baskett Butte. The trail crosses open areas of native prairie dominated by perennial bunch grasses.

For an overview of the refuge's northern half, continue uphill to the Van Duzer Winery by taking the gravel road off Smithfield Road, where you can enjoy a view of the grapevines and far-reaching vistas.

Columbia NWR
Othello, Washington

Channeled scablands, Columbia NWR

Gouged and ripped apart as if Thor in a rage had smashed the land with his hammer, the channeled scablands are among the most dramatic scenery in the West. Formed by the world's greatest known flood, Columbia NWR speaks of the West's wildest lands, a piece of the earth that people's best efforts couldn't quite tame. Here one sees creation at work in all its violence and austere beauty. The Drumheller Channels National Natural Landmark, including portions of this refuge, has been set aside to protect this extraordinary area.

HISTORY

The Spokane Flood, which occurred around 16,000 years ago, left behind a desolate and shattered desert where Columbia refuge now stands.

Salish Indians followed Crab Creek through the area (it ran only in wet seasons), but the Indians made no attempt to establish permanent camps here. Pioneers ranged cattle in the dry lands, which were soon overgrazed, and a few failed attempts at farming further decimated the land. The area might have remained a desert, but westerners do not allow water sources to go untapped. Impounded by a series of dams, the wild Columbia River was tamed. Construction began in 1934 on the Grand Coulee Dam (on the Columbia, upriver from what would become the refuge); and Columbia NWR was established in 1944 in conjunction with the related irrigation project.

The refuge includes 29,596 acres—23,000 acres of which are actively managed—making it one of Washington's largest refuges. It provides wildlife viewing opportunities for more than 80,000 visitors each year.

GETTING THERE

From Seattle drive 110 mi. east on I-90 to Vantage. Cross the Columbia River and take WA 26 east around 40 mi. to WA 24. Turn north and go about one-half mile to Othello. Turn east on 1st Ave. to headquarters or continue north on WA 24 (Broadway Ave.) and McManamon Rd. about 5 mi. to the refuge. From Spokane drive west on I-90 for around 90 mi. to Moses Lake, then turn south to follow WA 17 for 22 mi. toward Pasco. Turn west at road sign to Othello.

■ **SEASON:** Refuge open year-round, but approximately two-thirds of the property is closed from Oct. 1 to Feb. 28 to give waterfowl an undisturbed resting area.

■ **HOURS:** Refuge open 1 hour before sunrise to 1 hour after sunset. Office open Mon.–Thur., 7 a.m.–4:30 p.m., Fri. to 3:30 p.m.

■ **ADDRESS:** Columbia NWR, 735 East Main St., P.O. Drawer F, Othello, WA 99344

■ **TELEPHONE:** 509/488-2668

TOURING COLUMBIA

■ **BY AUTOMOBILE:** Automobiles are allowed on all paved and most gravel roads within the refuge. An extensive auto-tour route of 23 miles loops around the refuge. Drive north from Othello on Broadway Avenue, which turns into McManamon Road. Following McManamon Road to the right and turning right at Road H SE, O'Sullivan Dam Road and Morgan Lake Road puts you on a clockwise tour.

■ **BY FOOT:** There are three trails on Columbia NWR which lead hikers around 2.75 miles through a shrub-steppe environment, along Crab Creek and along Marsh Unit 2.

■ **BY BICYCLE:** Bicyclists may use all roads open to automobiles.

■ **BY CANOE, KAYAK, OR RAFT:** The Hutchinson-Shiner Lakes canoe area has a floating dock, and the boating area covers 2 miles.

WHAT TO SEE

■ **LANDSCAPE AND CLIMATE** Between 13 to 16 million years ago, the largest volcano in the Columbia Plateau erupted hundreds of times, smothering an area of thousands of square miles in lava.

Grand Coulee Dam transformed the Columbia River environs hereabouts from total desert into marshland containing 200 lakes and ponds (left in the aftermath of the Spokane Flood 16,000 years ago), still in the middle of a desert. Seepage from the dam, working its way through the lava fields, raised the area's water table and filled depressions in the lava, creating the maze of small lakes and ponds now found on the refuge. More lakes and ponds were formed by the damming of springs.

Lying in the rain shadow of the Cascade Range, Columbia refuge averages less than 8 inches of rain a year—although clouds and fog sometimes cover the area in winter and early spring. This desert country varies in elevation from 900 to 1,300 feet. Caution: Watch for blinding dust storms in spring. Summers are usually hot and very dry, with July temperatures ranging from 42 to 97 degrees. January temperatures run from 10 to 54 degrees.

■ **PLANT LIFE**

Arid lands In the desiccated soil of the refuge's arid lands, plants have adapted to a home where rain may not fall for six months. Greasewood has a resinous coating (produced in part by a scale insect) on its light green leaves that helps prevent evaporation. Its root system spreads far, searching out any available water, and its choice of habitat indicates soils with high alkalinity.

Growing to around 5 feet, greasewood is commonly found in the Great Basin, while the creosote bush, with which it is sometimes confused, grows in the south-

COLUMBIA NWR

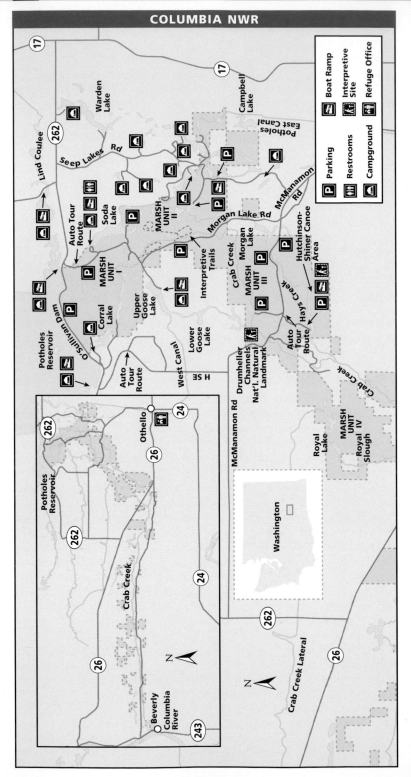

CHANNELED SCABLANDS The channeled scablands were formed by an unrivaled cataclysm in the earth's history that began around 16,000 years ago when a massive glacier advanced south out of Canada toward what is now Pend Oreille Lake.

One tongue of the glacier inched over a massive lava field, a solid sea of basalt covering more than 100,000 square miles in Idaho, Oregon, and Washington, including what is now Columbia NWR. In places the lava was more than 10,000 feet thick, indicative of the vast forces that formed the region.

The ice eventually dammed the Clark Fork River, creating a lake (now known as Glacial Lake Missoula) that covered 3,000 square miles, had half the volume of present-day Lake Michigan, and reached 2,000 feet in depth at the ice dam. When the dam breached, water ripped across the land at a rate estimated at 10 times the combined flow of all the rivers in the world—286 million cubic feet per second (cfs). (By comparison, the Colorado, which has the biggest white water in the West, flows at rates that can range between 2,000 cfs and 29,000 cfs. The Columbia averages around 255,000 cfs.)

The water was so powerful that when it scoured the lava field, it picked up and carried 30-cubic-foot blocks of basalt. It eroded canyons, formed cataracts, and laid down great ripple waves of gravel 20 to 30 feet high and 2 miles long. The hodgepodge of mesas, canyons, channels, and lakes left by the flood and surviving to our time offers endless opportunities for exploration.

west deserts. The creosote bush shares a name with the creosote used to preserve railroad ties and telephone poles, but the bush does not produce the preservative. The Spanish called it *hediondilla* ("little stinker"), and its pungent odor, particularly obvious just after a rain, will notify you of its presence.

Even though in summer most plants here lie dormant as the sun burns down onto Columbia's shrub-steppe lands, spring rains can turn the muted desert gray-greens into a riot of color. Look for the pink blooms of phlox in late April.

■ ANIMAL LIFE

Birds Spring—March and April—is the time to see the biggest variety of birds on the refuge as they fly through Columbia on their northern migration. (Much of the refuge is closed in winter, so visitors miss some of the southern migration.) Among the migrants are as many as 5,000 sandhill cranes, which stop off for around six weeks from early March to mid-April. May brings the shorebird and songbird migration to the refuge. Watch for the courtship dance of the western grebe, a long-necked bird with a cap of black feathers atop its white neck. The mating pair swim side by side, throwing their heads back as if they're throwing something away. They suddenly stand upright, keeping their heads and necks erect, and run forward on the water. Clark's grebes are common on Potholes Reservoir but are seldom seen on the refuge itself. The reservoir's southern edge forms the northern boundary of the refuge.

Summer begins early in Columbia. By mid-June broods of ducklings appear on the lakes. (Summer is not considered a good time for bird viewing because of the heat.) Some 6 or 7 miles north of the refuge is Washington's primary nesting site for the great egret, also seen during the summer. Look as well for swallows and

Western grebe

fledged birds of prey. The shorebird migration begins the first of July, and songbirds fly through starting in August.

By September and October the waterfowl have returned; peak viewing for mallards is in November. Tundra swans often winter at Columbia, but remember that many areas of the refuge are closed in winter to give the birds sanctuary.

Mammals You may spot mule deer, coyotes, and yellow-bellied marmots, and, in the shrub steppe, the Washington ground squirrel. Around water, look for river otters, beaver, muskrat, and raccoons. Refuge managers can provide guidance on how to recognize and differentiate tracks, scat, and middens.

Reptiles and amphibians Cold winters on the refuge limit the types of amphibians and reptiles found at Columbia. Bullfrogs, first seen near Migraine Lake in 1983, are now the most common amphibian. The tiger salamander, Pacific treefrog, and the Great Basin spadefoot toad may also be seen. Several lizards, the painted turtle and a few snakes live at Columbia. Warning: Watch in rocky areas and heavy vegetation for two venomous reptiles, the night snake (usually hidden during the day) and the western rattlesnake, which is active in late April through September. The coloration of the western rattlesnake varies greatly. It can be gray, greenish, brown, or black and often blends with its surroundings. This snake can always be recognized by the rattles on its tail. The night snake is gray or beige with dark gray or brown splotches.

Fish Most species of fish in refuge waters have arrived via the canal irrigation system from the Columbia, including Potholes Reservoir and Potholes Canal, and in Lower Crab Creek. Three species of trout—rainbow, brown, and cutthroat—plus whitefish, suckers, carp, bass, pumpkinseed sunfish, perch, and catfish all swim in refuge waters.

ACTIVITIES

■ **CAMPING:** Primitive Soda Lake Campground on the refuge has 10 covered picnic shelters, portable toilets, a gravel boat ramp, one campsite, and a portable toilet with wheelchair access. There is no water, sewer, electric, or garbage service. Access Soda Lake by turning east off the auto-tour route south of Pothole Reservoir.

COLUMBIA HUNTING AND FISHING SEASONS

Hunting
(Seasons may vary)

	Jan	Feb	Mar	Apr	May	Jun	Jul	Aug	Sep	Oct	Nov	Dec
geese	■									■	■	■
duck	■									■	■	■
coot	■									■	■	■
chukar										■	■	■
pheasant										■	■	■
quail										■	■	■
rabbit	■	■	■							■	■	■
deer										■		

Fishing

	Jan	Feb	Mar	Apr	May	Jun	Jul	Aug	Sep	Oct	Nov	Dec
bass			■	■	■	■	■	■	■			
rainbow trout			■	■	■	■	■	■	■			
German brown trout			■	■	■	■	■	■	■			
bluegill			■	■	■	■	■	■	■			
black crappie			■	■	■	■	■	■	■			
yellow perch			■	■	■	■	■	■	■			
walleye				■	■	■	■	■				
whitefish			■	■	■	■	■	■				
bubot			■	■	■	■	■	■	■			

In season, hunting is permitted on Wed., Sat., and Sun., as well as Thanksgiving, Christmas, and New Year's Day.

■ **WILDLIFE OBSERVATION:** Soda Lake Dam (on a refuge road) offers one of the better opportunities for viewing waterfowl. In April and May, Frenchman Hills (on nearby state land) blossoms with wildflowers. In May, after a wet winter, you may find the beautiful Mariposa lily. Note: While much of the refuge is closed during winter months to give sanctuary to the birds, a good viewpoint overlooks Royal Lake, where waterfowl are most concentrated. Access to this overlook is via Byers Road.

Watch for cliff swallows building their nests and swooping around the buttes while paddling Hutchinson-Shiner Lakes. There is no designated canoe trail.

■ **PHOTOGRAPHY:** At Drumheller Channels National Natural Landmark, don't miss a shot of the columnar basalt, tall, thin rectangular slabs of rock standing upright, formed during the cooling of the lava flows.

■ **HIKES AND WALKS:** The 1-mile Frog Lake Trail follows the drainage to Frog Lake, passing a variety of shrub-steppe plants such as greasewood and sagebrush. A .5-mile loop extension at the trail's end overlooks Seeps Lakes. The Marsh Trail loop (.75 mi.) circles two of the marsh impoundments—they are either kept flooded for the birds or allowed to dry up to encourage plant growth.

■ **SEASONAL EVENTS:** Late March: Sandhill Crane Festival, which includes seminars, art contests, field trips to view cranes and explore geology and local history. Festival information, Othello Chamber of Commerce, 800/684-2556 or 590/488-2683.

■ **PUBLICATIONS:** Refuge map.

Columbia River Gorge National Scenic NWRs

Steigerwald Lake NWR, Franz Lake NWR,
Pierce NWR
Stevenson, Washington

Canada geese

Most visitors to the Columbia River Gorge zip along I-84, stopping at pullouts along the south bank to view the great river, which cuts the only sea-level route from the Pacific Ocean through the Cascade Mountains. The drive through the Columbia River Gorge National Scenic Area begins near Troutman and continues east 150 miles to Boardman on I-84. The three refuges are across the river from the designated scenic area.

But a second, less traveled road (WA 14) following the river's north bank offers a glimpse of the lush riverside habitat as it must have appeared before the Columbia River was dammed into subservience and development took over. In the 38-mile drive between Portland and Stevenson, three national wildlife refuges preserve fragments of pristine environment. These are small, bucolic patches of woodland, fields, and wetlands. Currently closed to public use, these refuges can only be viewed from an overlook, a trail skirting the refuge's edge, or by an arranged visit.

GETTING THERE

From Portland drive east through Vancouver and follow WA 14 along the north shore of the Columbia River. From Olympia, drive south on I-5 to Vancouver and follow signs to WA 14.

■ **ADDRESS:** c/o Pierce NWR, 36062 SR 14, Stevenson, WA 98648-9541
■ **TELEPHONE:** 509/427-5208

Steigerwald Lake NWR
Washougal, Washington

WHAT TO SEE

One and a half square miles in size, Steigerwald became a refuge in 1986. To see wintering geese, walk the Columbia River Dike Trail, starting from Steamboat Landing State Park, at the junction of WA 14 and 15th St. in Washougal. More than 160 species of birds use the refuge, including purple martin, rufous humming-birds, great-horned owls, and up to 4,000 wintering Canada geese. Gibbons Creek flows through the refuge, supporting remnant runs of coho salmon and steelhead. A gateway center introducing visitors to the Columbia River Gorge and to wildlife preservation is planned for the refuge as well as a 2-mile interpretive trail.

Franz Lake NWR
Washougal, Washington

WHAT TO SEE

Wintering tundra swans and other waterfowl feed on large stands of refuge wapato (see Julia Butler Hansen NWR for a description of wapato) and coho salmon, and other juvenile salmonids rear in springs and seeps here.

Wetland plants include willow, wapato, bulrush, smartweed, and several sedges. Old-growth fir and cedar, willows, and cottonwoods add a shady canopy and shelter great blue herons, bandtailed pigeons, red-tailed hawks, Pacific treefrogs, and California ground squirrels. To see this 553-acre refuge, stop at the overlook near Milepost 32, just .25 mile west of the junction of Franz Road and WA 14.

Pierce NWR
Skamania, Washington

WHAT TO SEE

A forest of hardwoods—Oregon white oak, black cottonwood, and white ash—along the shore of the Columbia River shelters a lush undergrowth of Indian plum, snowberry, dogwood, wild rose, and blackberry.

The grasslands of this former cattle ranch include redtop, orchardgrass, meadow foxtail, and Ladino clover. The refuge was donated to the National Wildlife Service by Lena Pierce, who had observed a large increase in Canada geese (from around 20 to more than 1,000) after she and her husband began farming the land, inadvertently providing feed for the geese in the grazed pastures.

Western Canada geese brood and winter in the small refuge—336 acres—and Hardy Creek supports one of the last remaining chum salmon runs on the Columbia. Up to 15 bald eagles arrive each year to eat the salmon. Sixteen duck species visit Pierce. Mallards, northern pintails, American wigeons, and gadwalls are most likely to be seen.

To view this little gem, stop at Beacon Rock State Park (near Milepost 36 on WA 14) and hike to the summit of Beacon Rock—or follow Hamilton Mountain Trail, also in the park.

Conboy Lake NWR
Glenwood, Washington

Elk

The colossal, sprawling hulk of Mt. Adams, a 12,307-foot snow-capped volcano, dwarfs little Conboy Lake, nestled at its base. The lake is all that's left of a once extensive seasonal marsh filled each year by snowmelt from the surrounding Cascade Mountains. Ducks and geese stop by Conboy in February and March on their spring migration, and visitors come to thrill to the refuge's stunning scenery.

HISTORY

Settlers began arriving in the valley that held Conboy Lake in the 1870s and soon dug a ditch to drain the lake and extend their pastureland. But water from heavy rains and snowmelt kept the ditch from draining, and the lake continued to fill between mid-December and April. Conboy Lake refuge was established in 1964 to restore the lake, but until the entire lake bed has been purchased, drainage continues. About 3,800 people use the refuge every year.

GETTING THERE

From Portland, OR, take scenic WA 14 along the north bank of the Columbia River. Turn north at Underwood on WA 141 to Milepost 21, then east on the Glenwood-Trout Lake Hwy. about 9 mi. to Wildlife Refuge Rd.

From Yakima, drive 16 mi. south on I-82. At Toppenish, turn southwest for 48 mi. on US 97, then northwest on WA 142 for 34 mi. to Glenwood. Continue following above directions.

■ **SEASON:** Refuge open year-round.

■ **HOURS:** Open daily from sunrise to sunset.

■ **ADDRESS:** Conboy Lake NWR, 100 Wildlife Refuge Rd., P.O. Box 5, Glenwood, WA 98619-0005

■ **TELEPHONE:** 509/364-3410

TOURING CONBOY LAKE

■ **BY AUTOMOBILE OR BICYCLE:** County roads passing around and through the refuge are open to automobile touring and bicyclists.

■ **BY FOOT:** Willard Springs foot trail, a 2- to 3-mile loop with shortcuts, parallels the old lakeshore, providing spectacular views of Mt. Adams.

WHAT TO SEE

■ **LANDSCAPE AND CLIMATE** By late summer only the lowest parts of the lake hold water. The refuge—5,814 acres—is essentially flat, ranging in elevation from 1,820 to 1,850 feet.

■ **PLANT LIFE** The dense forest that climbs from the refuge up the slopes of Mt. Adams includes two pines—ponderosa and lodgepole—and two firs—Douglas and white. Willows, cottonwoods, and oaks dot the valley floor. An especially beautiful time in the refuge is fall, when the aspen turn yellow.

■ **ANIMAL LIFE**

Birds Canada geese, tundra swans, and mallard and pintail ducks are some of the 150 bird species seen on the refuge. Occasionally snow and white-fronted geese stop over during migration along with teal and wood ducks. Bald eagles, looking for a meal, arrive with the waterfowl. Best viewing to see these migrants is from February to April. Conboy Lake refuge is the only Washington refuge where greater sandhill cranes nest. Breeding populations have expanded from one pair in 1975 to 14 pairs in 1999.

Lodgepole pinecone

Mammals Look for elk during the fall on the refuge and in private meadows around the valley. Occasional sightings of river otter, bobcat, martin, mountain lion, and black bear have been made. Keep an eye open in forested areas for the rare chance to see one of these mammals.

HUNTING AND FISHING Parts of the refuge are open, Oct. through Jan., to the hunting of **deer, geese, common snipe, ducks, grouse,** and **coots.** There is limited fishing for **catfish** and **trout.**

Reptiles and amphibians The refuge is home to one of the largest populations of Oregon spotted frogs in the northwest.

ACTIVITIES

■ **PHOTOGRAPHY:** A good photograph can be made from mid- to late October by looking across the lake to the aspen grove with Mt. Adams in the background.

■ **PUBLICATIONS:** Refuge brochure, with map.

Grays Harbor NWR
Hoquiam, Washington

Western sandpipers, Grays Harbor NWR

More than a thousand western sandpipers skitter about the mudflats at Grays Harbor, persistently poking their thin beaks into the mud in search of worms, tiny crustaceans, and insects. By the time spring migration is over in May, hundreds of thousands of shorebirds will have stopped off at the harbor estuary to rest, feed, and store fat for their nonstop flight north, undeterred by the sewage lagoon (no bad odors here) and the airport that border the refuge. During spring migration, Grays Harbor is a birder's paradise, with peak viewing in late April and early May.

HISTORY

Grays Harbor refuge, a 1,500-acre property, is seen by some 5,600 visitors each year. Established by Congress in 1988, it has since been named as a site of international significance in the Western Hemisphere Shorebird Reserve Network.

GETTING THERE

From Olympia, drive west on US 101, US 12, and OR 8 to Aberdeen. Continue west on OR 109. Turn left on Paulson Rd. (leading to Bowerman Airport), then right on Airport Way. Park across from Lana's Hanger Café. The distance from Olympia is about 52 mi.

■ **SEASON:** Open year-round.
■ **HOURS:** Open daylight hours.
■ **ADDRESS:** Grays Harbor NWR, c/o Nisqually NWR, 100 Brown Farm Rd., Olympia, WA 98516. The refuge is administered from the Nisqually NWR and has no Visitor Center or other facilities.
■ **TELEPHONE:** 360/753-9467

TOURING GRAYS HARBOR

■ **BY AUTOMOBILE:** There is no auto route on the refuge.

■ **BY FOOT:** Jogging is not permitted on the refuge, but there is one walking trail leading to good views from the peninsula. When visiting, stay on the road or trail and off the marsh and tideflats.

■ **BY BICYCLE:** No biking at Grays Harbor.

■ **BY CANOE, KAYAK, OR BOAT:** The refuge does not allow boating, canoeing, or kayaking.

WHAT TO SEE

Flying from as far away as Argentina, some of the birds migrating through Grays Harbor refuge travel more than 15,000 miles each year. Grays Harbor Estuary is one of the four major staging areas for shorebirds in North America, and even though the refuge includes only 2 percent of the estuary's intertidal habitat, the hundreds of thousands of birds that stage at Grays Harbor use the refuge's mudflats.

Short-billed dowitcher

Some 24 species of shore-birds gather here. Dunlin (formerly called red-backed sandpipers) wheel and circle in such tight flocks that from a distance they resemble a fluttering cloud, their colors shifting like a kaleidoscope between dark and white plumage. During courting season in the Arctic, the males trail the females, trilling a low note that sounds like water drops falling into a bowl.

To see the dunlin and the other birds commonly found in the refuge—western sandpipers, short-billed and long-billed dowitchers, and semipalmated plovers—find a tide table and plan your visit during the two hours before and after high tide. The refuge mudflats are the last to be flooded in high tide and the first exposed as the tide ebbs, giving the birds extra feeding time.

You may see coyotes or black-tailed deer in the refuge uplands; red-tailed hawks, northern harriers, bald eagles, and peregrine falcons visit the refuge periodically.

ACTIVITIES

■ **CAMPING:** There is no camping on the refuge.

■ **SWIMMING:** The waters at this refuge are mudflats, not appropriate for swimming. Avoid the water of the sewage lagoon.

■ **HIKES AND WALKS:** The 1-mile Sandpiper Trail starts west of Lana's Hanger Café and proceeds to the tip of Bowerman Peninsula, where it becomes a .33-mile boardwalk. Walk west of Lana's Café through a gate, continue along the paved road and onto a trail leading through a shrubby haven for songbirds. The grassy meadow can be muddy (wear rubber boots). Follow the trail to the boardwalk.

■ **SEASONAL EVENTS:** April: Grays Harbor Audubon Society and the refuge sponsor a Shorebird Festival. Information: Grays Harbor Chamber of Commerce (360/532-1924).

HUNTING AND FISHING Not permitted on the refuge.

Julia Butler Hansen NWR for the Columbian White-tailed Deer

Cathlamet, Washington

Julia Butler Hansen NWR

The sparkle of sunlight on the breeze-rippled water of a quiet slough offers little evidence that only a half-mile away one of the country's mighty rivers is rushing toward the Pacific. As the Columbia River nears the ocean, its backwaters form an intricate pattern of tranquil sloughs, streams, and marsh. A corner of this wild and wet landscape has been saved in the Julia Butler Hansen NWR, a refuge devoted to the Columbian white-tailed deer. The Columbia River marks the boundary between Oregon and Washington, and the refuge is located in both states.

HISTORY

The Columbian white-tailed deer once ranged freely over two states, in the valleys near Roseburg, Oregon, and through the Willamette Valley to Puget Sound in Washington—a home range of more than 300 miles in length. The deer now survive only along the Umpqua River near Roseburg and at the upper end of the Columbia River estuary. Columbian White-tailed Deer NWR, on the shore and islands of the lower Columbia, was established in 1972 to protect around 230 of the remaining deer, one of 31 subspecies of the white-tailed deer in North America. The refuge (5,527 acres) was renamed after Julia Butler Hansen in 1988 to honor the late congresswoman and Washington state legislator.

GETTING THERE

The refuge borders the Columbia River in Washington and includes an island on the Oregon side of the Columbia. From Olympia drive 73 mi. south on I-5. Turn west on WA 4 to Longview. The highway takes city streets through Longview and goes through a park. When the road appears to branch, stay left. Continue 27 mi. on WA 4 through Cathlamet (pronounced Kath-LAM-et). About 2 mi. west of Cathlamet, cross a green truss bridge. Continue about .25 mi. and turn left on Steamboat Slough Rd. A brown sign will point (right) to the refuge office.

■ **SEASON:** Refuge open year-round.

■ **HOURS:** Refuge open daily between dawn and dusk. Office open Mon.–Fri., 7:30 a.m.–4 p.m.

■ **ADDRESS:** Julia Butler Hansen NWR for the Columbian White-tailed Deer, P.O. Box 566, Cathlamet, WA 98612

■ **TELEPHONE:** 360/795-3915

TOURING JULIA BUTLER HANSEN

■ **BY AUTOMOBILE:** A 9-mile auto-tour route loops around the refuge. Continue south on Steamboat Slough Road past headquarters. The road follows the west side of the mainland section of the refuge, ending at WA 4, where a right turn will take you back to the beginning of Steamboat Slough Road.

■ **BY FOOT:** Hiking is allowed only on Center Road, which cuts through the center of the refuge, ending at Steamboat Slough. The 3-mile (one-way) trail starts near refuge headquarters.

■ **BY BICYCLE:** Bicyclists may peddle the auto-tour route.

■ **BY CANOE, KAYAK, OR BOAT:** The extensive Columbia River Heritage Canoe Trail (for experienced canoeists) runs from Clatskanie to the John Day River and takes three to four days to paddle. One leg of the trail passes next to and through both the Julia Butler Hansen and Lewis and Clark refuges, allowing views of the refuges not visible from land. Launch at Cathlamet Marina for a day paddle through Elochoman and Steamboat sloughs to see the Julia Butler Hansen refuge. Although the route is marked, signs have disappeared; carry Marine Chart #18523 and pick up a brochure at refuge headquarters. If strong winds prevail, the route can be run upriver, using the winds and incoming tide instead of fighting them. For canoe rentals, call Skamokawa Paddle Center, 888/920-2777.

To visit the refuge's Tenasillahe (pronounced Ten-ah-SILL-ah-hee) Island on

Columbian white-tailed deer

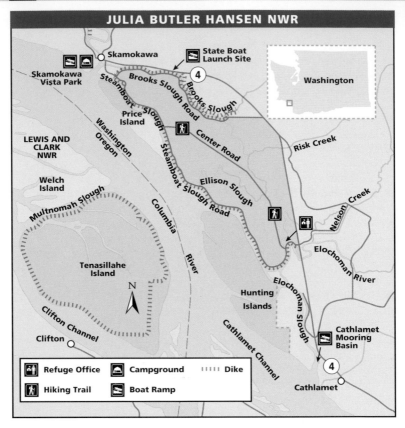

JULIA BUTLER HANSEN NWR

Skamokawa · State Boat Launch Site · Washington
Skamokawa Vista Park · Steamboat Slough · Brooks Slough Road · Brooks Slough · 4
LEWIS AND CLARK NWR · Price Island · Washington · Oregon · Center Road · Risk Creek
Welch Island · Multnomah Slough · Steamboat Slough Road · Ellison Slough · Nelson Creek
Tenasillahe Island · Columbia River · N · Elochoman River
Clifton Channel · Hunting Islands · Elochoman Slough · Cathlamet Mooring Basin
Clifton · Cathlamet Channel · Cathlamet · 4

Refuge Office · Campground · Dike
Hiking Trail · Boat Ramp

the Oregon side of the Columbia, you'll need a boat. Boat ramps: Washington Dept. of Wildlife boat launch on WA 4, between Cathlamet and Skamokawa; Skamokawa Vista Park; Cathlamet mooring basin—all on the Washington side of the Columbia. To launch from Oregon: Aldrich Point (end of Aldrich Point Road), north off US 30; or John Day boat launch, also along US 30. Both Oregon launch points are east of Astoria.

WHAT TO SEE

■ **LANDSCAPE AND CLIMATE** As the tide flows up the Columbia, it washes across the low-lying islands dotting the refuge's river estuary until only a few tufts of reeds nod above the water.

This is a land bathed in a marine climate of fog, mist, and rain—79 inches a year, with most of it falling between October and April. Summers are generally dry and pleasant. On the mainland, the diked floodplain is a mix of forested tidal swamps, brush thickets, and grazing fields. Twice a day tidal flow from the Pacific covers the refuge's low islands.

■ **PLANT LIFE**

Wetlands Wapato, the delta potato, was a mainstay in the diet of the Lewis and Clark expedition of 1804-1806. The explorers bought the tubers from native Indians. Easy to spot for its 10-inch leaves shaped like an arrowhead, the plant is now eaten by muskrats and ducks. (In China and Japan, wapato—also known as arrowhead—is grown and harvested for food.) Look for it in tidal mudflats and marshes.

Grasslands The refuge's grasslands are managed to produce feed for the deer. By grazing cattle and haying, grasses stay short. The best nutrition is found in new growth. Crops planted by refuge personnel keep the weeds down and provide extra food for wildlife. Because the deer don't stray far from shelter, parts of the open fields that were cleared of trees and brush by pioneers are being replanted with the same species of trees and brush cut down a hundred years ago. With new cover, the deer will be able to extend their feeding area.

Forest Trees typical of the coastal rain forest grow at Julia Butler Hansen—thick stands of Sitka spruce and black cottonwood, named for the appearance of its dark trunks. To identify Sitka spruce, touch a handful of its needles (gingerly). If the stiff needles hurt, it is Sitka spruce. Red alder, growing on the area's floodplain, fixes nitrogen in the soil and provides nourishment for a rich understory of ferns and grasses. Native Americans used a solution made from alder bark to clean wounds and as a medicine for tuberculosis. Red alder may have gotten its name from the use of its bark to make an orange or red dye. The tree's wood is considered the best for smoking salmon.

■ **ANIMAL LIFE**

Birds More than 175 species of birds have been seen on the refuge, and some 30,000 to 50,000 birds winter on the Columbian estuary. Ducks include shoveler, merganser, mallard, wigeon, greenwing, pintail, and greater and lesser scaup. Twenty pairs of great blue herons nest on the refuge; Canada geese and tundra swans winter on the lower Columbia—tundra swans can sometimes be seen eating wapato tubers. Around 30 pairs of bald eagles nest at Hanson refuge, too.

In summer the Virginia rail nests close to water's edge in salt marshes or on stream

Virginia rail

margins. Difficult to see because of its habit of hiding during the day, the rail ventures out at dusk to feed, its long slender bill and cinnamon breast distinguishing it from the black rail.

Mammals Bounding across a field, the white-tailed deer holds its 7-inch tail up and wags it from side to side, showing the tail's underside, which, unlike that of the mule deer, is white. Its scientific name, *odocoileus virginianus,* comes from the state of Virginia, where it was first studied. This once abundant species began a rapid decline in the late 1800s when its preferred habitat—grassland with nearby woodland—disappeared as farmers cleared the land for crops. By the 1930s, the whitetail was believed to be extinct, but the discovery of a remnant herd began efforts to save the species. A count done in 1997 found around 600 to 800 of the whitetails in

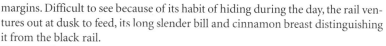

JULIA BUTLER HANSEN HUNTING AND FISHING SEASONS

Hunting
(Seasons may vary)

	Jan	Feb	Mar	Apr	May	Jun	Jul	Aug	Sep	Oct	Nov	Dec
geese	■									■	■	■
duck	■									■	■	■
coot	■									■	■	■
snipe	■									■	■	■

Fishing

	Jan	Feb	Mar	Apr	May	Jun	Jul	Aug	Sep	Oct	Nov	Dec
chinook salmon							■	■	■	■	■	■
coho salmon							■	■	■	■	■	■
sturgeon	■	■	■	■	■	■	■	■	■	■	■	■
steelhead	■	■	■	■	■	■	■	■	■	■	■	■

Hunting of geese, ducks, coots, and snipe is allowed on the refuge portion of Hunting Islands. Temporary blinds can be constructed by hunters but must be kept available for use on a first-come, first-served basis. Fishing in waters around the refuge includes Steamboat and Brooks sloughs and Elochoman and Columbia rivers.

the area, with about 400 of them living on the refuge, which is also home to Roosevelt elk.

Other mammals on the refuge include muskrats, coyotes, bobcats, river otters, and nutrias, a South American rodent brought to the Northwest to raise for its fur. Escaping the fur farms, nutrias have spread through the Northwest, competing with native species for nutritious water plants. Excellent swimmers and highly buoyant (nutrias can float with little motion), they stay hidden under marsh vegetation with only their eyes and nose above water.

Reptiles and amphibians Garter snakes are abundant on the refuge, sharing it with painted turtles, bullfrogs, and the Pacific tree frog.

Fish Chinook and coho salmon migrate up the Columbia, while steelhead, cutthroat, and the native bull trout swim refuge waters.

ACTIVITIES

■ **CAMPING:** Camping is permitted in nearby Skanokawa Vista Park, with RV hookups and tent sites (360/795-8605).

■ **SWIMMING:** No swimming is allowed on the refuge.

■ **WILDLIFE OBSERVATION AND PHOTOGRAPHY:** The best time to see the whitetails is September through May, in the early morning and evening. Steamboat Slough and Brooks Slough roads offer good viewing. An observation site for spotting the deer is located beside OR 4. You will get the best photographs of wildlife by staying in your car and using a telephoto lens for closeup shots.

■ **HIKES AND WALKS:** The 3-mile hike along Center Road, which is closed to automobiles, traverses some beautiful riverine landscape with thickets of alder, willow, and towering cottonwoods.

■ **PUBLICATIONS:** Refuge brochure.

Lewis and Clark NWR
Cathlamet, Washington

Harbor seal

As is nears the Pacific, the Columbia River slows, depositing great loads of silt and reshaping the ever-changing outlines of its delta islands. Lewis and Clark NWR, lying off the Columbia's shoreline in Washington, is composed of a number of low-elevation islands made up of tidal marshes and swamps surrounded by mud-flats and sandbars.

These are the islands the Lewis and Clark expedition saw as it approached the Pacific during its three-year exploration of the Northwest. "Rained all the after part of last night," William Clark wrote in his journal for November 5, 1805. "Rain continues this morning. I slept but verry little last night for the noise Kept up dureing the whole of the night by the Swans, Geese, white and Grey Brant Ducks etc., on a Small Sand Island close under the Larboard Side; they were emensely noumerous, and their noise horid. . . The day proved cloudy with rain the greater part of it, we are all wet cold and disagreeable."

HISTORY

Lewis and Clark NWR consists of 54.7 square miles (35,000 acres) and abuts Julia Hansen Butler refuge. Established in 1972 to preserve part of the Columbia's estuary and waters, the refuge includes 20 named islands amounting to about 8,300 acres, plus open water, sandbars, mudflats, and tidal marshes. More than 10,000 visitors tour the refuge annually.

GETTING THERE

From Olympia, Washington, drive 73 mi. south on I-5. Turn west on WA 4 to Longview. The highway takes city streets through Longview and goes through a park. When the road appears to branch, stay left. Continue on WA 4 through Cathlamet (pronounced Kath-LAM-et). About 2 mi. west of Cathlamet, cross a green truss bridge. Continue about .25 mi. and turn left on Steamboat Slough Rd. A brown sign will point (right) to the refuge headquarters.

■ **SEASON:** Refuge open year-round.

■ **HOURS:** Open daily during daylight hours. Headquarters open Mon.–Fri., 7:30 a.m.–4 p.m.

■ **ADDRESS:** Lewis and Clark NWR, c/o Julia Butler Hansen NWR for the Columbian White-tailed Deer, P.O. Box 566, Cathlamet, WA 98612-0566

■ **TELEPHONE:** 360/795-3915

TOURING LEWIS AND CLARK

■ **BY AUTOMOBILE:** This refuge consists entirely of islands. There are no roads and no foottrails.

■ **BY CANOE, KAYAK, OR BOAT:** This is a good refuge to see from the river's waters. Boat launching: From Astoria in Oregon, drive east on US 30. John Day boat launch: west bank of John Day River, west of the US 30 river crossing. Aldrich Point boat launch: Continue east on US 30 and turn north on Aldrich Point Rd. From Washington: Take WA 4 west from Longview to Cathlamet. Boat ramps are available at the Washington Dept. of Wildlife boat launch on WA 4, between Cathlamet and Skamokawa, at Skamokawa Vista Park, and at Cathlamet mooring basin. To approach boat ramps from Portland, drive north on US 30.

A portion of the Columbia River Heritage Canoe Trail traverses the length of the Lewis and Clark refuge, from the John Day River (boat ramp near river's outlet) past Welch Island. To access the route from the Oregon shore, go to Skamokawa off OR 4, where canoe rentals are available at Skamokawa Paddle Center (888/920-2777), and there is a launch site and camping at Vista Park. Warning: Strong winds, wakes from oceangoing freighters in the navigation channel, and fast-flowing tidal changes can make boating difficult and sometimes dangerous here. The crossing from Skamokawa to the refuge crosses the freighter channel. Be sure there is open space in both directions before attempting the crossing. Use tide tables and navigation charts (remembering that the sandbars will have changed shape since the charts were published). If your boat gets stuck in the mud, wait patiently for the next high tide.

WHAT TO SEE

All the environments that make an estuary the ideal habitat for waterfowl can be seen when you explore Lewis and Clark refuge by boat. The continual dredging of the Columbia to keep a shipping channel open has created uplands on several

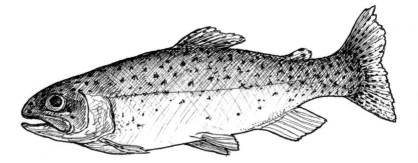

Steelhead trout

of the tidal islands where the silt is dumped. Waterfowl use the grass planted to stabilize these uplands for nesting and feeding.

In the deep water of the estuary where saltwater and freshwater mix, salmon and steelhead migrate upstream to mate, and the young fish swim downstream to the ocean. Worms, snails, and insects living in the mudflats provide meals for shorebirds during low tide, and juvenile fish use the shallow waters as a nursery. Tidal marshes—those covered with water twice daily during high tide—provide habitat for mammals and birds; and the tidal swamps (higher elevation marshes) are a suitable habitat for Sitka spruce, willow, and dogwood.

The best viewing of the 50,000 ducks, 10,000 Canada geese, and 1,000 tundra swans using the estuary during winter is between the months of October and April. Harbor seals haul out on the sandbars and mudflats; while beaver, raccoon, mink, and river otter also live on the islands. Look in the tallest trees for bald eagles; the refuge has 30 to 35 active nest sites.

HUNTING AND FISHING Hunting and fishing seasons are state-mandated. Hunting for **geese, ducks, coots,** and **snipe** is permitted.

You can also fish for **salmon, trout,** and **sturgeon.**

ACTIVITIES

■ **CAMPING:** Skamokawa Vista Park, with RV hookups and tent sites (360/795-8605), is on the Oregon shoreline off OR 4.

■ **SWIMMING:** There is no swimming allowed on the refuge. Sinkholes and riptides in the surrounding Columbia River make swimming treacherous.

Little Pend Oreille NWR
Colville, Washington

White-tailed deer

The ruins of 11 homestead and cabin sites scattered through Little Pend Oreille refuge are crumbling reminders of the pioneers who once attempted to live on this land—and who finally left it, to be reclaimed by the white-tailed deer and moose. Dense stands of ponderosa pine crowd the edges of fields cleared by the pioneers, the first who arrived to homestead in 1870. By the 1930s most home-steaders had been bought out by a federal resettlement plan meant to help farm-ers hurt by the Great Depression. In the forest, logging roads and clear-cuts indicate evidence of more recent human activity.

HISTORY

"Pend Oreille" is a contraction of the French *pendant d'oreille,* meaning "earring." Ear ornaments worn by Pend d'Oreille natives prompted 18th-century French trappers to give them their name. Sometimes called "The Forgotten Refuge," Little Pend Oreille (pronounced Pond-oh-ray) was established in 1939 as a game pre-serve for white-tailed deer. Most refuge land was acquired through the Federal Resettlement Administration, which retired marginal farmland. Management was turned over to the Washington Department of Wildlife in 1965 and returned to the U.S. Fish & Wildlife Service only in 1994. With 13 roads entering the refuge, little control over human visitation exists. Activities typical of contemporary western forests continue: logging, cattle grazing, hunting, fishing, and camping.

Little Pend Oreille encompasses nearly 63 square miles—one of Washington's biggest refuges—and welcomes some 30,000 visitors each year. The refuge is also used by an Air Force survival school and for search-and-rescue training. Proposed management plans, if adopted, may limit the refuge to more traditional wildlife-friendly uses.

GETTING THERE

From Spokane, go north 72 mi. on WA 395 to Colville. Turn east on WA 20 and drive about 6 mi. Turn right on the Artman-Gibson Rd. and go 1.7 mi., then turn left on the Kitt-Narcisse Rd. and drive 2.2 mi. until road forks. Stay right onto Bear Creek Rd. for 3.3 mi. to the refuge office, a log building on the right.

■ **SEASON:** Open year-round, but most refuge roads are closed from about Jan. 1 through mid-April to protect wintering wildlife.

■ **HOURS:** Open 24 hours.

■ **ADDRESS:** Little Pend Oreille NWR, 1310 Bear Creek Rd., Colville, WA 99114

■ **TELEPHONE:** 509/684-8384

TOURING LITTLE PEND OREILLE

■ **BY AUTOMOBILE, BICYCLE, OR FOOT:** Little Pend Oreille has 139 miles of roads, all open for hiking and mountain biking, if you don't mind encountering an occasional logging truck ripping by at full tilt (two roads are under road-use agreement with a private timber company). Refuge inholdings total 10 square miles, mainly industrial timberlands owned by Stimson Lumber and Boise Cascade. Pick up a map at headquarters showing which of the labyrinth of refuge roads are closed to motorized traffic.

■ **BY CANOE, KAYAK, OR BOAT:** Nonmotorized boats are welcome on Bayley and McDowell lakes.

WHAT TO SEE

■ **LANDSCAPE AND CLIMATE** Rising from the western lowlands (1,800 feet) to 5,610 feet atop Olson Peak, Little Pend Oreille's dramatic elevation change (4,210 feet) takes visitors through six plant communities with temperatures ranging from around 10 to 40 degrees (with 3 or 4 feet of snow) in January. By July temperatures have increased to a range of 50 to 100 degrees. Rainy seasons come

Rainbow trout

in spring and fall, with precipitation ranging from 22 inches of rain and snow at lower elevations to 34 inches in the higher country.

■ **PLANT LIFE** On a hot day the sweet scent of vanilla fills the air in the refuge's lowland ponderosa pine forest. Also called yellow pine (for the color of its vanilla-scented bark), the ponderosa is the most common of western conifers and is heavily logged. Climbing through the forest, you'll encounter Douglas fir, western larch, and lodgepole pine at midelevation and, in the high country, true fir, spruce, hemlock, and cedar.

■ **ANIMAL LIFE** The silence of Little Pend Oreille's deep forest may suddenly be broken by a *tap, tap, tap,* the only indication that one of the forest's quieter denizens is present and at work. The three-toed woodpecker, hunting its meal of insects hidden in the cracks of bark, likes burnt-over areas and often nests in the hole of a dead conifer. Look for the flash of a yellow cap and a series of black-and-white bars crossing its back.

ACTIVITIES

■ **CAMPING:** Of the refuge's five campgrounds, the most popular, Potter's Pond, has a fishing pier (handicapped-accessible) and allows boats equipped with electric motors and bait fishing for trout. All camps are primitive—bring water. The largest has seven sites.

■ **WILDLIFE OBSERVATION:** Driving one of the loop roads, with frequent stops to wander into the forest, offers the best chance to see some of the 180 species of birds spotted on the refuge. Look for waterfowl nesting in cavities near lakes and streams. Choice viewing areas for mammals are at the ponds and in streamside habitat (beaver) and in open fields (moose and white-tailed deer). There's a chance of viewing lynx, fisher, or marten in the forests.

Nisqually NWR
Olympia, Washington

Riverside, Nisqually NWR

Tucked between the metropolitan cities of Tacoma and Olympia and surrounded by a population of nearly 300,000, Nisqually refuge is a bucolic haven that recalls the quiet and simple life of the farm it once was. Refuge paths follow dikes through a bramble of berry bushes and sheltering trees as rain falls gently, glistening on leaves of wild ginger. In the winter, fog comes often to Nisqually, wrapping trees in a mantle of gray. The Nisqually River and McAllister and Red Salmon creeks thread through the refuge, making Nisqually a haven for migrating birds and fish and the people who come to see them.

HISTORY

Alson Brown was a Seattle lawyer who decided to try his hand at farming. In 1904 Brown bought 1,500 acres on the Nisqually (pronounced Nis-KWAL-ee) River delta and developed one of the most productive farms in the area. Hogs, dairy cows, bees, and chickens were raised to produce the eggs, meat, milk, cream, butter, honey, and sausage sold in Tacoma and Seattle. World War I sent Brown into bankruptcy after the collapse of his Austrian mining stock; and for the next 55 years his former farm was leased to various farmers. Today 2,973 acres of the Nisqually River delta make up the refuge. The land was purchased by the U.S. Fish & Wildlife Service at the urging of the Nisqually Delta Association, a citizens' group that prevented Seattle from turning the area into a dump and the Port of Tacoma from dredging it into a deep-water industrial port. Each year some 80,000 visitors arrive to see Nisqually, which became a refuge in 1974 and is one of the most visited of Washington refuges.

GETTING THERE

From Olympia drive east on I-5. Take Exit 114 (about 5 mi. east of Lacey) and turn north (left) under the freeway, following signs to the refuge. From Seattle, drive south on I-5. Take Exit 114, turn right, and follow signs to the refuge.

■ **SEASON:** Refuge open year-round.

■ **HOURS:** Open daily during daylight hours. Office open Mon.–Fri., 7:30 a.m.–4 p.m. Twin Barns Education Center, open to public Tues.–Sun., 9 a.m.–4 p.m.

■ **FEES:** The daily fee is $3 per family.

■ **ADDRESS:** Nisqually NWR, 100 Brown Farm Rd., Olympia, WA 98516

■ **TELEPHONE:** 360/753-9467

TOURING NISQUALLY

■ **BY AUTOMOBILE:** There are no roads on the refuge.

■ **BY FOOT:** Nisqually has seven miles of trails, including a .5-mile interpretive trail and 2 loop trails of 1 and 5.5 miles. Jogging, bicycles, and pets are not allowed. Three miles of the Brown Farm Dike Trail are closed from early October to mid-January.

■ **BY CANOE, KAYAK, OR BOAT:** A public boat ramp is located at Luhr Beach on the west bank of McAllister Creek, and boating is allowed on refuge waters outside Brown Farm Dike. Warning: Get a tide table and watch for hazardous tides and shallow water. Winds come up swiftly, creating choppy water if they're blowing against the tide.

WHAT TO SEE

■ **LANDSCAPE AND CLIMATE** Lying at the very southern tip of Puget Sound, the refuge spans the area where the freshwater of the Nisqually, rising on the southern slopes of Mount Rainier 78 miles away, flows into the sound's saltwater. Nisqually refuge includes the flat river delta and upland bluffs with an elevation rising from sea level to 300 feet.

Dense conifer forests on the bluffs above set off the mudflats, marshes, ponds, croplands, and grasslands of the nearly flat wetlands below. The Nisqually delta is one of the only sizable river deltas remaining in Washington (the others belong to the Columbia River, bordering Oregon, and up north at the Skagit River).

The entire topography of Nisqually's tidal estuary was changed in 1904 when farmer Alson Brown had his workers build a dike to create a freshwater area that was blocked off from the incoming tides. A sluice in the dike was opened to allow freshwater to flow into the estuary. It took

Boardwalk trail, Nisqually NWR

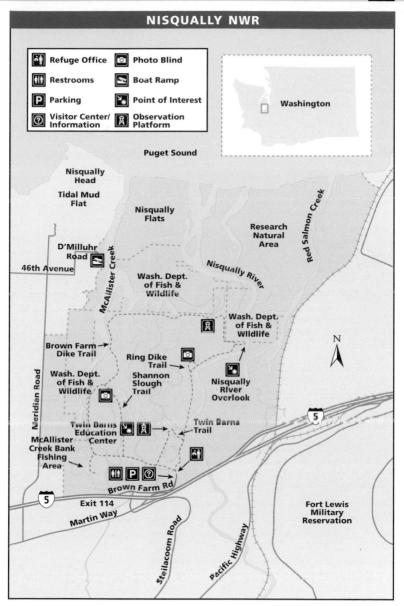

NISQUALLY NWR

Refuge Office

Restrooms

Parking

Visitor Center/
Information

Photo Blind

Boat Ramp

Point of Interest

Observation
Platform

Washington

Puget Sound

Nisqually
Head

Tidal Mud
Flat

Nisqually
Flats

Research
Natural
Area

Red Salmon Creek

D'Milluhr
Road

46th Avenue

McAllister Creek

Wash. Dept.
of Fish &
Wildlife

Nisqually River

Wash. Dept.
of Fish &
Wildlife

N

Brown Farm
Dike Trail

Ring Dike
Trail

Wash. Dept.
of Fish &
Wildlife

Shannon
Slough
Trail

Nisqually
River
Overlook

Meridian Road

Twin Barns
Education
Center

Twin Barns
Trail

5

McAllister
Creek Bank
Fishing
Area

5

Exit 114

Martin Way

Brown Farm Rd

Steilacoom Road

Pacific Highway

Fort Lewis
Military
Reservation

three years before the area was free enough of salt to grow crops. The dike remains today and separates freshwater marshes and grasslands from the saltwater estuary.

The climate is maritime, influenced by Puget Sound and the Pacific Ocean, with 49 inches of rain annually, 80 percent of it falling October through March. The average temperature in January is 37 degrees; in July, 63 degrees.

■ PLANT LIFE

Wetlands An odd parasitic plant called salt-marsh dodder pushes a thin orange stem out of the dirt, slowly twisting around until it latches onto one of the plants it likes—including lamb's-quarter, pickleweed, and marsh cudweed, all growing at

Nisqually. The dodder then grows suckers that insert themselves into the stem of the host plant and suck nourishment from it. The dodder eventually leaves the ground completely, flowers, and goes to seed.

Few plants grow in the mudflats, but beds of salt-marsh sand-spurry grow just below high-tide line.

Grasslands Fields of daffodils blooming in springtime are reminders of long-gone farming families, but the abundance of plant life, both native and introduced, is testament to the fertility of the soil. The refuge plant list includes 410 species. Fifty-three species of grass grow at the refuge, including introduced varieties such as sweet vernalgrass and orchard grass and natives that include nodding tristium and red fescue. Keep an eye pealed for poison oak, growing in clusters of three red-tinged leaves (when first leafing) that turn a deep, glossy green as they mature. Skunk cabbage starts its remarkable growth in early spring, and touch-me-nots bloom in late spring.

Skunk cabbage

Shrubs and small trees grow along the dike banks. Look for Oregon crab-apple, pear, evergreen, and Himalayan blackberry and wild rose. This shrub habitat, coupled with the adjacent riparian surge plain (an area that is intermittently inundated with water), supports the greatest variety of birds found on the refuge.

Woodlands The common and creeping snowberry are both found on the refuge, their white berries making a bright show in winter. Some native tribes considered the berries poisonous, while other tribes ate the berries. In the orchards remaining from farming days, you'll find some old European varieties of fruit trees. Red alder, black cottonwood, and western red cedar can be found throughout the refuge, including the bluffs overlooking the estuary, and one Douglas fir tree on the bluffs has an active bald eagle nest.

■ ANIMAL LIFE

Birds The red-throated loon, often seen at Nisqually in spring, fall, and winter, floats lazily on the water, then suddenly executes a swift and powerful dive, jetting with its webbed feet to follow every twist of its prey, then surfaces, holding a fish in its bill, ready to swallow. Pied-billed grebes and double-crested cormorants frequent Nisqually's waters all year as do Canada geese and great blue heron. Around 20,000 ducks winter at the refuge.

Shorebirds visiting the mudflats to eat shrimp, worms, and other invertebrates found there include dunlin, western sandpiper, killdeer, and long- and short-billed dowitchers. Black brant feed on the eelgrass beds in the mudflats.

Red-tailed hawks and northern harriers can be seen wheeling overhead throughout the year, and in the forest, downy woodpeckers, northern flickers, and red-breasted sapsuckers search for insects hidden in the bark.

Nisqually is rich in song-birds—look and listen for the black-capped chickadee, bushtit, and red-breasted nuthatch, as well as the Bewick's wren, visible year-round in the refuge.

Mammals Many of the Pacific Ocean's sea mammals pass through Puget Sound, and chances of seeing a gray whale or harbor porpoise from the refuge are good. An observation tower on the Brown Farm Dike Trail allows views toward the sound. Watch for harbor seals hauled out on exposed logs near the mouth of the Nisqually River. The California sea lion is occasionally seen here.

On land, look for the long-tailed weasel, with its short legs

Red-breasted nuthatch

and sharp claws; it may be spotted speeding through a field chasing its dinner, a gopher or rabbit. The weasel uses the skins of its victims to line its nest.

Other mammals commonly observed here are coyote, mink, and river otter. Also present but usually hidden are bobcats, common red foxes, raccoons, spotted and striped skunks, and ermine (also known as the short-tailed weasel).

Reptiles and amphibians Three species of garter snake—common, northwestern, and western—and the rubber boa live at Nisqually. Amphibians include the Pacific tree and red-legged frogs.

Fish The rich waters of the Nisqually estuary host a number of fish species, including the Chinook, pink, coho, chum, sockeye (Kokanee), and steelhead salmon, as well as as well as four varieties of trout—cutthroat, rainbow, brook and Dolly Varden, named after a character known for her colorful costume in the novel *Barnaby Rudge,* by Charles Dickens. Suckers, redside shiner, daces, squawfish, bass, crappie, perch, and catfish also inhabit the waters.

ACTIVITIES

■ **CAMPING AND SWIMMING:** No camping or swimming is allowed at or near the refuge.

■ **WILDLIFE OBSERVATION:** An observation tower, built by the Civilian Conservation Corps on the Brown Farm Dike Trail overlooking the estuary, can hold 8 to 10 people and is excellent for spotting waterfowl and shorebirds.

SCOURING RUSH The long-necked plesiosaur, with his sharp, pointy teeth and flipperlike feet, may have scratched his neck on an ancestor of the scouring rush that grows today in Nisqually. One of the world's longest surviving plants—it first appeared when the great swamp forests of the Carboniferous Period were forming massive deposits of coal, 330 to 280 million years ago—the scouring rush (also known as the horsetail) lived in swamps with the 34-foot-long plesiosaur, whose lamentable survival record was no match for the horsetail.

Of the 35 horsetail species that descended from the Carboniferous era and that grow in swamps throughout the world, the scouring rush is medium in size, reaching 5 feet. Its slender, stiff green stalk, banded in black and tan, contains so much silica that European cabinetmakers use the stalk to polish wooden floors and furniture.

Scouring rush gained the name "Dutch rush" after being imported from the Netherlands to England to polish pewter. Northwest native Indians used the plant to polish arrow shafts, canoes, and dishes and as decorations for baskets. If you're out of matches, try twirling the pointed head of the horsetail on a piece of wood until the friction causes a spark, a practice still in use among native tribes.

An observation platform near the Twin Barns provides viewing of songbirds, raptors, and waterfowl.

■ **PHOTOGRAPHY:** Photo blinds are located on the Ring Dike and Shannon Slough trails.

■ **HIKES AND WALKS:** The Twin Barns loop trail is a 1-mile boardwalk, wheelchair-accessible. The Brown Farm Dike Trail—5.5 miles—loops around the original dike built by Alson Brown's workers. It's one of the best trails in the Washington refuges, with views of both freshwater and saltwater marshes, grasslands, and luxuriantly growing shrubs, berry bushes, and wildflowers. On its western side, both Mount Rainier and the Olympic Mountains can be seen.

HUNTING AND FISHING The refuge is closed to hunting, but the closure area is adjacent to state lands where **waterfowl** hunting is allowed.

Protection Island NWR
Port Angeles, Washington

Protection Island NWR

Warped by ancient winds, the contorted outlines of Douglas firs tell stories of survival in a landscape blasted by harsh winter winds. Calm summer days give little inkling of winter's violent weather. Visiting Protection Island in spring—May 1, 1792—Captain George Vancouver was so impressed that he wrote: "our attention was immediately called to a landscape, almost as enchantingly beautiful as the most elegantly furnished pleasure grounds in Europe." The island retains its beauty, but its status today as protected nesting habitat for seabirds gives it its true importance. Of all the seabirds that frequent Puget Sound and the Strait of Juan de Fuca, 72 percent choose to nest on Protection Island.

HISTORY

Tiny Protection Island—1 square mile—became a refuge in 1982 by executive order of President Ronald Reagan. Named Isla de Carrasco in 1790 by the first Europeans to explore it, Protection Island was given its current name by Vancouver, who stopped by during his exploration of the Strait of Juan de Fuca while searching for the Northwest Passage.

GETTING THERE

There is no road or footpath access to the island. However, it can be viewed from boats, which must remain outside the 200-yard buffer zone around the island. From Olympia drive north on I-101 to Sequim (pronounced Skwim).

■ **SEASON:** The refuge can be seen all year from a boat.

■ **ADDRESS:** Protection Island NWR, c/o Washington Maritime NWR Complex, 33 South Barr Rd., Port Angeles, WA 98362-9202

■ **TELEPHONE:** 360/457-8451

TOURING PROTECTION ISLAND

■ **BY BOAT:** For boat tours around Protection Island: Call Sequim-Dungeness Valley Chamber of Commerce, 360/683-6197, or Jefferson County Visitor Center, Port Townsend, 360/385-2722. Binoculars or a spotting scope are necessary for a closeup look at the birds nesting on the island.

WHAT TO SEE

■ **LANDSCAPE AND CLIMATE** Bluffs reaching 210 feet dominate the island's central section. Protection Island lies in the rain shadow of the Olympic Mountains, receiving less than 18 inches of rain a year; but it seems wetter because of the heavy dew and fog in the area. Protection's climate is mild, with temperatures averaging 36 to 45 degrees in January and 51 to 72 in July.

■ **PLANT LIFE** Western red cedar and grand fir grow on Protection along with the Douglas fir. Willow, Douglas maple, oceanspray, and Nootka rose, with its pink blooms, also thrive on the island.

■ **ANIMAL LIFE**

Birds One of the two largest nesting colonies of rhinoceros auklets on the West Coast—17,000 pairs—inhabits the island, where they dig deep burrows for nesting. Look for a pigeon-sized bird (with an orange beak and white plumes around the eye) bobbing on the water near shore in the evening. The auklets feed at sea, then return to the waters around Protection Island, where they fly to their nests to feed their chicks.

Although it's difficult to distinguish among gulls, the largest nesting colony of glaucous-winged gulls in Washington— approximately 7,500 pairs—can be found on Protection Island, and chances are good that that's the gull you will see, feeding along the shore on dead fish, mussels, and clams. Other birds nesting on the island include pigeon guillemot, double-crested cormorants, tufted puffins, and black oystercatchers.

Looking at a seaside cliff filled with several species of seabirds is like glimpsing the balconies of a high-rise condo where each family has established its own living style. Protection Island's high, grassy slopes are a bird condo for seven species of birds. At the top are bald eagles. They build nests in large, old-growth trees and perch high up on sturdy, tall trees. Gulls make nests on the flat, grassy areas at the top of the cliff. Rhinoceros auklets burrow up to 11 feet into the hillside before laying one egg, which they incubate for about 45 days. Tufted puffins nest in burrows in the cliffs of the islands; they will burrow 3 to 6 feet into the hill before setting up housekeeping.

Dropping down to beach level, pigeon guillemots nest in the driftwood washed onto the beaches and piled along the cliff base. They share the driftwood with black oystercatchers, which build a pebble-lined hollow among the beach's rocks and driftwood.

Mammals Harbor seals get the basement apartment. They have their pups on the open beach. The island's two sandy spits, one at each end of the island, are favored by some 600 harbor seals, who come to Protection to haul out and pup.

Ridgefield NWR
Ridgefield, Washington

Ridgefield NWR

The oaks that dot the grassy knolls of Ridgefield seem rooted in time, their massive trunks witness to countless changing seasons. This autumn, just like hundreds of autumns past, geese have arrived to winter in this serene pastoral corner on the banks of the Columbia River. Ridgefield NWR is a lovely mix of scattered lakes and wetlands encircled by rolling hills brushed with brilliant spring wildflowers.

HISTORY

The violent earthquake that hit southern Alaska on March 27, 1964, is remembered for killing 131 people and wreaking enormous damage. It was also a major factor in the establishment of Ridgefield NWR and Oregon's three Willamette Valley refuges. Repeated shock waves from the earthquake lifted Alaska's Copper Delta 6 feet, transforming the marshy meadows—the traditional (and only) nesting grounds of the dusky Canada geese—into drier land covered with thickets of brush offering cover not for geese but coyotes and brown bear. The dusky population plummeted. Since the geese's only winter grounds are along the lower Columbia River and in the Willamette Valley, the four Oregon refuges were established to give the duskies a safe home during a portion of the year.

Ridgefield's 5,218 acres are seen by some 36,000 visitors annually.

GETTING THERE

From Portland drive north on I-205 about 14 mi. Take the Ridgefield exit and drive west 3 mi. to Ridgefield where signs give directions to the Carty and River S units of the refuge.

■ **SEASON:** Refuge open year-round.

■ **HOURS:** Refuge open daily from sunrise to sunset. Office open Mon.–Fri., 7 a.m.–3:30 p.m. There is no Visitor Center on the refuge.

■ **ADDRESS:** Ridgefield NWR, P.O. Box 457, 301 No. 3rd Ave., Ridgefield, WA 98642-0457
■ **TELEPHONE:** 360/887-4106

TOURING RIDGEFIELD

■ **BY AUTOMOBILE:** A 1.7-mile auto-tour route in the River S unit has four parking areas for wildlife observation and passes the large observation and photography blind. Turn west off So. 9th Street at the refuge sign to access the road.
■ **BY FOOT:** The 1.9-mile Oaks to Wetlands Wildlife Trail begins at the parking area for the Carty Unit, west off No. Main Street, at the refuge sign.
■ **BY BICYCLE:** Bicycles are permitted on the auto route.
■ **BY CANOE, KAYAK, OR BOAT:** Boaters can explore the Columbia and Lake rivers and Bachelor Slough. Oregon state waterways surround and bisect the refuge and offer closeup views of the wetlands you won't see by walking. Launch at the Ridgefield Marina.
■ **BY HORSEBACK:** Horses are allowed on the auto-tour route.

WHAT TO SEE

■ **LANDSCAPE AND CLIMATE** The climate along the lower Columbia River valley is warm and wet—exactly to the taste of the several million waterfowl that sensibly depart Alaska each fall. The 62 inches of rain, January temperatures that average only around 34 to 36 degrees, and lush bottomland lakes and sloughs at Ridgefield draw seven different species of Canada geese—30,000 of them—to the refuge each winter. July temperatures warm up to an average of 58 to 79 degrees. Ridgefield's 13 lakes rise and fall, their depth dependent on overflow from snowmelt pouring into the Columbia River. Outcroppings of basalt that were formerly quarried to pave Portland's streets form knolls in the Carty unit, bringing the refuge elevation from sea level up to a modest 40 feet.

Canada goose

■ **PLANT LIFE**
Wetlands Sometimes mistaken for a blanket of bright green algae covering a pond, duckweed is a perennial with one underwater root topped by a tiny leaf that floats on the water. Each minute leaf is only about 1/16-inch wide; both waterfowl and ducks like to eat it and the aquatic insects that live on its leaves. Duckweed grows in Ridgefield's marshes along with other typical wetland plants—wapato (duck potato), bulrush, horsetails, and water plantain.

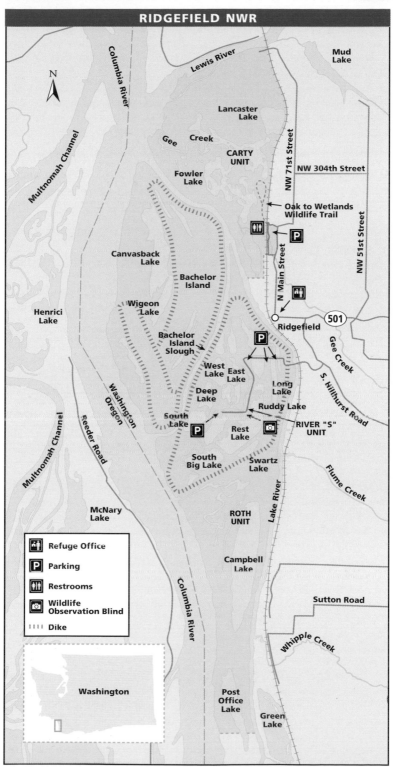

Grasslands Stands of beautiful hardwood trees dot the rolling terrain of Ridgefield, offering a pleasant contrast to the low-growing plants of the wetlands. Both Oregon white oak (also called garry oak) and Oregon ash are medium-sized trees, growing to about 80 feet high. The ash likes wet soil, surviving occasional flooding without dying, and can be seen in low-lying areas as well as on the slopes. Oaks prefer dry soil and grow on higher ground that doesn't flood. (In the parched lowland valleys of the West, they're considered a prime landscaping tree because they don't need summer watering.) Black cottonwood, widespread throughout the West, often signifies the presence of a water course or dry wash because of its preference for wet or moist soil. Reaching 160 feet in height, the cottonwood spreads a sticky resin on its buds and newly opened leaves. In spring the resin scents entire neighborhoods with its sweet fragrance.

Western red cedar and Douglas fir serve as a rich green background to the oaks and ash, and an understory of snowberry, roses, elderberry, and red osier dogwood create a low-lying canopy laced with flowers in season.

■ ANIMAL LIFE

Birds Around 30,000 geese visit Ridgefield each year. Seven species, including Canada, Ross', Emperor, cackling, great white-fronted, snow geese, and brant, fly out from the refuge in early morning to feed on refuge croplands. The geese are just a few of the 206 species of birds that migrate through or live on Ridgefield, but their impressive numbers make them a special refuge sight.

Cowbird

Sandhill cranes also winter on the refuge, along with 23 species of ducks.

Until the leaves drop in late autumn, the nests of the great blue heron rookery on Bachelor Island are difficult to see, but 500 nests have been counted on the island, which is reached only by boat and only from April 16 through September 30. The entire island is closed the remainder of the year to provide sanctuary during hunting and nesting season. The rookery houses the largest colony of great blue herons in the northwest. Sometimes mistaken for sandhill cranes, the heron, one of the most common western birds, is distinguished during flight by its folded-back neck; cranes fly with straight necks.

The wooded slopes of the Carty Unit are an excellent place to see and hear songbirds, both those that nest at Ridgefield and those flying through during migration. One of the nesters, the willow flycatcher (formerly called Traill's flycatcher) is a brash little bird, very aggressive in defending its territory. When angry, it fluffs up, and in flight will maneuver like a jet to threaten invaders.

Another nester, the yellow warbler, must watch for cowbirds. In spring the female cowbird looks for a warbler's nest where she can lay one of her own eggs after dumping one of the warbler's eggs. If the warbler catches the cowbird, she covers the egg with nesting material and lays a new batch of eggs of her own. If the warbler doesn't notice the strange egg, the baby cowbird hatches and is so much bigger than the warbler chicks that it crowds them out, and they starve. The warblers can be seen at Ridgefield, from April through September.

Mammals Black-tailed deer, Roosevelt elk, mountain lions, and coyotes are among the larger mammals living on Ridgefield. Look for beaver and nutria in the ponds and lakes. Nutrias *(coypus)*, originally from Argentina, are rodents that burrow into refuge dikes to make dens. Weighing from 5 to 25 pounds, they float easily and can even eat a diet of grass and leaves while lying on their backs in the water. Mountain lions are tawny in color and are 5 to 9 feet in length, weighing from 80 to 210 pounds. It would be strictly serendipity to see them at Ridgefield—and quite unlikely.

Reptiles and amphibians Look for western pond turtles and painted turtles basking on logs in the ponds.

Fish On the Columbia, chum, chinook, and coho salmon pass through the refuge, while the inland waters support carp, yellow bullhead, sculpin, pumpkinseed, chiselmouth, and 15 other species.

Painted turtles basking amid lily pads

RIDGEFIELD HUNTING AND FISHING SEASONS

Hunting
(Seasons may vary)

	Jan	Feb	Mar	Apr	May	Jun	Jul	Aug	Sep	Oct	Nov	Dec
geese	■									■	■	■
duck	■									■	■	■
coot	■									■	■	■

Fishing

	Jan	Feb	Mar	Apr	May	Jun	Jul	Aug	Sep	Oct	Nov	Dec
carp			■	■	■	■	■	■	■	■		
catfish			■	■	■	■	■	■	■			
crappie			■	■	■	■	■	■	■			
bluegill			■	■	■	■	■	■	■			

Waterfowl hunting is permitted on Mon., Wed., and Sat., using refuge blinds only.

ACTIVITIES

■ **CAMPING:** Nearby Paradise Point State Park (east of I-5, off Exit 16) has 70 sites and nine primitive walk-in sites.

■ **WILDLIFE OBSERVATION:** Best viewing for the greatest number of bird species occurs September through May, especially during spring and fall migration. The observation kiosk is outstanding for viewing waterfowl, while the Oaks to Wetlands Wildlife Trail leads by wooded areas where songbirds can be seen.

■ **PHOTOGRAPHY:** The roomy observation and photography blind at the edge of Rest Lake offers a chance for closeup shots of birds loafing on the lake. The blind is wheelchair-accessible.

■ **HIKES AND WALKS:** Although there is no formal trail along the banks of Bower Slough, walking is permitted there mid-April through September. Waterfowl can be observed away from the noise and fumes of vehicles.

■ **PUBLICATIONS:** Refuge brochure.

Turnbull NWR
Cheney, Washington

Refuge wetlands, Turnbull NWR

The silent waters of a hundred ponds and wetlands, hidden among Turnbull's scabrock (rock scoured clean by the great Spokane flood), create little portraits of tranquility for the visitor strolling along refuge paths. Birds like the ponds, too, because thousands of them—from 200 species—stop by Turnbull on their migrations each year, and more than 100 species stay to nest.

HISTORY

Turnbull became a refuge because its soil would not produce crops. By the 1920s, residents had drained the ponds to create farmland; but they soon discovered that unlike the rich loess soil to the south, blown in after explosions of ancient Mt. Mazama, their soil was barren. (Mt. Mazama's crater now holds Crater Lake.) Turnbull might have remained a maze of drainage ditches but for the determination of sportsmen, naturalists, and community activists, who realized the value of returning the land to its natural state and wanted to re-create what they had lost.

In 1937, after years of effort by the community, Turnbull became a refuge in fact as well as name. The community agreed that there should be no hunting or fishing on this 15,680-acre preserve. Each year about 24,000 visitors explore the 2,200 acres open to the public on the refuge, named for Cyrus Turnbull, a squatter who hunted game and sold it to railroad workers. The tracks of the old Burlington railroad line, which run through the refuge, are expected to be converted to a Rails to Trails path for bicyclists, horseback riders, and hikers.

GETTING THERE

From Spokane, drive south on I-90. At Exit 270 drive south on WA 904 to Cheney (pronounced CHEE-nee), a total of 15 mi. from Spokane. Turn south on Cheney-Plaza Rd., go 4 mi., then east 2 mi. on Smith Rd. to refuge headquarters.
■ **SEASON:** Refuge open year-round.

FIRE The ancient old-growth ponderosa pine forests—now mostly disappeared from the West—were spacious and sunny, with open vistas and a few huge trees dominating each acre. Fire created these open spaces by killing off seedlings; and the suppression of fire in western forests for the past 100 years has created vastly different forests, where an acre may have as many as 100 trees on it, all small and fighting for what sun they can reach, plus a heavy buildup of brush in the understory. When fire starts in these overgrown conditions, it can be catastrophic, decimating vast acreage. The devastating burns experienced in the West in the 1990s have changed the management of these forests.

Fires are now deliberately started—as the Indians used to do—to imitate natural burns, to return the understory and trees to their natural state. At Turnbull you can see the result of a prescribed burn along the north end of the auto route, where the fire burned some 80 percent of the trees, evidence of what fire can do to an overgrown forest. Birds are already nesting in the cavities of the dead snags, and, in another 200 years, Turnbull should look much as it did when the pioneers arrived in the 1880s.

An average of 480 wildfires strike the country's wildlife refuges each year, burning an average of 157,865 acres—more than 63 percent of the fires are ignited in Alaskan refuges. In addition, some 190,077 acres are deliberately burned on the refuges each year.

■ **HOURS:** Refuge open daylight hours 7 days a week. Office open Mon.–Fri. 7:30 a.m.–4 p.m. There is no Visitor Center on the refuge.
■ **FEES:** $3 per car, March 1–Oct. 31. Free entrance Nov.–Feb.
■ **ADDRESS:** Turnbull NWR, 26010 South Smith Rd., Cheney, WA 99004-9326
■ **TELEPHONE:** 509/235-4723

TOURING TURNBULL

■ **BY AUTOMOBILE:** Four observation stopoffs along the 5.5-mile auto-tour loop offer views of grasslands, ponderosa pine forest, and potholes, the steep-sided basins carved into rock by the grinding action of the Ice Age floods.
■ **BY FOOT:** Short trails, ranging from .25 to 1.5 miles, loop around lakes and ponds and follow a ridge through the refuge's pine forest, offering views of the extensive wetlands.
■ **BY BICYCLE:** The auto route is open to bicyclists.

WHAT TO SEE

■ **LANDSCAPE AND CLIMATE** Near the southern edge of the vast lands scoured by the great flood 15,000 years ago (See sidebar, Columbia NWR), Turnbull's landscape is a mix of rugged scabrock formations, rock cliffs, eroded basalt, grasslands, and ponderosa pine forest and aspen, with an elevation that varies little from 2,300 feet. Shallow depressions in the basalt, gouged by the flood, gradually eroded and filled, creating the refuge's 20 small lakes and more than 100 seasonal and semipermanent wetlands, including vernal pools that often dry up after several weeks or months.

January temperatures range, approximately, from a frigid minus 24 to 48 degrees; July temperatures run from 45 to 94 degrees. The refuge receives an average of 18 inches of precipitation annually, part of which falls as 44 inches of snow.

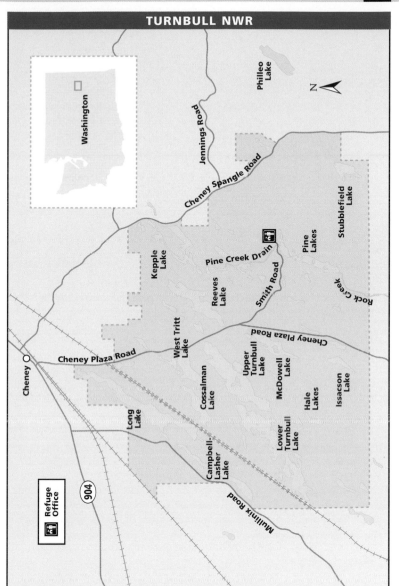

TURNBULL NWR

■ PLANT LIFE

Wetlands Turnbull served as a garden basket for the Spokane native Indians, who gathered wild onion, camas, bitterroot, kouse (a tubular plant resembling an onion), and kinnikinnick. Early visitors reported that the intense blue flowers of fields of the common camas, a member of the lily family, looked like a lake when seen from a distance. Indians gathered the bulbs, which are sweet when cooked for a long period. Warning: The death camas grows in similar areas and is extremely poisonous. Its flowers are white rather than blue.

Kinnikinnick, or the common bearberry, is a trailing evergreen with pinkish white flowers. Its berries are bright red and edible but rather tasteless. The fruits

Bitterroot

sometimes stay on the plant into the winter, providing a touch of bright color. Natives on the Pacific coast in Alaska, Washington, and Oregon dried the plant's leaves and smoked them.

The starchy root of the bitterroot plant is edible in spring but turns bitter in summer, giving the plant its common name. Its scientific name, *Lewisia rediviva,* came from Capt. Meriwether Lewis, who, with Capt. William Clark, led the first expedition across America to the Pacific Ocean. Bitterroot prefers rocky areas with little soil and brightens barren areas with its intense pink flowers.

Howellia is an aquatic plant on the federal endangered species list. It grows on the bottom of ponds in seasonal wetlands often bordered with aspen and is found at Turnbull and Ridgefield refuges and a few other sites in Montana and Idaho.

Grasslands Turnbull's meadows and grasslands are dominated by native bunchgrass, bluebunch wheatgrass, and Idaho fescue, but it is the wildflowers that visitors come to see. Starting in March with buttercups, the meadows are dotted with pink grass widow in March and April. Yellow bells bloom in April, and shooting stars, larkspur, Oregon grape, and balsamroot come out in May. May and June bring the blooms of the camas and wild onion, and the spectacular bitterroot blooms in June. With little leaf structure, bitterroot's pink flowers appear to spring full-grown out of the cracks in rocks. In July the pink blooms of the sticky geranium and wild rose blossom. The yellow plants wait for summer to dust the fields with blooms of Saint-John's-wort.

The refuge lands once housed 60 homesteads, and scattered through Turnbull are old apple trees and huge lilac bushes planted by the settlers.

Forest An understory of snowberry and native bunchgrasses grows in the ponderosa pine forest as well as pinegrass, which forms a beautiful light green solid mat. Other wetland and riparian trees and shrubs are the aspen, willow, red-osier dogwood, and cottonwood.

■ ANIMAL LIFE

Birds Sixteen species of ducks breed on the refuge, but best viewing for migrant species is in April through May and September through October. The refuge's single resident trumpeter swan stopped migrating after its mate was eaten by a coyote. Since then the swan stays until the ponds freeze in winter, when he disappears until the thaw.

Summer brings the house wrens, most energetic little birds. Look for a small bird of dust-brown color flitting in and out of tangled brush, chirping a loud and sprightly song or uttering a harsh and guttural scolding call. This tiny bird (4.5 to 5 inches) is quite bold and will chase other birds out of their nests and move in. If the hapless nesters protest, the wren will kill them if he can or will harass them by tipping their eggs out of the nest and bringing in his own nesting materials.

The refuge has 170 nesting boxes for western bluebirds and fledges more than 500 in a good year.

Mammals Looking like brown desert pincushion cacti, a mother porcupine and her offspring often appear on the headquarters' lawn. Munching on grass, they waddle across the lawn, then nod off for a rest. If you don't see them there, look for them near their natural habitat—trees, large rock crevices, and hollow logs in an open stand of conifers with a good understory of herbs, grasses, and shrubs.

A colony of Columbia ground squirrels also lives near headquarters with another colony at the restrooms. The squirrels live in underground burrows and generally remain in a state of torpor during the hot summer.

Mule deer

Early-morning visitors may see elk; other large animals include white-tailed and mule deer and coyotes in the upland areas of the refuge. In the ponds watch for river otter (found only in the Pine Creek wetland chain), mink, beaver, and muskrat.

Ten species of bats include the big brown and long-eared. Big brown bats roost in snags and dead-topped ponderosa pine trees, and the long-eared bat roosts in basalt rock formations.

Reptiles and amphibians Rubber boas and garter and bull snakes are found at Turnbull along with two frogs, the Columbian spotted and Pacific chorus. Rubber boas crawl into the burrows of mice and eat the baby mice after killing them by constriction. Long-toed and tiger salamanders can also be found at various spots on Turnbull refuge.

ACTIVITIES

■ **CAMPING:** Camping is available nearby. Ask at refuge headquarters for directions.

■ **SWIMMING:** No swimming is allowed on the refuge.

■ **WILDLIFE OBSERVATION:** Three environmental education sites along the auto-tour route offer a good starting point for viewing Turnbull's wildlife. Starting north from headquarters, stop at the east shore of Blackhorse Lake and hike out to Kepple Peninsula, or walk down to Kepple Overlook at the lake. At the west shore of Blackhorse Lake, there's an accessible boardwalk.

■ **PHOTOGRAPHY:** The refuge has one photography blind on Pine Lake.

■ **HIKES AND WALKS:** Visitors are free to walk off the trails in any areas open to the public. A trailhead along the auto-tour route north of headquarters will allow you to drop off hikers in your group to walk the .75-mile Thirty Acre Cutoff Trail and be picked up at the other end by those choosing to drive the loop.

■ **SKIING:** When adequate snow falls, the refuge is open for cross-country skiing.

■ **PUBLICATIONS:** Refuge brochure.

HUNTING AND FISHING
No hunting or fishing is allowed on this refuge.

Washington Maritime NWR Complex

Dungeness NWR, San Juan Islands NWR,
Washington Islands NWR
Port Angeles, Washington

Dungeness Sand Spit, Dungeness NWR

Dungeness NWR

Sequim, Washington

Painted in pale blues and grays, Dungeness Sand Spit lies like a frail finger stretched out along the shore. Logs are piled one on top of the other on the sand, like slumbering sea lions. The waters of Juan de Fuca Strait sneak onto the spit twice a day, surprising visitors who've never seen a 20-foot tidal change. The spit averages 300 feet wide along its 5.5-mile length but shrinks to 50 feet in width when the tide is in. The strait, which lies on the United States–Canada border, is Puget Sound's southern opening to the Pacific Ocean. This skinny finger of land is America's longest sand spit, lying along a wild shore shaped by tides and wind and the swift currents in the strait.

HISTORY

After a homesteader acquired land occupied by the S'Klallam native tribe, the local Indian agent told the S'Klallams to move to the Skokomish Indian Reservation. The S'Klallams preferred to remain in their home territory and attempted to live on the desolate Dungeness Spit from 1872 to 1874. Two years of hauling freshwater by canoe finished that attempt, and in 1874 the tribe pooled $500 in gold to buy 222 acres east of Dungeness, named Jamestown after Lord James Balch, who helped collect the money for the purchase. Graveyard Spit (a secondary spit formed on the south side of Dungeness) is a S'Klallam burial ground. Graveyard got its name after a massacre between tribes.

The spit became a small refuge in 1915. Upland woodlands on the bluff above were added to the refuge in the early 1970s, bringing the size to 1.2 square miles (768 acres). Some 110,000 visitors explore Dungeness each year.

GETTING THERE

From Seattle, take the ferry to Bainbridge Island, drive north on WA to the Hood Canal Bridge, cross the bridge and take OR 20 to US 101. Drive through Sequim, turn north on Kitchen-Dick Rd. and drive 3 mi. to Lotzgesell Rd. Turn east to the Dungeness Recreation Area. Continue through the recreation area to the refuge parking lot.

From Portland, drive north on I-5 to Olympia and follow signs to the Olympic Peninsula, Port Angeles, and US 101.

The Washington State ferries, which carry cars, ply between Seattle and Bainbridge Island or Bremerton, cutting some 130 mi. of driving, one-way; but weekend schedules are limited. Ferry schedules: 206/464-6400.

■ **SEASON:** Refuge open year-round.

■ **HOURS:** Open sunrise to sunset. Headquarters for the Washington Maritime NWR Complex, located in Port Angeles, is open Mon.–Fri., 7 a.m.–4:30 p.m. Visitors may pick up a refuge information sheet near the refuge entrance.

■ **FEES:** Entrance fee. $3 per family. Free entry for children under 16.

■ **ADDRESS:** Dungeness NWR, c/o Washington Maritime NWR Complex, 33 So. Barr Rd., Port Angeles, WA 98362

■ **TELEPHONE:** 360/457-8451

TOURING DUNGENESS

■ **BY AUTOMOBILE:** There are no roads in the refuge. Access is by foot.

■ **BY FOOT:** No trail follows the sand spit, but visitors are free to stroll along the 5.5-mile spit, as long as they keep to the side facing Juan de Fuca Strait. The inland sides of both Dungeness and Graveyard spits are closed at all times to protect nesting birds. A .4-mile trail leads through the upland forest to the bluff (80 feet, the highest point in refuge) overlooking the spit, then descends to the water at sea level.

■ **BY CANOE, KAYAK, OR RAFT:** Sea kayaks, canoes, and boats are allowed on refuge waters May 15 to September 30, but boaters should be aware of the 20-foot tidal changes, riptides, and waters can that suddenly turn choppy. The refuge waters are a no-wake zone, and there is a 100-yard buffer zone around all of Dungeness and Graveyard spits. The only boat landing zone on the refuge is open year-round opposite the New Dungeness Lighthouse on the bayside of Dungeness Spit. Advance reservations are required to land a boat at the lighthouse and may be obtained by calling the refuge office. Marine Drive has a public boat launch. Jet skiing and windsurfing are not allowed on refuge waters.

WHAT TO SEE

■ **LANDSCAPE AND CLIMATE** The piles of weather-beaten logs that hold down the sand at the spit and prevent it from blowing away in the wind arrived at Dungeness because of logging in the Pacific Northwest, and the heavy cutbacks in logging there may affect the spit's future. The logs, which uprooted from along the shore or worked loose from logging rafts, rode the currents and winds to the spit, where high tides rolled them onto the sand. The massive logs are strung out atop the spit and mark the demarcation between people and wildlife areas. As fewer logs roll in from the strait and as the slow aging of the log barrier continues, future generations will see a different spit, which is thought to have formed during the Vashon glacial era, 10,000 to 20,000 years ago. A longshore current flowing eastward—and prevailing northwesterly winds—caused drifting sediments to form the spit.

Summer days at Dungeness can be warm enough for a chilly dip in the strait (July temperatures average about 55 to 80 degrees), but harsh winds blow at any time of the year. Fog, mist, and rain bathe the refuge, which gets 18 to 20 inches of rain annually. Light snow usually falls by December, with January temperatures ranging from around 28 to 55 degrees.

■ PLANT LIFE

Tidelands The calm, sandy tidal flats of Dungeness' inner harbor provide an ideal environment for eelgrass, a slender, straplike plant that thrives in tidelands where freshwater and saltwater mix. The combination of sheltered tidal flats, protected by the refuge's spits, and of freshwater, from the Dungeness River outlet, have created one of the largest eelgrass beds along the West Coast.

Forest A dense stand of Douglas fir—and some red cedar, grand fir, and western hemlock—grows in the uplands. The 60-foot-tall western hemlock, with its graceful, drooping branches and scraggly, tipped-over tops, looks primeval; but strollers who visit the refuge's fog-bathed forest are actually seeing a second-growth forest that was intensively used by native people in the area and later logged.

Visitors to Dungeness in June may see hanging clusters of white Oceanspray blooms that seem to drift like clouds through the dark understory. The shrub's arching branches grow to around 4 feet, and its hard wood was used by natives to make many implements, including harpoon shafts and sticks used to hold salmon over a fire for cooking.

The Pacific madrone is a handsome native tree or large shrub used on the West Coast for landscaping. In Dungeness it grows tucked along the edges of

Old-growth forest

DUNGENESS NWR

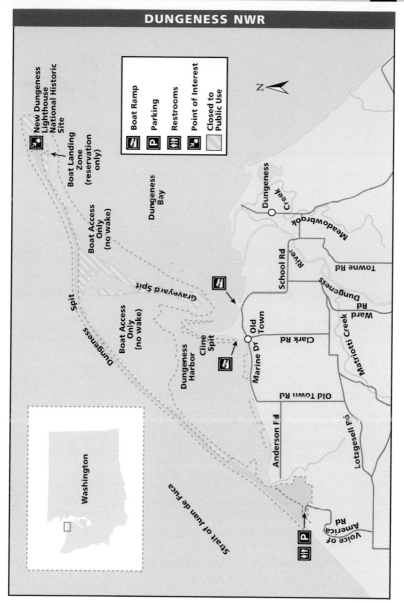

Map legend:
- Boat Ramp
- Parking
- Restrooms
- Point of Interest
- Closed to Public Use

New Dungeness Lighthouse National Historic Site

Boat Landing Zone (reservation only)

Dungeness Bay

Dungeness Creek

Meadowbrook

School Rd

River Rd

Towne Rd

Boat Access Only (no wake)

Graveyard Spit

Dungeness Rd

Ward Rd

Matriotti Creek

Spit

Dungeness

Boat Access Only (no wake)

Dungeness Harbor

Cline Spit

Old Town

Marine Dr

Clark Rd

Old Town Rd

Anderson Rd

Lotzgesell Rd

Washington

Strait of Juan de Fuca

Voice of America Rd

hemlock and alder stands, noticeable for its peeling reddish-brown bark, fall display of brilliant red and orange berries, and clusters of large, pinkish-white blooms in spring. Unless the birds eat them, the berries may last until December, making a colorful splash among the wintry greens.

■ ANIMAL LIFE

Birds For birds migrating along the Western Flyway, the serene and shallow harbor formed by the spit is a small natural sanctuary that offers shelter from the relentless winds. When the tide is out, there's a banquet of food to be gathered from the mudflats and shallow pools. Some 250 species of birds, a number of them dif-

Black brant

ficult to see elsewhere, take advantage of this tiny refuge, making it a prime destination for birders.

Dungeness has attracted more than 250 species, a number of them difficult to see elsewhere. Among the less common birds at Dungeness are the Pacific loon (formerly thought to be an Arctic loon) and the pelagic cormorant, which breeds along the West Coast from the Bering Sea to Baja California. About 1,500 black brant winter at Dungeness—from October through February—and by March the northbound migrant brant have arrived. In late April up to 8,000 black brant are busy eating eelgrass. The brant is a sea goose whose salt glands let it drink seawater and eat saltwater plants. In spring the upland forest is alive with birdsong. Listen for the *tree-tree-sweet* chant of MacGillivray's warbler and the slow, musical whistle of the solitary vireo. Flocks of shorebirds—dunlins numbering 2,000 to 3,000—winter at Dungeness along with black-bellied plovers, short-billed dowitchers, and sanderlings. All told, spring migration brings nearly 15,000 birds to the refuge, with peak numbers in March.

Land mammals Some 40 species of land mammals have been seen on the refuge, but visitors are most likely to glimpse raccoons or a shy black-tailed deer peering out from the underbrush along the trail to the overlook. Along the spit, look for river otters swimming in the bay or bounding along the shore.

Marine mammals The tip of Dungeness Spit past the lighthouse, off-limits to visitors, has historically served as a haulout and pupping site for harbor seals, with as many as 600 seals seen in the area. Gray whales pass through the strait and may be seen in spring and fall; at rare times the great black dorsal fins of a pod of killer whales (orcas) can be seen cutting in close formation through the water.

Reptiles and amphibians Rough-skinned newts live at Dungeness. The newts hide under rocks and in rotten wood, but from late December to July they head for water, where they breed.

Fish and invertebrates The inner harbor, with its dense eelgrass beds, is an important nursery for fish and provides protection for six varieties of salmon:

steelhead, cutthroat, chum, Chinook, coho, and Dungeness River pink. The harbor is also used by lingcod and Dolly Varden as a nursery. Dungeness crabs—famous for their succulence on the dinner table—inhabit the refuge waters. Younger crabs hide in the eelgrass while mature crabs prefer deeper water.

Both the native common Pacific littleneck and nonnative Manila (or Japanese littleneck) clams can be found at Dungeness. The Manila lives only 4 inches under sand, mud, or gravel and prefers the mid to high tidal zones. Accidentally introduced, it is displacing the Pacific littleneck. The Manila's thin shell can be drilled by Lewis's moonsnail, which then sucks out and dines on the unfortunate clam. Look for empty shells on the beach with a hole near the hinge edge of the shell.

ACTIVITIES

■ **CAMPING:** Camping is available at the adjacent Clallam County Dungeness Recreation Area (360/683-5847).

■ **SWIMMING:** Watch for swift, unpredictable currents and floating logs if you swim in the chilled waters of Juan de Fuca Strait. Sunbathing, jogging, and swimming are limited to the west end of the spit.

■ **WILDLIFE OBSERVATION:** Best sites for wildlife observation are along the spit. Remember that the inland side of the spit is closed to visitors.

■ **PHOTOGRAPHY:** Logs along the spit make a perfect natural blind for photography, allowing a good chance for shots of migratory and shore birds that frequent the tidal flats. For closeups you'll need a telephoto lens. In autumn the intense contrast of the madrone's red berries with the green understory makes a good shot, and in spring the blooms of both the madrone and seaspray offer excellent photo opportunities.

■ **HIKES AND WALKS:** Visitors must walk the .4-mile trail to see the spit. The first view of the spit, as strollers emerge from the bluff's encompassing hemlock forest, is breathtaking.

After walking the trail through the upland forest, be sure to continue to the first viewing platform, located on the path leading to the beach. Stand quietly and let the sounds and smells of Juan de Fuca Strait wash over you—the slap of lapping waves, the cries of the gulls, and the tangy smell of saltwater. Both viewing platforms on the trail have spotting scopes.

A 5-mile walk along the spit's outer edge leads to the New Dungeness Lighthouse, .33 mile from the end of the spit. Pick up a tide table in a local store and consult it before starting, or you might find yourself stranded at high tide, climbing back on the log barrier. The lighthouse, a National Historical Place, is maintained by members of the New Dungeness Chapter of the U.S. Lighthouse Society, who keep the lighthouse open to visitors and conduct daily tours.

■ **HORSEBACK RIDING:** A horse trail traverses the refuge uplands and then descends to the beach west of Dungeness Spit. The trail is open daily October 1 to May 14, weekdays only May 15 to September 30. Reservations for use of the trail are required (call the refuge office).

■ **PUBLICATIONS:** Refuge brochure and map.

> **HUNTING AND FISHING**
> There is no hunting on the refuge.
>
> Access to shell fishing areas east and west of Graveyard Spit is by boat only. **Crabbing** and **clamming** are permitted from May through Sept. All oysters are privately owned and may not be gathered.

Harbor seals

San Juan Islands NWR
Olympia, Washington

As the ferry plies the ancient passages between the San Juan Islands, fog and mist curl around the 468 rocks, reefs, and islands that dot Puget Sound. The silence shatters with the strident calls of gulls wheeling above the ferry. In the distance pigeon guillemots whistle and squeal. Eighty-three of the San Juan islands have been set aside as a wildlife refuge, a safe haven for the seabirds that nest and raise their young here.

HISTORY

The islands, established as a refuge in 1914, total only 448.5 acres, but almost 21,000 visitors come to the refuge each year. Only Matia and Turn islands are open to the public. Many visitors don't go ashore at all but instead view the wildlife from aboard a boat (boats must stay at least 200 yards offshore to avoid disturbing the birds).

GETTING THERE

Drive north from Seattle on I-5 and turn west on WA 532 to Anacortes. A Washington state ferry sails several times daily to Friday Harbor on San Juan Island. This one-hour, 45-minute cruise offers excellent opportunities to view wildlife—if your visit to San Juan Islands will not include chartering a boat or taking a wildlife tour. Check with San Juan Islands Chamber of Commerce (360/378-5240) for wildlife tour operators. Ferry information: 888/808-7977 (in Washington) or 206/464-6400 (elsewhere). Ferries are most likely to be full on weekends. If you're taking a car, make reservations. Walk-on passengers are usually accommodated. Warning: Strong riptides and a multitude of reefs, rocks, and islands make this no place for novice boaters.

■ **SEASON:** The refuge can be viewed year-round.

■ **HOURS:** The refuge office at Washington Maritime NWR Complex is open Mon.–Fri., 7:30 a.m.–4 p.m. There is no Visitor Center on the islands.

■ **ADDRESS:** San Juan Islands NWR, c/o Washington Maritime NWR Complex, 33 South Barr Rd., Port Angeles, WA 98362
■ **TELEPHONE:** 360/457-8451

WHAT TO SEE

■ **LANDSCAPE AND CLIMATE** Temperatures in the area average 35 to 45 degrees in January and 52 to 72 degrees in July. Because this Puget Sound refuge lies in the rain shadow of the Olympic Mountains (to the west), rain averages only 26 inches annually.

Riptides are a problem here. Picture a submerged sandbar lying near the shore with waves rolling over it in steady succession to break on shore and flow back to sea. If high seas cause the waves to roll in faster and higher, water piles up between the bar and shore faster than it can flow back to sea. The pressure of the accumulated water breaches the sandbar, and powerful currents pour through the breach, creating a riptide (also called a rip current). A swift riptide can catch a boat and quickly smack it against a rock or reef. Unwary swimmers may find themselves washed out to sea. (Since the rip current is usually narrow, swimmers should try to escape by swimming parallel to shore until they're out of the riptide.) Before venturing out on a boat or into the water, check with locals for known riptide areas.

■ **ANIMAL LIFE**
Birds Along the islands' high cliffs, you may spot bald eagles perching high in the tallest trees. Gulls, cormorants, and pigeon guillemots nest on rocky cliffs. Harbor seals haul out on rocky beaches and smaller rocks in the sound.
Marine mammals Transient pods of orcas (killer whales) swim through Puget Sound. If you're taking the ferry in summer, look for them as well as the three pods of 90 resident orcas that congregate to eat the spawning salmon. They're

Orca (killer) whale

easily recognized by their tall black fins cutting above the surface. Less easy to view is the minke, a solitary whale, the smallest of the baleen family. Look for a small, gray dorsal fin briefly cutting the water. Orcas and minkes are most likely to be seen between May and September. Watch for porpoises—both harbor and Dall's—taking exuberant leaps as they play. Sometimes river otters float past, swimming like dogs with their heads out of water.

ACTIVITIES

■ **CAMPING, HIKES, AND WALKS:** Visitors in private boats can anchor and go ashore to picnic, hike, and camp on the area's two Marine State Parks—all of Turn Island and 5 acres on Matia Island. Bring water—there's none on the islands—but toilets are available. A wilderness trail leads visitors on a tour of Matia Island. Most visitors, however, will see this refuge only from the ferryboat.

■ **BOATING:** If you come out to the islands by boat, be sure to observe the 200-yard limit for approaching wildlife. Baby seals may be drowned or crushed when adults stampede (if frightened), and baby birds and eggs are crushed, trampled, and preyed upon when adult birds panic and leave the nest.

■ **PUBLICATIONS:** *Seashore of the Pacific Northwest,* by Ian Sheldon (Lone Pine Publishing, Renton, WA, 1998)

Double-crested cormorant

Washington Islands NWR
Olympia, Washington

Waves rolling east across the Pacific shatter and roar on the craggy rocks, reefs, and islands—870 of them—along the wild and rainy ocean coastline of Washington's Olympic Peninsula. Three wildlife refuges—Flattery Rocks, Quillayute Needles, and Copalis—protect the million birds that stop off on the islands during their annual migrations or stay to nest and raise their young.

HISTORY

Flattery Rocks, Quillayute Needles and Copalis refuges were established as seabird sanctuaries in 1907 by President Theodore Roosevelt. Together they total just more than 486 acres.

GETTING THERE

Viewpoints for the islands can be accessed off side roads from US 101. Drive west 43 mi. from Port Angeles on US 101 to the first side road to Ozette. The best places to view the islands from shore (listed north to south) are as follows:

The narrow 57-mi. strip along the entire coast from Shi-Shi Beach south to South Beach is part of Olympic National Park. Warning: Be sure to carry a tide table, and don't try to walk around a point or headland on an incoming tide. People have lost their lives trying to outrun the water.

Ozette: East of Port Angeles, turn north off US 101 to WA 112. Follow 112 past Pillar Point and swing north again to stay on WA 112 at the T-intersection. The highway follows a section of the north shore of Lake Ozette. Continue to Ozette, where several trails (3 mi. one-way and 3.3 mi. one-way) lead to the beach.

Rialto Beach: From Port Angeles, drive west on US 101, passing Lake Crescent and Sappho. A forest service and national park service information station is located on the west side of the road past Tyee. At the four-corner intersection, turn west to Rialto Beach.

Second Beach: Follow instructions to Rialto Beach, but shortly past the four-corner intersection, swing left to La Push. A trailhead (.6 mi. one-way trail) before reaching La Push leads to Second Beach.

Ruby Beach: From Port Angeles, follow US 101 all the way to Ruby Beach, where US 101 closely follows the coast.

Kalaloch: Continue on US 101 past Ruby Beach to Kalaloch, where there's a national park service information station. Kalaloch Rocks can be seen slightly north of Kalaloch Lodge.

Tour boats leave occasionally from various locales to take passengers on wildlife tours around the islands. Tour-boat information: Forks Chamber of Commerce (360/374-2531).

■ **SEASON:** The islands can be viewed at any time of year, but none of them is open to the public.

■ **ADDRESS:** Washington Islands NWR, c/o Washington Maritime NWR Complex, 55 South Barr Rd., Port Angeles, WA 98362

■ **TELEPHONE:** 360/457-8451

WHAT TO SEE

■ **LANDSCAPE AND CLIMATE** The islands are usually bathed in rain, fog, or mist. Around 102 inches (that's 8.5 feet!) of rain fall along the coast each year. Driest months are June, July, and August, when rain totals around 3 inches per month.

Black oystercatchers

■ **PLANT LIFE** Rare surf grasses grow on the islands, which are mostly bare rocks, but what visitors aboard the tour boats will see is Sitka spruce and western red cedar, which grow on several of the islands.

■ **ANIMAL LIFE**

Birds Great colonies of cormorants—double-crested, Brandt's, and pelagic—nest on the islands. Known for their ability to dive from the surface of the water and swim underwater for extended lengths of time, cormorants are skilled fishers. You might see one breaking the surface with a fish in its beak, which the bird then tosses into the air before swallowing. Cormorants were used by fishermen in China, who buckled a ring around the lower part of their neck to prevent the birds from swallowing the fish. Trained to drive for fish and return them to their owners, the cormorants would perch on the bow of the boat and dive at a signal. The ringed collar was eventually loosened to allow the cormorant to eat some of the fish it caught.

Fork-tailed and Leach's petrels, sooty shearwaters, rhinoceros auklets, black oystercatchers, gulls, common murres, and tufted puffins are among the 14 species of birds breeding on the coastal rocks and islands.

Marine mammals Also watch for orcas (killer whales), gray and humpback whales, harbor seals, sea otters, and sea lions. To distinguish a harbor seal from a Steller's sea lion, look for color. The sea lion's coat is a yellowish cream color, and the harbor seal's coat is a dark color with light rings. Also consider weight: Harbor seals weigh around 180 pounds, while Steller's sea lions weigh in at approximately 1,245 pounds.

ACTIVITIES

■ **CAMPING:** A number of campgrounds can be found along the coast between Pacific Beach and Grayland.

■ **SWIMMING:** Check with local residents for safe swimming beaches.

■ **HIKES AND WALKS:** Various walks to viewing points are noted above under "Getting There."

Willapa NWR
Ilwaco, Washington

Wetlands, Willapa NWR

In shadows and stillness broken only by the dripping of water off a drooping branch, old-growth forest at Willapa refuge has survived the clear-cutting that has denuded much of the Willapa Hills. Secure on an island sanctuary surrounded by sometimes violent tides, the ancient forest bears witness to an age when these magnificent trees blanketed Washington's coastal lands.

Willapa refuge lies at the southern tip of Willapa Bay, separated from the Pacific Ocean only by the Long Beach Peninsula. In addition to its mainland units, the refuge includes Long Island, a large island in Willapa Bay.

HISTORY

Willapa NWR, established in 1937, protects habitats of migrating and wintering brant, ducks, and other waterfowl and shorebirds. The refuge consists of 13,677 acres and welcomes around 13,000 visitors annually.

GETTING THERE

From Portland, drive north on I-5 and exit west on WA 4 at Longview. Continue to the end of WA 4 and then go south on US 101 for about 5 mi. to refuge headquarters.

From Olympia, drive south on I-5, exit at Longview, and follow directions above to the refuge.

■ **SEASON:** Refuge open year-round.
■ **HOURS:** Refuge open daily from sunrise to sunset. Office open Mon.–Fri., 7:30 a.m.–4 p.m. (There is no Visitor Center on the refuge.)
■ **ADDRESS:** Willapa NWR, 3888 SR 101, Ilwaco, WA 98624-9707
■ **TELEPHONE:** 360/484-3482

TOURING WILLAPA

■ **BY FOOT:** Refuge trails total around 6.5 miles—plus 14 miles of gravel roads

WILLAPA NWR

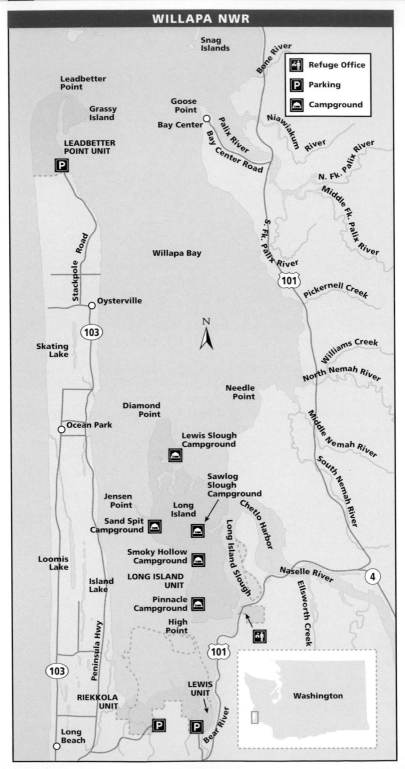

Snag Islands

Bone River

Refuge Office

Parking

Campground

Leadbetter Point

Grassy Island

Goose Point

Bay Center

Palix River

Niawiakum River

N. Fk. Palix River

LEADBETTER POINT UNIT

Bay Center Road

Middle Fk. Palix River

S. Fk. Palix River

Willapa Bay

Stackpole Road

101

Pickernell Creek

Oysterville

103

N

Williams Creek

North Nemah River

Skating Lake

Needle Point

Ocean Park

Diamond Point

Middle Nemah River

Lewis Slough Campground

South Nemah River

Jensen Point

Sawlog Slough Campground

Sand Spit Campground

Long Island

Chetlo Harbor

Loomis Lake

Smoky Hollow Campground

Long Island Slough

Naselle River

4

Island Lake

LONG ISLAND UNIT

Pinnacle Campground

Ellsworth Creek

Peninsula Hwy

High Point

101

103

LEWIS UNIT

RIEKKOLA UNIT

Long Beach

Bear River

Washington

on Long Island that can be hiked. Roads lead to the island's five campgrounds; and, since no public vehicles are allowed on the island, all make good hiking trails. Leadbetter Point, at the tip of Long Beach Peninsula (separating Willapa Bay from the Pacific Ocean), lies north of Leadbetter Point State Park. Trails through the park and point, administered jointly by the state park and refuge, total 5.2 miles. A .5-mile trail can be hiked at the Riekkola unit (through pastures at the south end of the bay).

■ **BY KAYAK OR BOAT:** Long Island, one of the refuge's six units, can be accessed only by boat or kayak. If you bring a boat, you can it launch at Nahcotta Mooring Basin or across US 101 from refuge headquarters. Warning: Boating can be difficult and sometimes dangerous here because of tidal flows and changing water levels. Swells can rise suddenly. Carry a tide table and don't venture onto the water unless you are experienced.

WHAT TO SEE

■ **LANDSCAPE AND CLIMATE** From open water to old-growth forest, the refuge is a microcosm of coastal environments, open water, mudflats, sand dunes, grasslands, and freshwater marsh. Rain comes heavily to this coast, often more than 100 inches a year, much of it falling during winter months. Old-growth cedars drip with moisture, the ground sinks and squishes with each step, and ferns grow out of fallen logs. In summer the rains come infrequently. Streams dry out, and ferns shelter under the spreading canopy of cedar and hemlock. Along Willapa Bay the mudflats stretch as far as the eye can see. The tide slides in, and the bay is once again a water world. Temperatures here are a cool 33 to 46 degrees in January and 52 to 68 degrees in July. The forested uplands of Long Island reach 250 feet, but this is a refuge defined chiefly by flatness, low rolling sand dunes, and water.

■ PLANT LIFE

Wetlands Flying south along the Pacific coast to their wintering grounds in Mexico, the brant, a type of seagoing geese, stop off at Dungeness NWR and then

Surf scoters

at Willapa. Both refuges have vast beds of eelgrass, one of the brant's favorite foods. In Willapa the eelgrass, growing at the lower levels of the intertidal zone, pollinates itself by forming pollen rafts that float across the water until they meet floating female stigmas. Underwater, pollen bundles looking like little brushes drift until they find their female counterparts.

Grasslands On the Riekkola Unit at the south end of the bay, grasslands have been established by diking tidelands, creating feeding pasture for migrating geese. Salt grass, growing on the sand dunes at the tip of Leadbetter Point, helps stabilize the shifting dunes.

Forest At the southern reach of the bay on Long Island is a dense forest of Sitka spruce and Washington's last and largest grove (274 acres) of old-growth western red cedar. The dominant tree in a red cedar–hemlock forest, these ancient cedars are magnificent, reaching heights of 100 to 175 feet with trunks that can measure 8 to 11 feet in diameter if the trees are left to live out their life span of 1,000 years. The branches of these venerable trees are so big that soil collects on their top sides, allowing a sky forest of shrubs and ferns to take root high in the air.

■ ANIMAL LIFE

Birds Of the six shearwaters that live at sea on the Pacific, the sooty shearwater—a 17-inch bird that gets its name from its dark, sooty brown color—is the one most likely to be seen in abundance at Willapa in summer and fall. The short-tailed shearwater is an occasional visitor to Willapa in winter, and the pink-footed shearwater is a rare visitor in fall. A Western Hemispheric Shorebird Reserve, Willapa Bay can have migrating populations of more than 100,000 shorebirds. The brown pelican and double-crested and brandt's cormorants are common through most of the year.

Among the 27 duck species using the Pacific Flyway, only the surf and white-winged scoter and red-breasted merganser commonly stop off at Willapa. The bay also hosts pintails, wigeon, canvasback, scaup, and green-winged teal.

An unusual and delightful bird to find in Willapa is the Steller's jay, an impudent creature that likes to perch on a branch overhead and squawk loudly at

Porcupine

intruders. An apt thief of camp table food, this jay is normally found in the high forests of northern California and is easily recognized by its blue color and top-knot (the only western jay with a crest). Look for it in autumn.

Mammals The Roosevelt elk inhabits the coastal rain forests from northern California to Vancouver Island in Canada. Adult bulls, weighing from 500 to 1,000 pounds, have great strength and can snap a 2-inch sapling simply by shaking it vigorously with their heads. Cows and bulls remain in separate herds except during mating, which can occasion brutal fights between competing bulls. In the bay look for sea lions, both Steller's and California, harbor and northern fur seals, and harbor porpoises. Gray whales pass by on their annual migrations.

Reptiles and amphibians Seven species of salamander live on the refuge. The three turtles that visit Willapa —loggerhead, green sea, and leatherback sea— are all on the endangered species list.

ACTIVITIES

■ **CAMPING:** Of the five primitive campgrounds on Long Island, Pinnacle Rock is nearest the boat landing, requiring a 2.5-mile backpack to reach. Smoky Hollow, also on the island's west side facing Willapa Bay, is about a 3-mile backpack. All campgrounds can be reached by boat at high tide. In summer, streams are dry, so bring water. Island water should be purified. Mainland camping: Fort Canby State Park (360/642-3078) near Ilwaco.

■ **SWIMMING:** No swimming is allowed on the refuge.

■ **WILDLIFE OBSERVATION:** Deer and elk may be seen in early morning or evening at Long Island's High Point Meadow. Smoky Hollow Marsh, Sawlog Slough, and the forest are excellent for birdwatching. On the mainland, look for peregrine falcons, trumpeter swans in the freshwater marshes of the Lewis Unit, and migrating Canada geese, ducks, and wading birds, all in the Riekkola Unit. Dunlins—15.5 percent of the Pacific Flyway population—winter on Willapa Bay. The dunlins, whimbrels, and godwits attract birders from throughout the region.

■ **PHOTOGRAPHY:** Some of the fallen trees and snags in Cedar Forest make

---

PORCUPINES There's no need for a porcupine to hurry—because if anything is unwise enough to chase him, he merely smacks the intruder with his 12-inch tail, driving in a number of sharp, barbed quills that work deeper and deeper into the unlucky victim. (Porcupines can't shoot their quills, as is commonly believed. They must make contact to drive them home.) Looking like an oversized pincushion, the porcupine likes to perch in trees and can sometimes be seen relaxing on a branch in one of Willapa's trees. A vegetarian, the porcupine eats twigs and leaves of shrubs as well as sedges, grasses, and wild flowers. In winter, when snow covers the ground, he scrapes the outer bark off trees and dines on the succulent inner bark. Baby porcupines weigh from 10 to 20 ounces at birth and come equipped with quarter-inch to 1-inch quills that they instinctively know how to erect. Although it would appear that porcupines have few enemies, they are attacked by the fisher and the mountain lion, which devour them, quills and all. Should you run over a porcupine with your car, it is wise to stop and pull out any quills embedded in your tires before they cause a flat.

WILLAPA HUNTING AND FISHING SEASONS

Hunting (Seasons may vary)	Jan	Feb	Mar	Apr	May	Jun	Jul	Aug	Sep	Oct	Nov	Dec
geese	■									■	■	■
duck	■									■	■	■
coot	■									■	■	■
ruffed grouse	■									■	■	■
blue grouse	■									■	■	■
Roosevelt elk									■		■	■
black-tailed deer									■		■	■
black bear								■	■	■	■	

Hunting is allowed on the Riekkola Unit on Wed. and Sat. only and only from designated blinds. Leadbetter Point Unit is open to waterfowl and coot hunting daily during season. Ruffed and blue grouse can be hunted only on Long Island and only with bow and arrow. Hunting for Roosevelt elk, black-tailed deer, and black bear is also limited to Long Island, using a bow and arrow only. Clamming and crabbing is permitted on some of the shore areas. Sportfishing for sturgeon and salmon is allowed; seasons fluctuate annually.

handsome shots. In the forest or meadows you might get a chance to photograph black bear as well as deer and elk.

■ **HIKES AND WALKS:** Long Island has one .75-mile trail, reached by a 2.5-mile walk along a gravel road from the ferry. The island's Trail of the Ancient Cedars passes trees that were growing 600 years before the Pilgrims arrived in the New World in 1620. Trailhead to the .75-mile trail is located off the gravel road 2.5 miles from the island's ferry landing at the south end of the island. On the trail shafts of light spill onto the lush undergrowth, and the massive trunks of the oldest trees reach 8 to 11 feet in diameter. Fallen trees along the trail may last for 400 to 500 years, storing water that carries the seedlings sprouted on them through the dry season. Cavities in the snags—the standing dead trees—serve as homes for woodpeckers, and owls and hawks use the snags as hunting perches. The trail passes a stand logged in the 1930s and one logged in the 1960s. Note the difference in the ground cover and thickness of the canopy in the logged areas. The ancient trees escaped clear-cutting because they were difficult to reach from shore, and because, starting in 1937 with the establishment of Willapa NWR, land acquisition by the U.S. Fish & Wildlife Service protected them. The last logging truck left Long Island only in 1993.

Appendix

NONVISITABLE NATIONAL WILDLIFE REFUGES

Below is a list of other national wildlife refuges in Oregon and Washington. Although these refuges are not open to the public, many can be viewed from a nearby road or from a boat.

Nestucca Bay NWR
c/o Oregon Coastal Refuges
2127 SE OSU Dr.
Newport, OR 97365-5258
541/867-4550

Siletz Bay NWR
c/o Oregon Coastal Refuges
2127 SE OSU Dr.
Newport, OR 97365-5258
541/867-4550

Three Arch Rocks NWR
c/o Oregon Coastal Refuges
2127 SE OSU Dr.
Newport, OR 97365-5258
541/867-4550

Copalis NWR
c/o Washington Maritime Complex
33 South Barr Rd.
Port Angeles, WA 98362-9202
360/457-8451

Flattery Rocks NWR
c/o Washington Maritime Complex
33 South Barr Rd.
Port Angeles, WA 98362-9202
360/457-8451

Pierce NWR
Columbia River Gorge Refuges
36062 SR 14
Stevenson, WA 98648-9541
509/427-5208

Protection Island NWR
c/o Washington Maritime Complex
33 South Barr Rd.
Port Angeles, WA 98362-9202
360/457-8451

Quillayute Needles NWR
c/o Washington Maritime Complex
33 South Barr Rd.
Port Angeles, WA 98362-9202
360/457-8451

Saddle Mountain NWR
c/o Hanford Complex
3520 Port of Benton Rd.
Richland, WA 99352
509/371-1801

Steigerwald Lake NWR
c/o Pierce NWR
Columbia River Gorge Refuges
36062 SR 14
Stevenson, WA 98648-9541
509/427-5208

FEDERAL RECREATION FEES

Some—but not all—NWRs and other federal outdoor recreation areas require payment of entrance or use fees (the latter for facilities such as boat ramps). There are several congressionally authorized entrance fee passes:

■ ANNUAL PASSES

Golden Eagle Passport Valid for most national parks, monuments, historic sites, recreation areas and national wildlife refuges. Admits the passport signee and any accompanying passengers in a private vehicle. Good for 12 months. Purchase at any federal area where an entrance fee is charged. The 1999 fee for this pass was $50.00

Federal Duck Stamp Authorized in 1934 as a federal permit to hunt waterfowl and as a source of revenue to purchase wetlands, the Duck Stamp now also serves as an annual entrance pass to NWRs. Admits holder and accompanying passengers in a private vehicle. Good from July 1 for one year. Valid for *entrance* fees only. Purchase at post offices and many NWRs or from Federal Duck Stamp Office, 800/782-6724, or at Wal-Mart, Kmart or other sporting good stores.

■ LIFETIME PASSES

Golden Access Passport Lifetime entrance pass—for persons who are blind or permanently disabled—to most national parks and NWRs. Admits signee and any accompanying passengers in a private vehicle. Provides 50% discount on federal use fees charged for facilities and services such as camping, or boating. Must be obtained in person at a federal recreation area charging a fee. Obtain by showing proof of medically determined permanent disability or eligibility for receiving benefits under federal law.

Golden Age Passport Lifetime entrance pass—for persons 62 years of age or older—to national parks and NWRs. Admits signee and any accompanying passengers in a private vehicle. Provides 50% discount on federal use fees charged for facilities and services such as camping, or boating. Must be obtained in person at a federal recreation area charging a fee. One-time $10.00 processing charge. Available only to U.S. citizens or permanent residents.

For more information, contact your local federal recreation area for a copy of the *Federal Recreation Passport Program* brochure.

VOLUNTEER ACTIVITIES

Each year, 30,000 Americans volunteer their time and talents to help the U.S. Fish & Wildlife Service conserve the nation's precious wildlife and their habitats. Volunteers conduct Fish & Wildlife population surveys, lead public tours and other recreational programs, protect endangered species, restore habitat, and run environmental education programs.

The NWR volunteer program is as diverse as are the refuges themselves. There is no "typical" Fish & Wildlife Service volunteer. The different ages, backgrounds, and experiences volunteers bring with them is one of the greatest strengths of the program. Refuge managers also work with their neighbors, conservation groups, colleges and universities, and business organizations.

A growing number of people are taking pride in the stewardship of local national wildlife refuges by organizing nonprofit organizations to support individual refuges. These refuge community partner groups, which numbered about 200 in 2000, have been so helpful that the Fish & Wildlife Service, National Audubon Society, National Wildlife Refuge Association, and National Fish & Wildlife Foundation now carry out a national program called the "Refuge System Friends Initiative" to coordinate and strengthen existing partnerships, to jump start new ones, and to organize other efforts promoting community involvement in activities associated with the National Wildlife Refuge System.

For more information on how to get involved, visit the Fish & Wildlife Service Homepage at http://refuges.fws.gov; or contact one of the Volunteer Coordinator offices listed on the U.S. Fish & Wildlife General Information list of addresses below or the U. S. Fish & Wildlife Service, Division of Refuges, Attn: Volunteer Coordinator, 4401 North Fairfax Drive, Arlington, VA 22203; 703/358-2303.

U.S. FISH & WILDLIFE GENERAL INFORMATION

Below is a list of addresses to contact for more inforamation concerning the National Wildlife Refuge System.

U.S. Fish & Wildlife Service Division of Refuges

4401 North Fairfax Dr., Room 670
Arlington, Virginia 22203
703/358-1744
Web site: fws.refuges.gov

F & W Service Publications:

800/344-WILD

U.S. Fish & Wildlife Service Pacific Region

911 NE 11th Ave.
Eastside Federal Complex
Portland, OR 97232-4181
External Affairs Office: 503/231-6120
Volunteer Coordinator: 503/231-2077
The Pacific Region office oversees the refuges in California, Hawaii, Idaho, Nevada, Oregon, and Washington.

U.S. Fish & Wildlife Service Southwest Region

500 Gold Ave., SW
P.O. Box 1306
Albuquerque, NM 87103
External Affairs Office: 505/248-6285
Volunteer Coordinator: 505/248-6635
The Southwest Region office oversees the refuges in Arizona, New Mexico, Oklahoma, and Texas.

U.S. Fish & Wildlife Service Great Lakes–Big Rivers Region

1 Federal Dr.
Federal Building
Fort Snelling, MN 55111-4056
External Affairs Office: 612/713-5310
Volunteer Coordinator: 612/713-5444
The Great Lakes-Big Rivers Region office oversees the refuges in Iowa, Illinois, Indiana, Michigan, Minnesota, Missouri, Ohio, and Wisconsin.

U.S. Fish & Wildlife Service Southeast Region

1875 Century Center Blvd.
Atlanta, GA 30345
External Affairs Office: 404/679-7288
Volunteer Coordinator: 404/679-7178
The Southeast Region office oversees the refuges in Alabama, Arkansas, Florida, Georgia, Kentucky, Louisiana, Mississippi, North Carolina, South Carolina, Tennessee, and Puerto Rico.

U.S. Fish & Wildlife Service Northeast Region

300 Westgate Center Dr.
Hadley, MA 01035-9589
External Affairs Office: 413/253-8325
Volunteer Coordinator: 413/253-8303
The Northeast Region office oversees the refuges in Connecticut, Delaware, Massachusetts, Maine, New Hampshire, New Jersey, New York, Pennsylvania, Rhode Island, Vermont, Virginia, West Virginia.

U.S. Fish & Wildlife Service Mountain-Prairie Region

P.O. Box 25486
Denver Federal Center
P. O. Box 25486
Denver, CO 80225
External Affairs Office: 303/236-7905
Volunteer Coordinator: 303/236-8145, x 614
The Mountain-Prairie Region office oversees the refuges in Colorado, Kansas, Montana, Nebraska, North Dakota, South Dakota, Utah, and Wyoming.

U.S. Fish & Wildlife Service Alaska Region

1011 East Tudor Rd.
Anchorage, AK 99503
External Affairs Office: 907/786-3309
Volunteer Coordinator: 907/786-3391

NATIONAL AUDUBON SOCIETY WILDLIFE SANCTUARIES

National Audubon Society's 100 sanctuaries comprise 150,000 acres and include a wide range of habitats. Audubon managers and scientists use the sanctuaries for rigorous field research and for testing wildlife management strategies. The following is a list of 24 sanctuaries open to the public. Sanctuaries open by appointment only are marked with an asterisk.

EDWARD M. BRIGHAM III ALKALI LAKE SANCTUARY*
c/o North Dakota State Office
118 Broadway, Suite 502
Fargo, ND 58102
701/298-3373

FRANCIS BEIDLER FOREST SANCTUARY
336 Sanctuary Rd.
Harleyville, SC 29448
843/462-2160

BORESTONE MOUNTAIN SANCTUARY
P.O. Box 524
118 Union Square
Dover-Foxcroft, ME 04426
207/564-7946

CLYDE E. BUCKLEY SANCTUARY
1305 Germany Rd.
Frankfort, KY 40601
606/873-5711

BUTTERCUP WILDLIFE SANCTUARY*
c/o New York State Office
200 Trillium Lane
Albany, NY 12203
518/869-9731

CONSTITUTION MARSH SANCTUARY
P.O. Box 174
Cold Spring, NY, 10516
914/265-2601

CORKSCREW SWAMP SANCTUARY
375 Sanctuary Rd. West
Naples, FL 34120
941/348-9151

FLORIDA COASTAL ISLANDS SANCTUARY*
410 Ware Blvd., Suite 702
Tampa, FL 33619
813/623-6826

EDWARD L. & CHARLES E. GILLMOR SANCTUARY*
3868 Marsha Dr.
West Valley City, UT 84120
801/966-0464

KISSIMMEE PRAIRIE SANCTUARY*
100 Riverwoods Circle
Lorida, FL 33857
941/467-8497

MAINE COASTAL ISLANDS SANCTUARIES*
Summer (June–Aug.):
12 Audubon Rd.
Bremen, ME 04551
207/529-5828

MILES WILDLIFE SANCTUARY*
99 West Cornwall Rd.
Sharon, CT 06069
860/364-0048

NORTH CAROLINA COASTAL ISLANDS SANCTUARY*
720 Market St.
Wilmington, NC 28401-4647
910/762-9534

NORTHERN CALIFORNIA SANCTUARIES*
c/o California State Office
555 Audubon Place
Sacramento, CA 95825
916/481-5440

PINE ISLAND SANCTUARY*
P.O. Box 174
Poplar Branch, NC 27965
919/453-2838

RAINEY WILDLIFE SANCTUARY*
10149 Richard Rd.
Abbeville, LA 70510-9216
318/898-5969 (Beeper: leave message)

RESEARCH RANCH SANCTUARY*
HC1, Box 44
Elgin, AZ 85611
520/455-5522

RHEINSTROM HILL WILDLIFE SANCTUARY*
P.O. Box 1
Craryville, NY 12521
518/325-5203

THEODORE ROOSEVELT SANCTUARY
134 Cove Rd.
Oyster Bay, NY 11771
516/922-3200

LILLIAN ANNETTE ROWE SANCTUARY
44450 Elm Island Rd.
Gibbon, NE 68840
308/468-5282

SABAL PALM GROVE SANCTUARY
P.O. Box 5052
Brownsville, TX 78523
956/541-8034

SILVER BLUFF SANCTUARY*
4542 Silver Bluff Rd.
Jackson, SC 29831
803/827-0781

STARR RANCH SANCTUARY*
100 Bell Canyon Rd.
Trabuco Canyon, CA 92678
949/858-0309

TEXAS COASTAL ISLANDS SANCTUARIES
c/o Texas State Office
2525 Wallingwood, Suite 301
Austin, TX 78746
512/306-0225

BIBLIOGRAPHY AND RESOURCES

Aquatic and Marine Biology

Armstrong, Robert. *Alaska's Fish: A Guide to Selected Species*, Anchorage: Alaska Northwest Books, 1996.

Field, Carmen and Conrad. *Alaska's Seashore Creatures: A Guide to Selected Marine Invertebrates*, Anchorage: Alaska Northwest Books, 1999.

Flaherty, Chuck. *Whales of the Northwest: A Guide to Marine Mammals of Oregon, Washington and British Columbia*, Seattle: Cherry Lane Press, 1990.

Ford, John K. B. *Transients: Mammal-Hunting Killer Whales of British Columbia, Washington, and Southeastern Alaska*, Seattle: University of Washington Pr., 1999.

Sheldon, Ian. *Seashore of the Pacific Northwest*, Vancouver, Canada: Lone Pine Publishing, 1998.

Wynne, Kate. *Guide to Marine Mammals of Alaska*, Fairbanks: Alaska Sea Grant Program, University of Alaska, 1997.

Audio Recordings

Peyton, Leonard. *Bird Songs of Alaska*, Ithaca, N.Y.: Cornell Laboratory of Ornithology, 1999.

Birds

Armstrong, Robert. *Alaska's Birds: A Guide to Selected Species*, Anchorage: Alaska Northwest Books, 1994.

Armstrong, Robert. *Guide to the Birds of Alaska*, Anchorage: Alaska Northwest Books, 1998.

Baron, Nancy. *Birds of the Pacific Northwest Coast*, Renton, Wash.: Lone Pine Publishing, 1997.

Field Guide to the Birds of North America, 3rd Edition, National Geographic Society: Washington, D.C. 1999.

Isleib, Pete and Brina Kessel. *Birds of the North Gulf Coast: Prince William Sound Region, Alaska*, Fairbanks: University of Alaska Press, 1989.

Kerlinger, Paul. *How Birds Migrate*, Mechanicsburg, Pa.: Stackpole Books, 1995.

Kessel, Brina. *Birds of the Seward Peninsula*, Fairbanks: University of Alaska Press, 1989.

MacRae, Diann. *Birders Guide to Washington*, Houston: Gulf Publishing Co., 1995.

Stromsen, N. *A Guide to Alaska Seabirds*, Anchorage: Alaska Natural History Association, 1995.

Wassink, Jan L. *Birds of the Pacific Northwest Mountains: The Cascade Range, the Olympic Mountains, Vancouver Island and the Coast Mountains*, Missoula, Mont.: Mountain Press, 1995.

Botany

Atkinson, Scott. *Wild Plants of the San Juan Islands*, Seattle: Mountaineers Books, 1993.

Franklin, Jerry E. *Natural Vegetation of Oregon and Washington*, Corvallis, Ore.: Oregon State University Press, 1998.

Guard, B. Jennifer. *Wetland Plants of Oregon and Washington*, Redmond, Wash.: Lone Pine Publishing, 1995.

Kari, Priscilla. *Tanaina Plantlore: Dena'ina K'et'una*, Anchorage: Alaska Native Language Center/Alaska Natural History Association, 1995.

Pojar, Jim and Andy MacKinnon, editors. *Plants of the Pacific Northwest Coast— Washington, Oregon, British Columbia & Alaska*, Redmond, Wash.: Lone Pine Publishing, 1994.

Pratt ,Verna. *Field Guide to Alaskan Wildflowers*, Anchorage: Alaskrafts, Inc., 1989.

Schofield, Janice. *Alaska's Wild Plants: A Guide to Alaska's Edible Harvest*, Anchorage: Alaska Northwest Books, 1993.

Viereck, Leslie. *Alaska Trees and Shrubs*, Fairbanks: University of Alaska Press, 1986.

Wiedemann, Alfred M. *Plants of the Oregon Coastal Dunes*, Corvallis, Ore.: Oregon State University Press, 1999.

White, Helen. *Alaska and Yukon Wild Flowers Guide*, Anchorage: Alaska Northwest Books, 1996.

Cultural and Environmental History

The Alaska Almanac, 20th Anniversary Edition, Anchorage: Alaska Northwest Books, 1996.

Carpenter, Cecilia Svinth. *They Walked Before: the Indians of Washington State*, Tacoma, Wash.: Tahoma Publishing, 1989.

Carrey, Johnny and Cort Conley. *River of No Return*, Cambridge, Md.: Backeddy Books, 1978.

Douthit, Nathan. *A Guide to Oregon South Coast History: Traveling the Jedediah Smith Trail*, Corvallis, Ore.: Oregon State University Press, 1999.

Durbin, Kathie. *Tree Huggers: Victory, Defeat & Renewal in the Northwest Ancient Forest Campaign*, Seattle: Mountaineers Books, 1996.

Halliday, Jan. *Native Peoples of Alaska: A Traveler's Guide to Land, Art and Culture*, Seattle: Sasquatch Books, 1998.

Hudson, Ray. *Moments Rightly Placed: An Aleutian Memoir*, Seattle: Epicenter Press, 1998.

Huntington, Sidney as told to Jim Reardon. *Shadows on the Koyukuk: An Alaskan Native's Life Along the River*, Anchorage: Alaska Northwest Books, 1993.

Komar, Paul D. *The Pacific Northwest Coast: Living With the Shores of Washington and Oregon*, Durham, N.C.: Duke University Press, 1998.

Kremers, Carolyn. *Place of the Pretend People: Gifts from a Yup'ik Eskimo Village*, Anchorage: Alaska Northwest Books, 1996.

Lewis, Capt. Meriwether and Capt. William Clark, edited by Bernard DeVoto. *The Journals of Lewis and Clark*, Boston: Houghton Mifflin Co., 1953.

Mitchell, Donald Craig. *Sold American: The Story of Alaska Natives and Their Land, 1967-1959*, Hanover, N.H.: University Press of New England, 1997.

Muir, John. *Letters from Alaska*, Madison, Wis.: University of Wisconsin Press, 1993.

Nelson, Richard. *Make Prayers to the Raven: A Koyukon View of the Northern Forest*, Chicago: University of Chicago Press, 1986.

Oregon's Living Landscape: Strategies and Opportunities to Conserve Biodiversity, Corvallis, Ore.: a Defenders of Wildlife Publication, Oregon State University Press, 1998.

Ritter, Harry. *Alaska's History: The People, Land, and Events of the North Country*, Anchorage: Alaska Northwest Books, 1999.

Vancouver, Capt. George. *A Voyage of Discovery to the North Pacific Ocean and Round the World (1791-1795)*, out of print.

Wells, Gail. *The Tillamook: A Created Forest Comes of Age*, Corvallis, Ore.: Oregon State University Press, 1999.

Geology

Alaska's Glaciers, Vol. 9, No. 1, Anchorage: Alaska Geographic Society, 1993.

Alaska's Volcanoes, Vol. 18, No. 2, Anchorage: Alaska Geographic Society, 1991.

Alt, David D. and Donald W. Hyndman. *Roadside Geology of Oregon*, Missoula,

Mont.: Mountain Press Publishing Co., 1998.

Alt, David D. and Donald W. Hyndman. *Roadside Geology of Washington*, Missoula, Mont.: Mountain Press Publishing Co., 1998.

Burns, Robert E. *The Shape and Form of Puget Sound*, Seattle: University of Washington Press, 1985.

Connor, Cathy and Daniel O'Haire. *Roadside Geology of Alaska*, Missoula, Mont.: Mountain Press Publishing Co., 1998.

Mueller, Margaret. *A Guide to Washington's South Cascades' Volcanic Landscapes*, Seattle: Moutaineers Books, 1995.

Wiley, Sally D. *Blue Ice in Motion: The Story of Alaska's Glaciers*, Anchorage: Alaska Natural History Association, 1995.

Mammals

Carraway, Leslie N. *Land Mammals of Oregon*, Berkeley, Calif.: University of California Press, 1998.

Mammals of Alaska: A Comprehensive Guide, Anchorage: Alaska Geographic Society, 1996.

Maser, Chris. *Mammals of the Pacific Northwest*, Corvallis, Ore.: Oregon State University Press, 1998.

Melham, Tom. *Alaska's Wildlife Treasures*, Washington, D.C.: National Geographic Society, 1994.

Moose, Caribou and Muskox, Vol. 23, No. 4, Anchorage: Alaska Geographic Society, 1997.

Sherwonit, Bill and Tom Walker. *Alaska's Bears*, Anchorage: Alaska Northwest Books, 1998.

Smith, Dave and Tom Walker. *Alaska's Mammals: A Guide to Selected Species*, Anchorage: Alaska Northwest Books, 1998.

Outdoor/Natural History Writings

Jans, Nick. *The Last Light Breaking: Living Among Alaska's Inupiat Eskimos*, Anchorage: Alaska Northwest Books, 1993.

Lopez, Barry. *Arctic Dreams*, New York: Bantam, 1996.

Lord, Nancy. *Fishcamp: Life on an Alaskan Shore*, Washington, D.C.: Island Press, 1997.

MacLeish, Sumner. *Seven Words for Wind: Essays & Field Notes from Alaska's Pribolof Islands*, Seattle: Epicenter Press, 1997.

McPhee, John. *Coming Into the Country*, New York: Noonday Press, 1977.

Marshall, Robert. *Alaska Wilderness: Exploring the Central Brooks Range*, Berkeley, Calif.: University of California Press, 1970.

Nelson, Richard. *Island Within*, New York: Vintage Books, 1991.

Miller, Debbie S. *Midnight Wilderness: Journeys in Alaska's Arctic National Wildlife Refuge*, 10th Anniversary Edition, Anchorage: Alaska Northwest Books, 2000.

Muir, John. *Travels in Alaska*, New York: Houghton Mifflin, 1998.

Murie, Margaret. *Two in the Far North*, 35th Anniversary Edition, Anchorage: Alaska Northwest Books, 1997.

Stuck, Hudson. *Ten Thousand Miles with a Dog Sled*, Lincoln, Neb.: University of Nebraska Press; 1988.

Regional/State Guides

Chasen, Daniel Jack. *The Smithsonian Guides to Natural America: the Pacific Northwest Washington and Oregon*, Washington, D.C.: Smithsonian Books, 1995.

Jettmar, Karen. *The Alaska River Guide*, Anchorage: Alaska Northwest Books,

1998.

La Tourette, Joe. *Washington Wildlife Viewing Guide: The Watchable Wildlife Series*, Helena, Mont.: Falcon Publishing Co., 1992.

Littlepage, Dean, *Hiking Alaska: A Falcon Guide*, Helena, Mont.: Falcon Publications, 1997.

Lund, Annabel M. and Michelle Sydeman. *Alaska Wildlife Viewing Guide*, Helena, Mont.: Falcon Publications, 1996.

O'Clair, Rita, Robert Armstrong, and Richard Carstensen. *The Nature of Southeast Alaska*, Anchorage: Alaska Northwest Books, 1997.

Perry, John. *The Sierra Club Guide to the Natural Areas of Oregon and Washington*, San Francisco: Sierra Club Books, 1997.

Pielou, E.C. *A Naturalist's Guide to the Arctic*, Chicago: University of Chicago Press; 1994.

Yuskavitch, James A. *Oregon Wildlife Viewing Guide: The Watchable Wildlife Series.*, Helena, Mont.: Falcon Publishing Co., 1994.

Reptiles and Amphibians

Nussbaum, Ronald A., Edmund D. Brodie, and Robert M. Storm. *Amphibians and Reptiles of the Pacific Northwest*, Moscow, Id.: University of Idaho Press, 1983.

Storm, Robert M. and William P. Leonard, editors. *Reptiles of Washington and Oregon: Trailside*, Seattle: Seattle Audubon Society, Wash., 1995.

GLOSSARY

'A'a Rough, sharp lava.

Accidental A bird species seen only rarely in a certain region and whose normal territory is elsewhere. *See also* occasional.

Acre-foot The amount of water required to cover one acre one foot deep.

Alaska National Interest Lands Conservation Act (ANILCA) A monumental land conservation act passed by Congress in 1980, setting aside more than 100 million acres of Alaskan national parks, monuments, preserves, wildlife refuges, forest, and wilderness lands, including 26 additions to the National Wild and Scenic River System.

Alaska Native Claims Settlement Act (ANCSA) A 1971 federal act granting 44 million acres and nearly $1 billion to Alaska Native Indian, Eskimo, and Aleut people.

Alaska Natives Alaskans of Native descent, including Athabascan Indians, Inupiat and Yupik Eskimos, Aleut, Tlingit, Haida, and Tsimshian peoples.

Aleut An Alaska Native group of people from southwest Alaska and the Aleutian Islands.

Alkali sink An alkaline habitat at the bottom of a basin where there is moisture under the surface.

Alluvial Clay, sand, silt, pebbles and rocks deposited by running water. River floodplains have alluvial deposits, sometimes called alluvial fans, where a stream exits from mountains onto flatland.

Aquifer Underground layer of porous water-bearing sand, rock, or gravel.

Arctic Circle The latitude at which the sun never sets on the day of summer solstice (June 20 or 21), and never rises on winter solstice (December 21 or 22), approximately 66.5 degrees north of the equator.

Arthropod Invertebrates, including insects, crustaceans, arachnids, and myriapods, with a semitransparent exoskeleton (hard outer structure) and a segmented body, with jointed appendages in articulated pairs.

Athabascan Indians An Alaska Native group of people living largely in the interior, with seven subgroups speaking 11 identified languages.

ATV All-terrain vehicle. *See also* 4WD and ORV.

Backhand tributary A tributary that flows in a reversed direction from the main river.

Baleen Flexible, bonelike straps in a whale's mouth used to strain food from the seawater.

Barrier island Coastal island produced by wave action and made of sand. Over time the island shifts and changes shape. Barrier islands protect the mainland from storms, tides, and winds.

Basking The habit of certain creatures such as turtles, snakes, or alligators to expose themselves to the pleasant warmth of the sun by resting on logs, rocks, or other relatively dry areas.

Biome A major ecological community such as a marsh or a forest.

Blowout A hollow formed by wind erosion in a preexisting sand dune, often due to vegetation loss.

Bog Wet, spongy ground filled with sphagnum moss and having highly acidic water.

Boreal forest Forested regions in the northern parts of the temperate zone, characterized by coniferous species such as fir, pine, and spruce.

Bottomland Low-elevation alluvial area, close by a river. Sometimes also called "bottoms."

Brackish   Water that is less salty than seawater; often found in salt marshes, mangrove swamps, estuaries, and lagoons.

Breachway   A gap in a barrier beach or island, forming a connection between sea and lagoon.

Bushwhack   To hike through territory without established trails.

Cambium   In woody plants, a sheath of cells between external bark and internal wood that generates parallel rows of cells to make new tissue, either as secondary growth or cork.

Canopy   The highest layer of the forest, consisting of the crowns of the trees.

Carnivore   An animal that is primarily flesh-eating. *See also* herbivore and omnivore.

Channeled scablands   Rugged land in eastern Washington formed by a great flood.

Circumpolar   Common features and characteristics of the region encircling the poles, above the Arctic Circle, or below the Antarctic Circle.

Cirque   A glacial-carved basin on a mountain that is shaped like a half bowl.

Climax   In a stable ecological community, the plants and animals that will successfully continue to live there.

Colonial birds   Birds that live in relatively stable colonies, used annually for breeding and nesting.

Competition   A social behavior that organizes the sharing of resources such as space, food, and breeding partners when resources are in short supply.

Coniferous   Trees that are needle-leaved or scale-leaved; mostly evergreen and cone-bearing, such as pines, spruces, and firs. *See also* deciduous.

Cordgrass   Grasses found in marshy areas, capable of growing in brackish waters. Varieties include salt-marsh cordgrass, hay, spike grass, and glasswort.

Crust   The outer layer of the earth, between 15 to 40 miles thick.

Crustacean   A hard-shelled, usually aquatic, arthropod such as a lobster or crab. *See also* arthropod.

DDT   An insecticide (C14H9Cl5), toxic to animals and human beings whether ingested or absorbed through skin; particularly devastating to certain bird populations, DDT was generally banned in the U.S. in 1972.

Deciduous   Plants that shed or lose their foliage at the conclusion of the growing season, as in "deciduous trees," such as hardwoods (maple, beech, oak, etc.). *See also* coniferous.

Delta   A triangular alluvial deposit at a river's mouth or at the mouth of a tidal inlet. *See also* alluvial.

Dominant   The species most characteristic of a plant or animal community, usually influencing the types and numbers of other species in the same community.

Ecological niche   An organism's function, status, or occupied area in its ecological community.

Ecosystem   A mostly self-contained community consisting of an environment and the animals and plants that live there.

Eelgrass beds   A submerged marine plant with long leaves; grows in abundance; important food source for geese and other waterfowl.

Emergent plants   Plants adapted to living in shallow water or in saturated soils such as marshes or wetlands.

Endangered species   A species determined by the federal government to be in danger of extinction throughout all or a significant portion of its range (Endangered Species Act, 1973). *See also* threatened.

Endemic species Species that evolved in a certain place and live naturally nowhere else. *See also* indigenous species.

Epiphyte A type of plant (often found in swamps) that lives on a tree instead of on the soil. Epiphytes are not parasitic; they collect their own water and minerals and perform photosynthesis.

Esker An extended gravel ridge left by a river or stream that runs beneath a decaying glacier.

Estuary The lower part of a river where freshwater meets tidal saltwater. Usually characterized by abundant animal and plant life.

Evergreen A tree, shrub, or other plant whose leaves remain green through all seasons.

Exotic A plant or animal not native to the territory. Many exotic plants and animals displace native species.

Extirpation The elimination of a species by unnatural causes, such as overhunting or overfishing.

Fall line A line between the piedmont and the coastal plain below which rivers flow through relatively flat terrain. Large rivers are navigable from the ocean to the fall line.

Fauna Animals, especially those of a certain region or era, generally considered as a group. *See also* flora.

Fjord A glacially carved valley, with steep, high slopes, that has been invaded by the sea.

Fledge To raise birds until they have their feathers and are able to fly.

Floodplain A low-lying, flat area along a river where flooding is common.

Flora Plants, especially those of a certain region or era, generally considered as a group. *See also* fauna.

Flyway A migratory route, providing food and shelter, followed by large numbers of birds.

Forb Any herb that is not in the grass family; forbs are commonly found in fields, prairies, or meadows.

4WD Four-wheel-drive vehicle. *See also* ATV.

Frond A fern leaf, a compound palm leaf, or a leaflike thallus (where leaf and stem are continuous), as with seaweed and lichen.

Glacial outwash Sediment dropped by rivers or streams as they flow away from melting glaciers.

Glacial till An unsorted mix of clay, sand, and rock transported and left by glacial action.

Gneiss A common and rather erosion-resistant metamorphic rock originating from shale, characterized by alternating dark and light bands.

Grassy bald A summit area devoid of trees due to shallow or absent soil overlying bedrock (ledge).

Greentree reservoir An area seasonally flooded by opening dikes. Oaks, hickories, and other water-tolerant trees drop nuts (mast) into the water. Migratory waterfowl and other wildlife feed on the mast during winter.

Habitat The area or environment where a plant or animal, or communities of plants or animals, normally live, such as an alpine habitat.

Hammock A fertile spot of high ground in a wetland that supports the growth of hardwood trees.

Hardwoods Flowering trees such as oaks, hickories, maples, and others, as opposed to softwoods and coniferous trees such as pines and hemlocks.

Herbivore An animal that feeds on plant life. *See also* carnivore and omnivore.

Heronry   Nesting and breeding site for herons.

Herptiles   The class of animals including reptiles and amphibians.

Holdfast   The attachment, in lieu of roots, that enables seaweed to grip a substrate such as a rock.

Hot spot   An opening in the earth's interior from which molten rock erupts, eventually forming a volcano.

Hummock   A rounded knoll or mound underlain by permafrost.

Humus   Decomposed leaves and other organic material found, for instance, on the forest floor.

Impoundment   A man-made body of water controlled by dikes or levees.

Indigenous species   Species that arrived unaided by humans but that may also live in other locations.

Inholding   Private land surrounded by federal or state lands such as a wildlife refuge.

Intertidal zone   The beach or shoreline area located between low and high tide lines.

Introduced species   Species brought to a location by humans, intentionally or accidentally; also called nonnative or alien species. *See also* exotic.

Inupiat Eskimo   An Alaska Native group of people of northern and northwest Alaska, speaking the Inupiaq language.

Lichen   A ground-hugging plant, usually found on rocks, produced by an association between an alga, which manufactures food, and a fungus, which provides support.

Loess   Deep, fertile, and loamy soil deposited by wind, the deepest deposits reaching 200 feet.

Magma   Underground molten rock.

Management area   A section of land within a federal wildlife preserve or forest where specific wildlife management practices are implemented and studied.

Marsh   A low-elevation transitional area between water (the sea) and land, dominated by grasses in soft, wet soils.

Mast   A general word for nuts, acorns, and other food for wildlife produced by trees in autumn.

Meander   A winding stream, river, or path.

Mesozoic   A geologic era, 230-265 million years ago, during which dinosaurs appeared and became extinct, and birds and flowering plants first appeared.

Midden   An accumulation of organic material near a village or dwelling; also called a shell mound.

Migrant   An animal that moves from one habitat to another, as opposed to resident species that live permanently in the same habitat.

Mitigation   The act of creating or enlarging refuges or awarding them water rights to replace wildlife habitat lost because of the damming or channelization of rivers or the building of roads.

Moist-soil unit   A wet area that sprouts annual plants, which attract waterfowl. Naturally produced by river flooding, moist-soil units are artificially created through controlled watering.

Moraine   A formation of rock and soil debris transported and dropped by a glacier.

Muskeg   A grassy bog, often studded with tussocks, that is underlain with permafrost. Short plants, berry bushes, and spindly black spruce are associated with this marshy terrain that covers much of Alaska.

Neotropical   New world tropics, generally referring to central and northern South America, as in *neotropical* birds.

Nesting species Birds that take up permanent residence in a habitat.

Occasional A bird species seen only occasionally in a certain region and whose normal territory is elsewhere.

Oceanic trench The place where a sinking tectonic plate bends down, creating a declivity in the ocean floor.

Old field A field that was once cultivated for crops but has been left to grow back into forest.

Old-growth forest A forest characterized by large trees and a stable ecosystem. Old-growth forests are similar to precolonial forests.

Omnivore An animal that feeds on both plant and animal material. *See also* carnivore and herbivore.

ORVs Off-road vehicles. *See also* 4WD and ATV.

Oxbow A curved section of water (once a bend in a river) that was severed from the river when the river changed course. An oxbow lake is formed by the changing course of a river as it meanders through its floodplain.

Passerine A bird in the *Passeriformes* order, primarily composed of perching birds and songbirds.

Peat An accumulation of sphagnum moss and other organic material in wetland areas, known as peat bogs.

Permafrost Ground that stays frozen year round. The arctic region of Alaska is covered with continuous permafrost, beginning at about one foot below the surface and extending down as deep as 2,000 feet.

Petroglyph Carving or inscription on a rock.

Pahoehoe Smooth lava.

Photosynthesis The process by which green plants use the energy in sunlight to create carbohydrates from carbon dioxide and water, generally releasing oxygen as a by-product.

Pictograph Pictures painted on rock by indigenous people.

Pit-and-mound topography Terrain characteristic of damp hemlock woods where shallow-rooted fallen trees create pits (former locations of trees) and mounds (upended root balls).

Plant community Plants and animals that interact in a similar environment within a region.

Pleistocene A geologic era, 1.8 million to 10,000 years ago, known as the great age of glaciers.

Prairie An expansive, undulating, or flat grassland, usually without trees, generally on the plains of mid-continent North America. In the southeast, "prairie" refers to wet grasslands with standing water much of the year.

Prescribed burn A fire that is intentionally set to reduce the buildup of dry organic matter in a forest or grassland, to prevent catastrophic fires later on or to assist plant species whose seeds need intense heat to open.

Proclamation area An area of open water beside or around a coastal refuge where waterfowl are protected from hunting.

Rain shadow An area sheltered from heavy rainfall by mountains that, at their higher altitudes, have drawn much of the rain from the atmosphere.

Raptor A bird of prey with a sharp curved beak and hooked talons. Raptors include hawks, eagles, owls, falcons, and ospreys.

Rhizome A horizontal plant stem, often thick with reserved food material, from which grow shoots above and roots below.

Riparian The bank and associated plant life zone of any water body, including tidewaters.

Riverine Living or located on the banks of a river.

Rookery A nesting place for a colony of birds or other animals (seals, penguins, others).

Salt marsh An expanse of tall grass, usually cordgrass and sedges, located in sheltered places such as the land side of coastal barrier islands or along river mouths and deltas at the sea.

Salt pan A shallow pool of saline water formed by tidal action that usually provides abundant food for plovers, sandpipers, and other wading birds.

Scabrock Rock scoured clean by the great Spokane flood.

Scat Animal fecal droppings.

Scrub A dry area of sandy or otherwise poor soil that supports species adapted to such conditions, such as sand myrtle and prickly pear cactus, or dwarf forms of other species, such as oaks and palmettos.

Sea stack A small, steep-sided rock island lying off the coast.

Second growth Trees in a forest that grow naturally after the original stand is cut or burned. *See also* old growth.

Seeps Small springs that may dry up periodically.

Shorebird A bird, such as a plover or sandpiper, frequently found on or near the seashore.

Shrub-Steppe Desertlike lands dominated by sagebrush, tumbleweed and other dry-weather-adapted plants.

Slough A backwater or creek in a marshy area; sloughs sometimes dry into deep mud.

Spit A narrow point of land, often of sand or gravel, extending into the water.

Staging area A place where birds rest, gather strength, and prepare for the next stage of a journey.

Subarctic region The area immediately outside (south of) the Arctic Circle, with similar climatic conditions and characteristics.

Subsistence In Alaska this term often refers to a way of life whereby people hunt, fish, or cultivate much of their food and other resources from the land nearby their homes.

Successional Referring to a series of different plants that establish themselves by territories, from water's edge to drier ground. Also, the series of differing plants that reestablish themselves over time after a fire or the retreat of a glacier.

Sump A pit or reservoir used as a drain or receptacle for liquids.

Swale A low-lying, wet area of land.

Swamp A spongy wetland supporting trees and shrubs (as opposed to a marsh, which is characterized by grasses). Swamps provide habitat for birds, turtles, alligators, and bears and serve as refuges for species extirpated elsewhere. *See also* extirpated.

Test The hard, round exoskeleton of a sea urchin.

Threatened species A species of plant or animal in which population numbers are declining, but not in immediate danger of extinction. Threatened species are protected under the Endangered Species Act of 1973. *See also* endangered species.

Tuber A short, underground stem with buds from which new shoots grow.

Tundra A layer of vegetation over permanently frozen subsoil. The northern third of Alaska, and much of its interior, is covered with wet, moist, or alpine tundra. *See also* permafrost.

Tussock Knobby, vegetated mounds of cotton grass that make walking across the tundra difficult.

Understory Plants growing under the canopy of a forest. *See also* canopy.

Vascular plant A fern or another seed-bearing plant with a series of channels for conveying nutrients.

Vernal pool Shallow ponds that fill with spring ("vernal") rains or snowmelt and dry up as summer approaches; temporary homes for certain amphibians.

Wader A long-legged bird, such as a crane or stork, usually found feeding in shallow water.

Wetland A low, moist, area, often marsh or swamp, especially when regarded as the natural habitat of wildlife.

Wilderness Area An area of land (within a national forest, a national park, or a national wildlife refuge) protected under the 1964 Federal Wilderness Act. Logging, construction, and use of mechanized vehicles or tools are prohibited here, and habitats are left in their pristine states. "Designated Wilderness" is the highest form of federal land protection.

Wrack line Plant, animal, and unnatural debris left on the upper beach by a receding tide.

Yup'ik Eskimo Alaskan Native people associated with western and southwest Alaska, divided into three regional and language groups.

INDEX

ACKNOWLEDGMENTS

The writing of a book like this doesn't get done without a lot of help. I can't list the hundred or so U.S. Fish & Wildlife personnel from California, Hawaii and Midway—and Alaska, Washington, and Oregon (I've written two books in this series)—who answered my endless questions and showed me their refuges, expressing a pride in them that was contagious; but I can offer a big thank-you, because without them these books wouldn't have been written.

I do want to mention three behind-the-scenes people who toil away without getting the recognition they deserve: Will Balliett, editor extraordinaire, who can take the worst piece of banal writing and turn it into prose that sparkles; David Emblidge, the editor who envisioned these books in the first place and whose eagle-eyed overview carried the series through to completion; and Don Young, who edited the California & Hawaii book and prevented any number of gaffes from getting into print.

I'd also like to thank two good friends, Jan and Bob Burns, who pitched in when this project seemed overwhelming. Bob's extensive knowledge of plants and birds added immensely to the book, and Jan's logistical help assured that visits to the California and Hawaii refuges went smoothly.

To the readers, I want to say this: Go see these refuges. They're special.

—Loren Mac Arthur

I'd like to thank all of the refuge managers and their staff for assisting with research, answering countless questions, and reviewing all the draft text. In light of a busy field season, I especially appreciated the time and efforts that many individuals contributed to this project. Perhaps more importantly, I would also like to acknowledge the extraordinary animals that live in Alaska's special refuges. Last, thanks to all those individuals who had the vision and dedication in working to pass the 1980 Alaska National Interest Lands Conservation Act, which established or enlarged Alaska's 16 national wildlife refuges, protecting some of the greatest wilderness and wildlife populations remaining on the planet.

—Debbie S. Miller

ABOUT THE AUTHORS

Loren Mac Arthur has been a U.S. Forest Service naturalist interpreter in Alaska, a features writer and editor on California newspapers, and a nationally published freelance writer, working in adventure travel and natural history. For this book, she has written the Pacific Northwest Regional Overview, all refuges in Washington and Oregon, all sidebars in Washington and Oregon, as well as Alaska's Kenai NWR, Tetlin NWR, and the "Mosquitoes" sidebar in Kenai.

Debbie S. Miller is a 25-year Alaska resident who has authored two books on the Arctic National Wildlife Refuge as well as many award-winning nature books for children. For this book, she has described all of the Alaska refuges except Kenai NWR and Tetlin NWR. For her work as a teacher, nature writer, and wilderness advocate, she received the 1999 Refuge Hero Award from the U.S. Fish & Wildlife Service. She lives in Fairbanks with her husband, Dennis, a wildlife survey pilot, and their two daughters, Robin and Casey, who love exploring Alaska with her.

PHOTOGRAPHY CREDITS

We would like to thank the U. S. Fish & Wildlife Service for letting us publish photos from their collection, as well as the other contributing photographers for their wonderful imagery. The pages on which the photos appear are listed after each contributor.

Dan Gibson: 5

John & Karen Hollingsworth: 4, 6, 14, 22, 23, 24, 25, 26, 27, 29, 30, 33, 34, 39, 40, 46, 77, 83, 91, 94, 95, 97, 102, 109, 112, 118, 120, 126, 131, 136, 142, 148, 151, 155, 157, 163, 165, 171, 181, 183, 188, 192, 193, 195, 203, 205, 211, 213, 217, 219, 224, 226, 235

Gary Kramer: xiv, 7, 8, 50, 54, 56, 74, 80, 106, 116, 122, 124, 125, 127, 129, 135, 139, 145, 146, 147, 152, 153, 161, 166, 174, 175, 180, 186, 199, 202, 214, 223, 228, 230, 232, 233, 237

Omni-Photo Communications: 64, 115, 134, 140, 178, 238

U.S. Fish & Wildlife Service: ii-iii, 18-19, 20, 35, 37, 43, 47, 49, 53, 59, 62, 66, 67, 70, 72, 73, 84, 87, 89, 100, 159, 169, 190, 194, 206, 208

NATIONAL AUDUBON SOCIETY
Mission Statement

The mission of National Audubon Society, founded in 1905, is to conserve and restore natural ecosystems, focusing on birds, other wildlife, and their habitats for the benefit of humanity and the earth's biological diversity.

One of the largest, most effective environmental organizations, Audubon has more than 560,000 members, numerous state offices and nature centers, and 500+ chapters in the United States and Latin America, plus a professional staff of scientists, lobbyists, lawyers, policy analysts, and educators. Through our nationwide sanctuary system we manage 150,000 acres of critical wildlife habitat and unique natural areas for birds, wild animals, and rare plant life.

Our award-winning Audubon magazine, published six times a year and sent to all members, carries outstanding articles and color photography on wildlife and nature, and presents in-depth reports on critical environmental issues, as well as conservation news and commentary. We also publish Field Notes, a journal reporting on seasonal bird sightings continent-wide, and Audubon Adventures, a bimonthly children's newsletter reaching 500,000 students. Through our ecology camps and workshops in Maine, Connecticut, and Wyoming, we offer professional development for educators and activists; through Audubon Expedition Institute in Belfast, Maine, we offer unique, traveling undergraduate and graduate degree programs in Environmental Education.

Our acclaimed World of Audubon television documentaries on TBS deal with a variety of environmental themes, and our children's series for the Disney Channel, Audubon's Animal Adventures, introduces family audiences to endangered wildlife species. Other Audubon film and television projects include conservation-oriented movies, electronic field trips, and educational videos. National Audubon Society also sponsors books and interactive programs on nature, plus travel programs to exotic places like Antarctica, Africa, Australia, Baja California, Galapagos Islands, Indonesia, and Patagonia.

For information about how you can become an Audubon member, subscribe to Audubon Adventures, or learn more about our camps and workshops, please write or call:

National Audubon Society
Membership Dept.
700 Broadway
New York, New York 10003
212/979-3000
http://www.audubon.org/audubon

JOIN THE NATIONAL AUDUBON SOCIETY—RISK FREE!

Please send me my first issue of AUDUBON magazine and enroll me as a temporary member of the National Audubon Society at the $20 introductory rate—$15 off the regular rate. If I wish to continue as a member, I'll pay your bill when it arrives. If not, I'll return it marked "cancel," owe nothing, and keep the first issue free.

____ Payment Enclosed   ____ Bill Me

Name _____

Street _____

City _____

State/zip _____

Please make checks payable to the National Audubon Society. Allow 4–6 weeks for delivery of magazine. $10 of dues is for AUDUBON magazine. Basic membership, dues are $35.

Mail to:

NATIONAL AUDUBON SOCIETY
Membership Data Center
PO Box 52529
Boulder, CO 80322-2529